# Pay without Performance

# Pay without Performance

*The Unfulfilled Promise of Executive Compensation*

**Lucian Bebchuk and Jesse Fried**

**Harvard University Press**

Cambridge, Massachusetts, and London, England | 2004

*Library of Congress Cataloging-in-Publication Data*

Bebchuk, Lucian
   Pay without performance: the unfulfilled promise of executive compensation /
   Lucian Bebchuk and Jesse Fried.
      p. cm.
   Includes bibliographical references and index.
   ISBN 0–674–01665–3 (alk. paper)
      1. Executives—Salaries, etc. 2. Corporate governance. I. Fried, Jesse II. Title.
   HD4965.2.B43 2004
   331.2'816584—dc22      2004052253

*For Alma, Alon, and Yonatan*
—L.B.


*For Naomi, Joshua, Avital, and Ayelet*
—J.F.

# Contents

## Part IV. Going Forward

# Preface

**A** WAVE OF corporate scandals that began in late 2001 shook confidence in the performance of public company boards and drew attention to potential flaws in their executive compensation practices. There is now recognition that many boards have employed compensation arrangements that do not serve shareholders' interests. But there is still substantial disagreement about the scope and source of such problems and, not surprisingly, about how to address them.

Many take the view that concerns about executive compensation have been exaggerated. Some of these observers believe that flawed compensation arrangements have been limited to a small number of firms and that most boards have carried out effectively their role of setting executive pay. Others concede that flaws in compensation arrangements have been widespread, but maintain that these flaws have resulted from honest mistakes and misperceptions on the part of boards seeking to serve shareholders. In this view, now that the problems have been recognized, corporate boards can be expected to fix them on their own.

Our aim in this book is to persuade readers that such complacency is hardly warranted. Flawed compensation arrangements have been widespread, persistent, and systemic, and they have stemmed from defects in the underlying governance structure that enable executives to exert considerable influence over their boards. Given executives' power, directors could not have been expected to engage in arm's-length bargaining with executives over their compensation. The absence of effective arm's-length dealing under today's system of corporate governance—not temporary mistakes or lapses of judgment—has been the primary source of problematic compensation arrangements.

Another, broader aim of this book is to contribute to a better understanding of some basic problems of the corporate governance system. Our study of executive compensation opens a window through which we can examine our current reliance on boards to act as guardians of shareholders' interests. Our corporate governance system gives boards substantial power and counts on them to monitor and supervise the company's managers. As long as it is believed that corporate directors carry out their tasks for the benefit of shareholders, current governance arrangements—which insulate boards from intervention by shareholders—appear acceptable. Our work casts doubt on the validity of this belief and on the wisdom of insulating boards from shareholders.

By providing a full account of how and why boards have failed to serve their critical role in the executive compensation area, we hope to contribute to efforts to improve compensation practices and corporate governance more generally. Understanding the source of existing problems is essential for assessing reforms. Some observers now concede that boards have not been sufficiently attentive to shareholders' interests, but argue that an increase in the role of independent directors—facilitated by recently adopted stock exchange requirements—will make such problems a matter of the past. But this is not the case. Our analysis indicates that, to address the identified problems, directors must be made not only more independent of insiders but also more dependent on shareholders. We therefore put forward reforms that would reduce boards' insulation from shareholders. Such reforms may well offer the most promising route for improving executive compensation and corporate governance.

---

This book builds on our 2001 study with David Walker, "Executive Compensation in America: Managerial Power or Extraction of Rents?" which was published in 2002 in the *University of Chicago Law Review* under the title "Managerial Power and Rent Extraction in the Design of Executive Compensation." It also draws on another piece by the two of us, "Executive Compensation as an Agency Problem," which was published in the *Journal of Economic Perspectives* in the summer of 2003. As we indicate at various points throughout the book, we also build on other work that we have done on corporate governance.

In the course of writing this book, we have incurred considerable debts that we wish to acknowledge. Special thanks go to David Walker, our coauthor on the 2001 study. David worked on the first stage of this study and made an important contribution to its development. In the fall of 2000, he entered legal practice for two years, and the demands of this practice prevented him from continuing to work with us. His sound judgment and insights contributed much to our 2001 study, and we very much missed them after he left.

We are also grateful to many individuals for their valuable discussions and comments on drafts of this book or the earlier pieces on which it draws. These individuals include Marc Abramowitz, Yitz Applbaum, Adi Ayal, Franklin Ballotti, Oren Bar-Gill, Lisa Bernstein, Margaret Blair, Victor Brudney, Brian Cheffins, Steve Choi, Bob Cooter, Brad DeLong, Mel Eisenberg, Charles Elson, Allen Ferrell, Merritt Fox, Jeff Gordon, Mitu Gulati, Dan Halperin, Assaf Hamdani, Sharon Hannes, Henry Hansmann, Paul Hodgson, Marcel Kahan, Louis Kaplow, Ira Kay, Reinier Kraakman, Stuart Gillan, Michael Levine, Saul Levmore, Patrick McGurn, Bob Monks, Kevin Murphy, Richard Painter, Adam Pritchard, Mark Roe, David Schizer, Steve Shavell, Andrei Shleifer, Eric Talley, Timothy Taylor, Randall Thomas, Detlev Vagts, Steve Vogel, Michael Wachter, Michael Waldman, Ivo Welch, and David Yermack.

We also received very useful suggestions from participants in workshops at various universities and conferences. Thanks go to workshop participants at Boalt Hall, Harvard Law School, the Kennedy School of Government at Harvard, Harvard Business School, the American Association of Law Schools Business Law Panel on Executive Compensation, the Berkeley Business Law Journal symposium on "The Role of Law in the Creation of Long-term Shareholder Value," and the University of Chicago Law Review symposium on "Management and Control of the Modern Business Corporation."

We are also indebted to many research assistants who have greatly helped us in this project: Alex Aizin, Chris Busselle, Erin Carroll, Misun Isabelle Chung, Lubov Getmansky, Miranda Gong, Nicholas Hecker, Matthew Heyn, Ryan Kantor, Jason Knott, Karen Marciano, Matthew McDermott, Selena Medlen, Jay Metz, Aaron Monick, Jeff Wagner, and Dan Wolk. For their valuable help and for their dedication we are grateful to the assistants we had while working on the book, especially Madeline Burgess, Julie Johnson, and Anita Sarrett. Our presentation was substantially improved by the careful copyediting done by Alexandra McCormack, Jean Martin, Emily Ogden, and Moshe Spinowitz.

For financial support, we wish to thank the John M. Olin Center for Law, Economics, and Business at Harvard Law School; the Harvard Law School; the Berkeley Committee on Research; and the Boalt Hall Fund. Lucian Bebchuk wishes to thank Robert Clark and Elena Kagan, his former and current deans at Harvard Law School, and Professor Steve Shavell, the director of the Olin Center, for their encouragement and support. Jesse Fried is similarly indebted to Herma Hill Kay, John Dwyer, and Robert Berring, his former and current deans at Boalt Hall.

We owe a large debt to our wives, Alma Cohen and Naomi Fried, who have provided a critical and constant source of support, advice, and understanding. Our children—Alon and Yonatan in the case of Lucian, and Joshua, Avital, and Ayelet in the case of Jesse—have been somewhat less understanding, but their sweetness has added much to our lives during the period in which we worked on this book.

June 2004

In judging whether Corporate America is serious about reforming itself, CEO pay remains the acid test. To date, the results aren't encouraging.

Warren Buffett, letter to shareholders of
Berkshire Hathaway, Inc., February 2004

# Introduction

Is it a problem of bad apples, or is it the barrel?
Kim Clark, Dean of the Harvard
Business School, 2003

DURING THE EXTENDED bull market of the 1990s, executive compensation at public companies—companies whose shares are traded on stock exchanges—soared to unprecedented levels. Between 1992 and 2000, the average real (inflation-adjusted) pay of chief executive officers (CEOs) of S&P 500 firms more than quadrupled, climbing from $3.5 million to $14.7 million.[1] Increases in option-based compensation accounted for the lion's share of the gains, with the value of stock options granted to CEOs jumping ninefold during this period.[2] The growth of executive compensation far outstripped that of compensation for other employees. In 1991, the average large-company CEO received approximately 140 times the pay of an average worker; in 2003, the ratio was about 500:1.[3]

Executive pay has long attracted much attention from investors, financial economists, regulators, the media, and the public at large. The higher CEO compensation has climbed, the keener that interest has become. Indeed, one economist has calculated that the dramatic growth in executive pay during the 1990s was outpaced by the increase in the volume of research papers on the subject.[4]

Executive compensation has also long been a topic of heated debate. The rise in pay has been the subject of much public criticism, which further intensified following the corporate governance scandals that began erupting in late 2001. But the evolution of executive compensation during the past two decades has also had powerful defenders. In their view, despite some lapses, imperfections, and cases of abuse, executive arrangements have largely been shaped by market forces and boards loyal to shareholders.

1

Our main goal in this book is to provide a full account of how managerial power and influence have shaped the executive compensation landscape. The dominant paradigm for financial economists' study of executive compensation has assumed that pay arrangements are the product of arm's-length bargaining—bargaining between executives attempting to get the possible deal for themselves and boards seeking to get the best possible deal for shareholders. This assumption has also been the basis for the corporate law rules governing the subject. We aim to show, however, that the pay-setting process in publicly traded companies has strayed far from the arm's-length model.

Our analysis indicates that managerial power has played a key role in shaping managers' pay arrangements. The pervasive role of managerial power can explain much of the contemporary landscape of executive compensation. Indeed, it can explain practices and patterns that have long puzzled financial economists studying executive compensation.

We seek to contribute to a better understanding of the flaws in current compensation arrangements and in the corporate governance processes generating them. Such an understanding is necessary for addressing these problems. We show that recent corporate governance reforms, which seek to increase board independence, would likely improve matters but that much more needs to be done. And we put forward reforms that, by making directors more accountable to shareholders, would reduce the forces that have in the past distorted compensation arrangements.

## The Official View and Its Shortcomings

Part I discusses the shortcomings of the "official" view of executive compensation. According to this view, which underlies existing corporate governance arrangements, corporate boards operate at arm's length from the executives whose pay arrangements they decide. Seeking to serve shareholders, directors design cost-effective compensation arrangements that provide executives with incentives to increase shareholder value.

Recognition of managers' influence over their own pay has been at the heart of the criticism of executive compensation in the media and by shareholder activists.[5] However, the premise that boards negotiate pay arrangements at arm's length from executives has long been and remains a central tenet in the corporate world and in most research on executive compensation. Holders of the official view believe it provides a good approximation of reality. When faced with practices that are hard to reconcile with arm's-length contracting, they seek to explain these "deviant" examples as "rotten apples" that do not represent the entire barrel or as the result of temporary lapses, mistakes, or misperceptions that, once identified, will promptly be corrected by boards.

In the corporate world, the official view serves as the practical basis for legal rules and public policy. It is used to justify directors' compensation decisions to shareholders, policymakers, and courts. These decisions are portrayed as being made largely with shareholders' interests at heart and therefore deserving of deference.

The official view's premise of arm's-length bargaining has also been shared by most of the research on executive compensation. Managers' influence over directors has been recognized by those writing on the subject from a legal, organizational, or sociological perspective.[6] But most of the research on executive pay (especially empirical research) has been done by financial economists, and the premise of arm's-length bargaining has guided most of their work. Some financial economists, whose studies we discuss later, have reported findings they viewed as inconsistent with arm's-length contracting.[7] However, the majority of work in the field has assumed arm's-length bargaining between boards and executives.

In the paradigm that has dominated financial economics, which we label the "arm's-length bargaining" approach, the board of directors is viewed as operating at arm's length from executives and seeking to maximize shareholder value. Rational parties transacting at arm's length have powerful incentives to avoid inefficient provisions that shrink the pie produced by their contractual arrangements. The arm's-length contracting approach has thus led researchers to believe that executive compensation arrangements will tend to increase value, which is why we have used the terms "efficient contracting" or "optimal contracting" to label this approach in some of our earlier work.[8]

Financial economists, both theorists and empiricists, have largely worked within the arm's-length model in attempting to explain common compensation arrangements as well as variation in compensation practices among firms.[9] In fact, upon discovering practices that appear inconsistent with the cost-effective provision of incentives, financial economists have often labored to come up with clever explanations for how such practices might be consistent with arm's-length contracting after all. Practices for which no explanation has been found have been considered "anomalies" or "puzzles" that will ultimately either be explained within the paradigm or disappear.

The official arm's-length story is neat, tractable, and reassuring. However, as we explain in part I, this model has failed to account for the realities of executive compensation. Directors have had various economic incentives to support, or at least go along with, arrangements favorable to the company's top executives. Various social and psychological factors—collegiality, team spirit, a natural desire to avoid conflict within the board team, and sometimes friendship and loyalty—have also pulled board members in that direction. Although many directors own shares in their firms, their financial incentives to avoid arrangements favorable to executives have been too weak to induce them to take the personally costly, or at the very least unpleasant, route of haggling with their CEOs. Finally, limitations on time and resources have made it difficult for even well-intentioned directors to do their pay-setting job properly.

Some writers have argued that even if directors are subject to considerable influence from corporate executives, market forces can be relied on to force boards and executives to adopt the compensation arrangements that arm's-length bargaining would produce. Our analysis, however, finds that market forces are neither sufficiently finely tuned nor sufficiently powerful to compel such outcomes. The markets for capital, corporate control, and managerial labor do impose *some* constraints on executive compensation. These constraints are hardly stringent, however, and they permit substantial deviations from arm's-length contracting.

A realistic picture of the incentives and circumstances of board members, then, reveals myriad incentives and tendencies that lead directors to behave very differently than expected under the arm's-length model. Recent reforms, such as the new stock exchange listing requirements that seek to limit CEOs' ability to financially reward independent directors, may weaken some of these factors but will not eliminate them. Without additional reforms, the pay-setting process will continue to deviate substantially from the arm's-length model.

## Power and Pay

After analyzing the shortcomings of the arm's-length contracting view, we turn in part II to the managerial power perspective on executive compensation. The same factors that limit the usefulness of the arm's-length model suggest that executives have had substantial influence over their own pay. Compensation arrangements have often deviated from arm's-length contracting because directors have been influenced by management, sympathetic to executives, insufficiently motivated to bargain over compensation, or simply ineffectual in overseeing compensation. Executives' influence over directors has enabled them to obtain "rents"—benefits greater than those obtainable under true arm's-length bargaining.

Although top executives generally have some degree of influence over their board, the extent of their influence depends on various features of the firm's governance structure. The managerial power approach predicts that executives who have more power vis-à-vis their boards should receive higher pay—or pay that is less sensitive to performance—than their less powerful counterparts. A substantial body of evidence does indeed indicate that pay has been higher, and less sensitive to performance, when executives have more power.

There are, of course, limits to the arrangements that directors will approve and executives will seek. Markets, such as the market for corporate control, might penalize boards that allow pay arrangements that appear egregious. Directors and executives might in such a case also bear social costs. The constraints imposed by markets and by social forces are far from tight, however, and they permit substantial deviations from arm's-length outcomes. The adoption of arrangements favoring executives is unlikely to impose substantial economic or social costs if the arrangements are not patently abusive or indefensible.

One important building block of the managerial power approach is that of "outrage" costs. When a board approves a compensation arrangement favorable to managers, the extent to which directors and executives bear economic and social costs will depend on how the arrangement is perceived by outsiders whose views matter to the directors and executives. An arrangement that is perceived as outrageous might reduce shareholders' willingness to support incumbents in proxy contests or takeover bids. Outrage might also lead to shareholder pressure on managers and directors, as well as possibly embarrass directors and managers or harm their reputations. The more outrage a compensation arrangement is expected to generate, the more reluctant directors will be to approve it and the more hesitant managers will be to propose it in the first place.

The critical role of outsiders' perception of executives' compensation and the significance of outrage costs explain the importance of yet another component of the managerial power approach: "camouflage." The desire to minimize outrage gives designers of compensation arrangements a strong incentive to try to obscure and legitimize—or, more generally, to camouflage—both the level and performance-insensitivity of executive compensation. Camouflage thus allows executives to reap benefits at the expense of shareholders. More importantly, attempts to camouflage can lead to the adoption of inefficient compensation structures that harm managers' incentives and, in turn, company performance, imposing even greater costs on shareholders.

We present evidence that compensation arrangements have often been designed with an eye to camouflaging rent and minimizing outrage. Firms have systematically taken steps that make less transparent both the total amount of compensation and the extent to which it is decoupled from managers' own performance. Managers' interest in reduced transparency has been served by the design of numerous compensation practices, such as postretirement perks and consulting arrangements, deferred compensation, pension plans, and executive loans. Overall, the camouflage motive turns out to be quite useful in explaining many otherwise puzzling features of the executive compensation landscape.

## Performance Pay and the Unfulfilled Promise of Executive Pay

Those applauding the rise in executive compensation have stressed the benefits to shareholders from strengthening managers' incentives to increase shareholder value. Indeed, in the beginning of the 1990s, prominent financial economists such as Michael Jensen and Kevin Murphy urged shareholders to be more accepting of large pay packages that would provide high-powered incentives.[10] Shareholders, it was argued, should care much more about providing managers with sufficiently strong incentives than about the amounts spent on executive pay.

Indeed, throughout the past decade, shareholders have often accepted the increase in executive pay as the price of improving managers' incentives. Higher compensation has been presented as essential for improving managers' incentives and therefore worth the additional cost. Unfortunately, however, much of the additional value provided to executives has not actually been tied to their own performance. Shareholders have not received as much bang for their buck as possible.

As we describe in part III, managers have used their influence to obtain higher compensation through arrangements that have substantially decoupled pay from performance. Firms could have generated the same increase in incentives at a much lower cost, or they could have used the amount spent to obtain more powerful incentives. Executive pay is much less sensitive to performance than has commonly been recognized.

Although equity-based compensation has recently drawn the most attention, much executive pay comes in forms other than equity, such as salary and bonus. The evidence indicates that cash compensation—including bonuses—has been at best weakly correlated with firms' industry-adjusted performance. Such compensation has been generously awarded even to managers whose performance was mediocre relative to other executives in their industry. Furthermore, financial economists have paid little attention to the other forms of non-equity compensation that managers frequently receive, such as favorable loans, pensions and deferred compensation, and various perks. These less-noticed forms of compensation, which can be substantial, have tended to be insensitive to managerial performance.

In light of the historically weak link between non-equity compensation and managerial performance, shareholders and regulators wishing to make pay more sensitive to performance have increasingly looked to, and encouraged, equity-based compensation—that is, compensation based on the value of the company's stock. Most equity-based compensation has taken the form of stock options—options to buy a certain number of company shares for a specified price (the "exercise" or "strike" price). We strongly support equity-based compensation, which in principle can provide managers with desirable incentives. Unfortunately, however, managers have been able to use their influence to obtain option arrangements that have deviated substantially from arm's-length contracting in ways that favor the managers. Our analysis indicates that equity-based plans have enabled executives to reap substantial rewards even when their performance was merely passable or even poor.

For instance, firms have failed to filter out stock price rises that are due largely to industry and general market trends and thus are unrelated to managers' own contribution to shareholder value. Although there is a whole range of ways in which such windfalls could be filtered out, a large majority of firms have continued to cling to conventional option plans under which most of the equity-based compensation paid to managers is not tied to their own performance. In addition, firms have given executives broad freedom to unload options and shares, a practice that has been beneficial to executives but costly to shareholders. Unfortunately, most of the boards now changing their equity-based compensation plans in response to outside pressure are still choosing to avoid plans that would effectively eliminate such windfalls. Rather, they are moving to plans, such as those based on restricted stock, that fail to eliminate, and sometimes even increase, these windfalls.

## Alternative Critiques of Executive Compensation

Criticism of executive compensation practices can come from a variety of methodological and ideological perspectives. It is important to make clear at the outset how our take on the subject differs from other types of criticism. Indeed, in some respects, our positions are closer to those of supporters of current pay arrangements than to those of other critics of these arrangements.

To begin, there is the "moral," "fairness-based"—and, some might say, "populist"—opposition to large amounts of pay. In this view, putting aside practical consequences, paying executives hundreds of times what other employees get is inherently unfair and unacceptable.

Our own criticism does not come from this perspective. Our approach is completely pragmatic and consequentialist, focusing on shareholder value and the performance of corporations (and, in turn, the economy as a whole). We would accept compensation at current or even higher levels as long as such compensation, through its incentive effects, actually serves shareholders. We are concerned, however, that the compensation arrangements that have been in place do not meet this standard.

It is also important to distinguish our position from the view that financial incentives are not very important in motivating top executives and that enhancing shareholder value therefore does not call for large pay packages. At least since the first half of the past century, some industrial psychologists have maintained that corporate executives, who are all materially well off anyway, are primarily moved by such factors as the need for esteem, self-actualization, and so forth.[11] In this view, "The real driving force which motivates the typical executive . . . is not money, but the deep inner satisfaction that he is doing a tough job well."[12] Accordingly, increasing the pay of already well-paid managers, it is argued, does not affect performance and is simply a waste of shareholder money.

In contrast to this view, we share the assumption of defenders of current pay arrangements that executives are influenced by financial incentives. We agree that paying generously to provide desirable incentives can be a good compensation strategy for shareholders. Indeed, the fact that executives (as well as directors) are influenced by financial incentives and have an interest in increasing their own pay actually plays an important role in our analysis. Our concern is simply that executives have partly taken over the compensation machine, leading to arrangements that fail to provide managers with desirable incentives.

Finally, it is worth emphasizing that our criticism of executive pay arrangements does not focus on the amount of compensation received by executives. In our view, high absolute levels of pay do not by themselves imply that compensation arrangements deviate from arm's-length contracting. Our conclusion that such deviations have been common is based primarily on an analysis of the processes by which pay is set, as well as on examining the inefficient, distorted, and nontransparent structure of pay arrangements. For us, the "smoking gun" of managerial influence on pay is not high pay but rather such things as evidence linking the relationship between power and pay, the systematic use of compensation practices that obscure the amount and performance insensitivity of pay, and the showering of gratuitous benefits on departing executives.

## The Stakes

How important is the subject of executive pay? Why should one read a whole book on the subject? Some might wonder whether executive compensation has a significant economic impact on the corporate sector. The problems existing in the area of executive compensation, it might be argued, do not substantially affect shareholders' bottom line and are thus mainly symbolic.

Even if symbolism were unimportant, however, the subject of executive compensation is of substantial practical importance for shareholders and policymakers. Flaws in compensation arrangements impose substantial costs on shareholders. To begin with, there is the excess pay that managers receive as a result of their power, that is, the difference between what managers' influence enables them to obtain and what they would get under arm's-length contracting. As a current study by Yaniv Grinstein and one of us seeks to document in detail,[13] the amounts involved are hardly pocket change for shareholders.

During the five-year period 1998–2002, the compensation paid to the top five executives at each company in the widely used ExecuComp database, aggregated over the 1500 companies in the database, totaled about $100 billion (in 2002 dollars). And the capitalized present value of aggregate top-5 compensation in publicly traded U.S. companies is rather substantial. During the past ten years, the growth rate of aggregate executive compensation has kept pace with that of total stock market capitalization. Assuming that aggregate executive compensation continues to grow in tandem with market capitalization or that managers' share of aggregate corporate profits remains at current levels, the capitalized present value of aggregate top-5 compensation in publicly held U.S. firms could be on the order of half a trillion dollars. Thus, if compensation could be cut without weakening managerial incentives, the gain to investors would not be merely symbolic. It would have real practical significance.

Furthermore, and perhaps even more important, managers' influence on compensation arrangements dilutes and distorts the incentives that they produce. In our view, the reduction in shareholder value caused by these inefficiencies—rather than that caused by excessive managerial pay—could well be the biggest cost arising from managerial influence over compensation.

We discuss two incentive problems that current pay arrangements have been producing. First, compensation arrangements have been providing weaker incentives to reduce managerial slack and to increase shareholder value than would be the case under arm's-length contracting. Both the non-equity and equity components of managerial compensation have been more severely decoupled from managers' contribution to company performance than superficial appearances might suggest. Making pay more sensitive to performance may well benefit shareholders substantially.

Second, prevailing compensation practices have also created perverse incentives. For example, managers' ability to unload options and shares has provided them with incentives to misreport results, suppress bad news, and choose projects and strategies that are less transparent to the market. Improving compensation schemes could thus considerably benefit shareholders by reducing the costs resulting from such distorted behavior.

## Going Forward

In part IV, we turn to some of the implications of our analysis, both for executive compensation and for corporate governance more generally. Given the difficulty of achieving an arm's-length relationship between boards and managers, it is important that shareholders scrutinize executive compensation for inefficient pay structures. Our analysis highlights the types of schemes that institutional investors should support. Such investors should, for example, pressure firms to use equity-based schemes that filter out windfalls, tie pay tightly to management's own performance, and substantially limit managers' freedom to unload equity incentives.

Because outside monitoring and pressure can serve as a check on managerial rent extraction, our analysis implies that compensation arrangements should be highly transparent. It is not enough for information to be in the public domain and fully accessible and understood by a limited number of market professionals. Given the importance of outsiders' perceptions and scrutiny, transparency is critical for reducing the extent to which managers' influence distorts compensation arrangements.

Getting compensation arrangements to be more consistent with arm's-length contracting and getting boards to be more effective monitors of managers generally are likely to be more difficult than many expect. Recent reforms require companies listed on the major stock exchanges (the New York Stock Exchange, NASDAQ, and the American Stock Exchange) to have a majority of independent directors—directors who are not otherwise employed by the firm or in a business relationship with it. These companies must also staff compensation and nominating committees with such directors and submit equity compensation plans to a shareholder vote. Our analysis indicates that even though these reforms are likely to be beneficial, they cannot be relied on to produce the kind of arm's-length relationship between directors and executives on which our corporate governance system relies.

What else should be done? To induce boards to perform their critical role well, we should focus not only on insulating directors from the influence of executives, but also on reducing their current insulation from shareholders. While we should lessen directors' dependence on executives, we should also seek to increase directors' dependence on shareholders.

Even in the wake of poor performance and shareholder dissatisfaction, directors now face very little risk of being ousted in a proxy contest or a hostile takeover. This state of affairs should not continue. To improve the performance of corporate boards, arrangements that insulate directors from removal by either a proxy fight or a takeover should be eliminated or reduced. Additionally, boards should not have veto power—which current corporate law grants them—over changing the governance arrangements in the company's charter.

Although we do sketch out some of the implications of our analysis, our aim in this book is not to offer a fully detailed blueprint for changes in pay arrangements and corporate governance. Rather, we focus on some prior and crucial steps: demonstrating that, contrary to the official story of executive compensation, boards have not been bargaining at arm's length with managers over their pay; explaining how managerial influence and rent seeking have played important roles in shaping executive compensation; and providing a full account of the range and adverse consequences of the resulting deviations from arm's-length bargaining.

This is an area in which the very recognition of problems may help to alleviate them. Managers' ability to influence pay structures depends on the extent to which the resulting distortions are not too apparent to market participants—especially institutional investors. Thus, recognition of how managerial influence can produce substantial deviations from efficient contracts may serve as a useful check simply by reducing managers' ability to camouflage rents.

To address the problems that we examine in corporate governance, additional structural reforms in the allocation of power between boards and shareholders are necessary. To make such reforms possible, shareholders and public officials must have a fuller understanding of how pervasive, systemic, and costly the current flaws in governance have been. Helping to bring about such an understanding is a main aim of this book.

# Part I

## The Official View and Its Shortcomings

# 1

# The Official Story

The board of directors is the oversight mechanism charged
with monitoring management and providing shareholders
with accountability.
Ira Millstein, "The Professional Board," 1995

**W**E SHOULD START by describing briefly the "official" view of executive compensation—that boards, bargaining at arm's length with CEOs, negotiate pay arrangements designed to serve shareholders' interests. This view underlies corporate law's approach to executive compensation, helps legitimize compensation arrangements, and informs much of the large body of research on executive compensation carried out by financial economists.

## The Agency Problem

Our focus in this book is on publicly traded American companies without a controlling shareholder. This diffuse ownership structure is the norm in the United States, though not in other countries.[1] The dispersion of shareholder interests was first documented in 1932 by Adolph Berle and Gardiner Means in their classic study *The Modern Corporation and Private Property*,[2] and it remains the dominant form of ownership among publicly traded companies in the United States.

The dispersed owners of a typical publicly traded company cannot monitor or direct managers' actions, so the executives who exert day-to-day control in such companies often have considerable discretion. In such a situation, ownership and control are separated. Shareholders own the company, but the managers exercise a substantial amount of control over how it is run.

The separation of ownership and control creates what financial econ-

15

omists call an "agency relationship": a company's managers act as agents of its shareholders. The principals (the shareholders) cannot directly ensure that the agents (the managers) will always act in the principals' best interests. As a result, the manager-agents, whose interests do not fully overlap those of the shareholder-principals, may deviate from the best course of action for shareholders. This is called the "agency problem."[3] Managers' departures from shareholder-regarding strategies in turn may involve "inefficient" behavior—behavior that reduces the size of the corporate pie. The reductions in aggregate company value caused by such deviations are called "agency costs."

The agency problem can affect a wide variety of managerial choices: how much effort to exert, how many perks to consume, and which strategic and business choices to make for the company. In each instance, managers' interests may not match those of shareholders. Consider, for example, decisions about how much effort to exert. Because managers will bear the entire cost of their own effort, but will not fully enjoy its benefit to the company, they will tend to exert less effort than is optimal. On the other hand, because managers will fully enjoy the perks they consume while not bearing their entire cost, they will have an incentive to consume too much.

Managers' private interests may also distort business decisions that affect company size. CEOs may engage in empire building, which can increase their prestige, perks, compensation, and other private benefits.[4] Because managers derive more private benefits from being at the helm of a larger company, they may make acquisitions and additional investments that reduce shareholder value. They may also fail to reorganize and reduce the scope of operations when downsizing is called for. Moreover, to avoid company contraction and perhaps also to facilitate future empire building, managers may retain too much cash, failing to distribute excess funds to shareholders even when their firms do not have profitable investment opportunities.[5]

Agency problems are likely to affect other business decisions as well. Overall, managers may run companies in ways that are personally more satisfying or convenient even if they come at the expense of shareholders. They may be tempted to pursue pet projects, for example, or they may fail to take actions that are personally costly, such as firing mediocre subordinates who also happen to be their friends.

Finally, managers may continue to run their companies even when they are no longer the best people for the job.[6] They may turn down attractive acquisition offers or block takeover attempts that would increase shareholder value but cost them their positions. And they have an incentive to take entrenching actions (such as adopting antitakeover measures) that make it more difficult to replace them.

## The Board as Guardian of Shareholder Interests

The official theory of executive compensation recognizes that there is an agency problem in publicly traded companies with separation of ownership and control. This agency problem is supposed to be addressed by the board's supervision and monitoring of managers. Under the rules of corporate law, the power to run the company is not given to the CEO and other officers. Rather, this power is vested in the board, under whose direction the business and affairs of the corporation are supposed to be managed.[7]

Although the board has formal authority and control, directors are not expected to manage the company themselves. The directors of publicly traded companies have other primary careers and thus do not perform their board roles full-time. In addition, many directors sit on more than one board. Directors are therefore generally expected to delegate ongoing management to the company's officers and especially to the CEO. But the board's power to intervene is supposed to keep managers in line. The threat of board intervention is expected to curb managers' tendency toward self-serving behavior, thereby reducing agency costs.[8]

After selecting and hiring executives, directors are therefore supposed to monitor their performance, replacing them as necessary. Major corporate decisions, such as how to respond to an acquisition offer, are ultimately reviewed by the board, which has full power to accept or reject management's recommendations.

In carrying out its supervisory duties, the board must be guided by the interests of the corporation and its shareholders. The directors have a fiduciary duty to the company and its shareholders. In addition to this duty, the directors are assumed to have an incentive to serve shareholder interests. Failure to do so, it is widely believed, may lead shareholders to replace the board by voting in a different slate of directors or by selling their shares to a hostile acquirer.

## Arm's-Length Bargaining over Compensation

Given executives' natural interest in being paid more and working less, permitting them to set their own pay would obviously generate large agency costs. Therefore, the board is directly entrusted with these decisions. Under the official theory of executive compensation, the board is assumed to bargain at arm's length with executives over their pay, solely with the interests of the corporation and its shareholders in mind. That premise underlies corporate law's treatment of board compensation decisions. Following a strong presumption that directors exercise their business judgment to serve shareholders, courts generally defer to boards' decisions on compensation issues. As the Delaware Supreme Court recently wrote, "The size and structure of executive compensation are inherently matters of judgment" that are entitled to "great deference" by the courts.[9]

The same premise underlies most of the large volume of research that financial economists have done on executive compensation. The dominant model in the economics literature assumes that, in negotiating compensation, directors take an independent position vis-à-vis executives. The board is viewed as bargaining with management with the exclusive goal of serving shareholder interests. In an effort to understand executive compensation practices, financial economists have done substantial work within this model of arm's-length bargaining.[10] Even after the wave of corporate scandals that began erupting in late 2001, financial economists have continued to use arm's-length contracting as the main lens through which to view compensation arrangements.

## Efficient Contracting and Paying for Performance

What would characterize an executive compensation arrangement produced by arm's-length bargaining between the executive and a board seeking to maximize shareholder value? To begin with, the contract must provide enough value to induce the executive to accept and remain in the position being offered. Thus, the contract must provide benefits whose value meets or exceeds the value of the other opportunities available to the candidate (the executive's "reservation value").

In addition, when rational, self-interested buyers and sellers transact, their contracts tend to avoid inefficient terms, that is, terms that reduce the size of the pie produced by the contractual arrangement and shared by the transacting parties. Thus, for example, employment contracts tend to take advantage of forms of compensation that are tax subsidized and thus can increase the parties' combined wealth, and tend to avoid ways that impose an unnecessary tax cost and therefore reduce the parties' combined wealth. For this reason, when studying compensation arrangements from the perspective of the arm's-length model, financial economists have viewed terms that seem inefficient as puzzling and have sought to show that they might be value enhancing after all.

Economists have long believed that efficient compensation contracts should link pay with performance to provide executives with desirable incentives. Indeed, according to the standard view, the compensation arrangement is an important mechanism for reducing agency costs. And the significance of the agency problem makes it crucial to use this instrument effectively.

Directors have neither the time nor the information necessary to monitor all managerial actions to ensure that they benefit shareholders. Given the considerable discretion inherent in a CEO's position, inducing the CEO to focus on shareholder interests and avoid self-serving choices is therefore important. The board can influence the CEO to behave in this manner by designing a compensation arrangement that provides the CEO with an incentive to increase shareholder value. Thus, it is argued, a well-designed compensation scheme can make up for the fact that directors cannot directly monitor or evaluate many of their top executives' decisions. Such a well-designed scheme can substantially reduce agency costs, improve performance, and increase shareholder value.[11]

Linking compensation to performance may require a company to increase an executive's level of compensation because pay that is sensitive to performance is less valuable to managers than fixed pay with the same expected value. Because the company's performance will depend on some future factors beyond the executive's control, tying a manager's compensation to performance makes the level of compensation uncertain. Managers are generally risk averse—they value a dollar paid with certainty more than they value variable pay with an expected value of a dollar (e.g., a 50 percent chance of receiving two dollars). This risk aversion makes performance-based compensation worth less to an executive. Everything being equal, it would take more performance-based compensation than fixed compensation to meet the executive's reservation value. As long as managers' incentives are important, however, an efficient contract can be expected to provide a major part of its compensation in ways that induce and reward performance. For this reason, economists have long emphasized the importance of increasing the sensitivity of compensation to performance.[12]

Indeed, the incentive benefits of performance-based pay might be substantial enough to make it desirable for shareholders to pay their top executives more than the "reservation wage" needed to hire and retain them.[13] It would be worth granting, say, another $1,000,000 of performance-based compensation if the effect of the stronger incentives on the executive's behavior is expected to increase the value of the company by more than $1,000,000. Importantly, however, such an increase in compensation beyond the executive's reservation wage could serve shareholders only if it were given in a performance-based form.

In examining whether the empirical reality has been consistent with arm's-length contracting, it will be useful to focus on the structure of executive compensation. Because a board seeking to maximize shareholder value may set high levels of compensation, such levels do not by themselves demonstrate a departure from arm's-length contracting. Under the arm's-length contracting view, however, there is little reason to expect the widespread persistence of arrangements that, by distorting incentives or otherwise, compensate managers in an inefficient way. Thus, evidence that such arrangements are widespread and persistent will be a more telling sign of departures from the arm's-length model than absolute amounts could be.

## It's the Market

Defenders of existing compensation practices often try to base their case on analogies to other markets for talent. For example, while testifying before a U.S. Senate committee, noted compensation consultant Ira Kay argued that "the CEO labor market meets all of the criteria of any market."[14] In this view, compensation arrangements are the outcome of market interactions, a product of the combined forces of the supply of and demand for managerial talent. Executive compensation arrangements produced by this process, it is argued, are not more problematic, and should not be questioned more, than the compensation arrangements obtained by other highly paid individuals, such as star athletes and famous movie actors.

### Are CEOs like Star Athletes?

The analogy to star athletes is one that defenders of existing pay practices often seek to invoke.[15] After all, star athletes are a rather popular and admired group, and reports about their high salaries are commonly greeted with awe and approval rather than with outrage. Furthermore, the compensation of star athletes climbed dramatically during the 1990s.[16] Thus, defenders of current executive pay practices can assert that the meteoric rise in executive pay is simply part of the broader phenomenon of the rise in the value of special talent that has also manifested itself in other markets. The rise in executive pay, so the argument goes, is no more problematic than the fact that top basketball center Shaquille O'Neal is paid much more than earlier great centers such as Bill Russell and Wilt Chamberlain.

But the process generating the compensation of, say, O'Neal is quite different from that producing the compensation arrangements of, say, Disney CEO Michael Eisner. Those invoking the market analogy implicitly rely on the premise of arm's-length bargaining, which is valid for athletes but not for executives. When an athlete's compensation arrangements are set, there is little doubt that the club's manager is negotiating with the athlete at arm's length. The manager is seeking to serve the club's interests, not those of the individual player. And when transactions occur between independent buyers and sellers, the invisible hand of the market tends to produce efficient arrangements.

Indeed, it is worth noting that although star athletes are highly paid, some more than the average S&P 500 CEO, their compensation arrangements lack the features of executive pay arrangements that managerial influence produces. After the compensation packages of star athletes are negotiated, clubs have little reason to try to camouflage the amount of pay and to channel pay through arrangements designed to make the pay less visible. While athletes are paid generously during the period of their contracts, clubs generally do not provide them with a large amount of compensation in the form of postretirement perks and payments. Clubs also generally do not provide athletes with complex deferred-compensation arrangements that serve to obscure total pay. And when clubs get rid of players, they do not generally provide them with large gratuitous payments in addition to the players' contractually entitled payouts. As we shall see, however, these are all common practices in the area of executive compensation. Executives are not like star athletes.

### Is It Possible for Most Executives to Be Overpaid?

Defenders of current pay arrangements also argue that the only way to assess whether an individual is overpaid is by reference to the compensation paid to others in the same market. One cannot judge a compensation arrangement, it is argued, outside the context of the particular market in which it is set. In this view, it is impossible, by definition, for most executives to be paid too much. Furthermore, in this view, compensation arrangements should not be seen as problematic as long as boards use market surveys to set compensation in line with that paid to executives of other publicly traded companies.

It is true that, by definition, most CEOs cannot be compensated above the median level of their peer group. But boards acting at arm's length should be doing more than ensuring that the compensation they set can be defended as being in line with market levels. Boards acting at arm's length are supposed to try to get, against the background of market conditions, the best outcome for shareholders.

Furthermore, in the absence of an arm's-length bargaining process, concerns about executive compensation arrangements cannot be assuaged by a determination that all executives get similar packages. The absence of arm's-length bargaining could still mean that managers are paid too much or paid in inefficient ways. In such a market, compensation levels could be higher than those that would prevail if arm's-length bargaining shaped the market. Thus, when the market as a whole is distorted by the absence of arm's-length bargaining, general conformity to market terms cannot allay concerns about the amount and structure of compensation.

In the end, then, the validity of the arguments for deference to market outcomes depends on whether those outcomes are largely generated by arm's-length negotiations between executives and self-interested purchases of their services. The critical question, which we will consider next, is whether the arm's-length model is a sufficiently accurate reflection of reality.

# 2

## Have Boards Been Bargaining at Arm's Length?

> The directors of [joint stock] companies, however, being the managers rather of other people's money than of their own . . . cannot well be expected . . . [to] watch over it with the same anxious vigilance [as the owners themselves].
>
> Adam Smith, 1776

THE ARM'S-LENGTH CONTRACTING view recognizes that executives do not automatically serve shareholders. It concedes that executives might well act in ways that suit their own interests—a tendency that proper incentives and board oversight are supposed to curb. But the arm's-length model implicitly assumes that, unlike corporate executives, corporate directors can be relied on to serve shareholders.

Given that executives do not instinctively seek to maximize shareholder value, however, there is no reason to expect a priori that directors will act in this way. Directors' own incentives and preferences do matter. Directors have financial and nonfinancial incentives to favor, or at least to get along with, executives. A variety of psychological and social factors reinforce these incentives. Because directors hold only a tiny fraction of the firm's shares, their holdings are insufficient to outweigh their incentives and tendencies to side with executives. In any event, directors have thus far had neither the time nor the information necessary to serve shareholder interests when determining executive compensation.

The pay-setting process is, of course, better in some firms than in others. However, significant deviations from arm's-length contracting have been common in widely held public companies. And while recently adopted stock exchange requirements will probably somewhat improve pay-setting processes, they are unlikely to eliminate substantial and widespread deviations from arm's-length contracting.

## The Pay-Setting Process

We begin our exploration of the limitations of the arm's-length model with a brief description of the pay-setting process in large public corporations. The board of directors is responsible for determining the compensation of the CEO and other top executives.[1] Boards of large public companies delegate to compensation committees the task of working out the critical details of executive compensation arrangements.

The compensation committee has typically been composed of three or four directors.[2] For some time now, most directors serving on compensation committees have been "independent." Directors are generally considered independent if they are not current or former employees of the firm and are not affiliated with the firm other than through their directorship. The Investor Responsibility Research Center reported that 73 percent of the S&P 1500 compensation committees surveyed during 2002 were fully independent.[3]

Tax rules and court decisions have contributed to the widespread use of compensation committees made up exclusively of independent directors. Since 1994, the federal tax code has penalized corporations lacking such committees; publicly traded corporations have not been permitted to deduct pay in excess of $1 million annually per executive unless the excess compensation either consists of options or is based on the achievement of performance goals that have been established by a compensation committee composed solely of independent directors.[4] Courts have generally upheld compensation arrangements recommended to the board by a compensation committee composed of independent directors. Thus, the use of such a committee has largely insulated board compensation decisions from judicial review.[5]

Although already very common, the presence of independent directors on boards and on compensation committees in particular is expected to grow because of the listing requirements adopted by the NYSE, NASDAQ, and AMEX and approved by the Securities and Exchange Commission (SEC) in 2003.[6] These new provisions require the boards of most publicly traded companies to have a majority of independent directors.[7] Under the NYSE rules, each company must have a compensation committee composed only of independent directors. Under the rules of the other two exchanges, the CEO's compensation must be determined or recommended to the board by a majority of independent directors or a compensation committee composed solely of such directors. The stock exchange requirements also establish standards for determining independence.

Although these new requirements have attracted a great deal of attention, it is important to keep in mind that they merely make mandatory a practice that most public companies already have been following for some time. Thus it seems unlikely that these new requirements, by themselves, will greatly change the relationship between executives and their boards. Indeed, there are good reasons to doubt that the mere presence of independent directors on the board and on the compensation committee can ensure a pay-setting process that approximates arm's-length bargaining.

## Directors' Desire to Be Reelected to the Board

A director receives a number of benefits from serving on a board. First, a board seat provides direct financial benefits. In most cases, these benefits are likely to be economically significant to the director. Like executive pay, director pay rose dramatically with the stock market. In 2002, director compensation averaged $152,000 in the largest 200 companies and $116,000 in the largest 1,000 companies.[8] There are often additional perks and indirect benefits; for example, directors of UAL Corp. (which owns United Airlines) can fly United free of charge, and directors of Starwood Hotels get complimentary nights in company hotels.[9] Moreover, a board seat often provides directors with prestige and with valuable business and social connections. The financial and nonfinancial benefits of holding a board seat give directors a strong interest in keeping their positions.

That directors have a desire to be reelected is clear. The question, then, is what incentives this desire provides. According to the official view, the desire to be reelected by shareholders should make directors attentive to shareholder interests; the better their performance, the argument goes, the more likely they are to win reelection.

In reality, however, candidates placed on the company's slate by the board have been virtually assured of being reelected. Dissident shareholders contemplating putting forward their own director slate have confronted substantial obstacles.[10] As a result, the director slate proposed by the company has almost always been the only one on the ballot. In a recent empirical study of the seven-year period 1996–2002, we document that, outside the context of hostile takeovers, the incidence of electoral challenges to the board's slate was practically nonexistent—no more than two a year among firms with a market capitalization exceeding $200 million.[11]

The key to a board position is, therefore, getting one's name on the company slate. And, at least thus far, CEOs have had considerable and sometimes decisive influence over the nomination process.[12] Most boards have had a nominating committee, but while compensation committees have for some time been composed mostly of independent directors, this has not been true for nominating committees. Indeed, CEOs have often served on these panels.[13] A 2002 survey found that among the S&P 1500 firms that had a nominating committee, only 50 percent were fully independent.[14]

Even CEOs not formally serving on the nominating committee have had a significant influence on the nomination process.[15] Boards and nominating committees have been unlikely to nominate a director clearly opposed by the CEO. At a minimum, CEOs have had considerable power to block nominations. Thus, sparring with the CEO over executive compensation could have only hurt a director's chances of being renominated to the board. "Going along" with the CEO's pay arrangement has been a much safer strategy.

Under the NYSE's new listing requirements, the firm must have a nominating committee staffed solely with independent directors. NASDAQ's new listing provisions require that director nominees be selected or recommended either by a majority of the independent directors or by a nominating committee composed solely of such directors.[16] These requirements might significantly reduce CEOs' influence over the nomination process. But taking care not to upset the compensation apple cart may well remain the best bet for remaining on a company's slate.

Even if the CEO's power over director nomination declines, the CEO's wishes can be expected to continue to influence the decisions of the nominating committee; after all, the directors appointed to the board will have to work with the CEO. Indeed, experts interviewed by the *Wall Street Journal* have advised boards to consult with management on the independent nominating committee's choices. And, as a lawyer who has served on the boards of several public companies said, "I think as a practical matter, few new directors would accept without knowing that the CEO is enthusiastic about the decision.... No one likes to go to the boardroom thinking they've been imposed on the CEO."[17]

Even if the CEO had no influence over nominations, fighting with the CEO over the amount or performance sensitivity of compensation might be viewed unfavorably by independent directors on the nominating committee. These directors might prefer to exclude an individual whose poor relationship with the CEO undermines board collegiality. They might also wish to avoid the friction and unpleasantness likely to accompany disputes over the CEO's compensation. Finally, the directors might side with the CEO for other reasons to be discussed below.

To be sure, the effect of the new stock exchange regulations boosting the role of independent directors in the nominating process will become clear only with time. At this stage, however, it appears likely that as long as the key to board appointment remains being on the company's slate, the safest strategy for directors wishing to keep their board seats will be to avoid challenging CEO compensation. This state of affairs would be likely to change, we believe, only under fundamental reforms that give shareholders a more meaningful role in the selection of directors.

## CEOs' Power to Benefit Directors

Putting aside the issue of reelection to the board, directors, including independent directors, have other economic incentives to be on good terms with the CEO. CEOs have a great deal of power apart from their influence over board nominations. They have substantial control over the firm's resources, and their position sometimes gives them significant influence outside the firm. CEOs can use this power to benefit individual directors directly or indirectly. In the past, CEOs have displayed considerable willingness to use their power to reward friendly directors in myriad ways. And the new stock exchange criteria for "independent directors," discussed in detail below, reduce but do not eliminate the CEO's ability to benefit independent directors.

### Current and Past Practices

In the wake of the high-profile corporate scandals beginning in late 2001, evidence emerged suggesting that some CEOs had effectively bought off directors by providing them individually with special perks or monetary benefits.[18] While the practice of business dealings with directors has received much attention in the cases of companies tainted by scandal such as Enron, WorldCom, and Tyco, it has hardly been limited to such companies. Many other firms have also engaged directly and indirectly in such business dealings.[19] For example, Verizon's 2001 board included an executive director of Boston Consulting Group, which received $3.5 million from Verizon for services in 2000; the CEO of a railroad that was paid $650,000 by Verizon for services and products; and two attorneys from law firms that provided Verizon with legal services. Bank of America's 2001 board included high-ranking officials from three property businesses that received $3.47 million from the bank in rental fees the previous year.

Companies expend billions of dollars annually on charitable contributions,[20] and CEOs have used their power to direct contributions to benefit directors. It has been common practice for companies to make charitable contributions to nonprofit organizations that employ or are headed by a director. Verizon contributed hundreds of thousands of dollars annually to the National Urban League, whose head sat on Verizon's board.[21] Oracle, which has on its board three Stanford University professors and a Stanford alumnus who is active in the university's affairs, has been making large contributions to the university.[22] Furthermore, to reward directors who are not employed by charities, CEOs have used their power to direct contributions to those directors' favored charitable organizations.[23] Enron, for example, donated millions of dollars to some of its directors' favorite causes.[24]

### The New Independence Standards and Their Limits

The listing standards adopted by the stock exchanges in 2003 will in the future place some limits on CEOs' ability to reward independent directors.[25] However, these standards leave CEOs with substantial power in this area. To begin with, the rules do not prohibit a firm from giving directors compensation on top of their director fees; rather, they only limit the amount of such compensation. Under the NYSE listing standards, for example, directors can still be considered independent even if they receive up to $100,000 a year in such additional compensation, hardly a negligible amount for many directors.[26] Moreover, under the NYSE requirements, compensation given to an immediate family member who is a nonexecutive employee of the company would not count toward this $100,000 limit.[27]

Similarly, the new stock exchange requirements limit but do not prohibit business dealings between a company and a firm associated with one of its independent directors. Under the NYSE standards, a director who is an officer or an employee of another business is presumed to be independent as long as the other business receives from the company less than $1 million annually (and less than 2 percent of the other firm's gross revenues).[28] Business dealings below this ceiling might well be economically significant for many directors. Consider a partner in a large New York law firm who is both a director of a company and one of its outside lawyers, for which the partner's law firm receives $900,000 each year. This amount of business might well matter to the director, even if it represents less than 2 percent of his or her law firm's gross revenues.

Now consider a member of a company's board who is a partner in a law firm that is not currently providing services to the company. This lawyer still has an economic incentive to remain on good terms with the CEO because the company could be a future client. Fighting with the CEO over compensation is hardly a good way to get the company's legal business. Of course, if the company ends up giving a large amount of business to the lawyer's firm—say, work on acquisitions with many millions in fees—then the partner will no longer be able to qualify as an independent director. The point, however, is that the possibility of such future business might affect the lawyer's economic incentives even while the lawyer is still an independent director. This point also highlights how difficult it is to prevent directors who have ties to a business from being influenced by the CEO's power over the company's resources.

As for charitable contributions, the NYSE standards make it clear that the $1 million limit on business dealings does not apply to charitable contributions. A director who is an officer or employee of a charitable organization can still be considered independent even if the firm on whose board the director sits contributes more than $1 million to that organization. The only requirement is that the contributions be disclosed.[29] And even disclosure is not necessary when the firm contributes to a charitable organization at the suggestion of a director who is not an officer or an employee of that organization.

Should the above problems be addressed by tightening the tests of director independence? When we examine the subject of future reforms in the concluding chapter, we argue that even complete director independence from executives would be insufficient to ensure board accountability to shareholders; some dependence on shareholders is essential. For the purpose of understanding the current landscape of executive compensation, however, it is important to recognize that director independence has in the past been compromised by CEOs' ability to confer significant rewards on directors, and that recent reforms diminish but do not eliminate their ability to do so.

## Interlocks

When a director is an executive at a firm on whose board the CEO sits, the CEO has another channel for rewarding the director. In this case, the

CEO can benefit the director by using whatever influence the CEO has as a member of the other company's board.

The considered case—usually referred to as "interlocking directors"— is not as rare as one might imagine. According to one study, in approximately one out of every 12 publicly traded firms, the board is "current CEO–interlocked"—that is, the CEO of Firm A sits on the board of Firm B, and the CEO of Firm B sits on the board of Firm A.[30] The study also finds that, as might be expected, CEO pay has been larger in companies with interlocking directors.

The new stock exchange requirements reduce but do not eliminate the potential influence of interlocks on independent directors. Under these requirements, a director of Firm A who is an executive of Firm B cannot be considered independent if A's CEO (or any other of its executives) serves on B's compensation committee. However, the director of Firm A can be considered independent if A's CEO serves on Firm B's board but not on B's compensation committee. The presence of Firm A's CEO on Firm B's board might well still have an effect on the director's interests; A's CEO could be an important voice on B's board either for or against decisions favored by the director. For this reason, we expect that the practice of interlocking directors will continue to provide CEOs with another source of influence over certain directors.

### Director Compensation

Directors have a natural interest in their own compensation, which CEOs may be able to influence. As the company leader, usually as a board member, and often as board chair, the CEO has some say over director compensation. Although recommendations concerning director compensation are usually made by the compensation committee, the CEO can choose to either discourage or encourage director pay increases. Independent directors who are generous with the CEO might reasonably expect the CEO to use his or her bully pulpit to support higher director compensation. At a minimum, generous treatment of the CEO contributes to an atmosphere that is conducive to generous treatment of directors.

A study by Ivan Brick, Oded Palmon, and John Wald finds that companies with higher CEO compensation have had higher director compensation as well.[31] To be sure, high CEO and director compensation may reflect the fact that a firm is particularly difficult to run, that there is a shortage of people capable of running it, or that the firm is doing so well that the board believes both the CEO and its own members should be rewarded. But this study rejects these alternative explanations after finding that excess CEO and director compensation has been negatively associated with firm performance. This finding leads the researchers to conclude that collusion between directors and CEOs has driven the link between high director pay and high CEO pay.

## Social and Psychological Factors

Putting aside economic incentives and the desire to be renominated to the board, there are various social and psychological factors that encourage directors to go along with compensation arrangements that favor the company's CEO and other senior executives. These social and psychological factors reinforce the economic incentives to favor executives and can also affect directors who are not significantly influenced by such economic incentives. Most directors are likely to be subject to at least some of the social and psychological factors discussed below.

### Friendship and Loyalty

Let us start with social and psychological factors that operate on directors as soon as they begin serving on the board. Many independent directors have some prior social connection to, or are even friends with, the CEO or other senior executives.

Even directors who did not know the CEO before their appointment may well have begun their service with a sense of obligation and loyalty to the CEO. The CEO often will have been involved in bringing the director onto the board—even if only by not blocking the director's nomination. With such a background, directors often start serving with a reservoir of good will toward the CEO, which will contribute to a tendency not to bargain aggressively with the CEO over pay. This kind of reciprocity is expected and observed in many social and professional contexts. Not surprisingly, Brian Main, Charles O'Reilly, and James Wade find that compensation committees whose chairs have been appointed after the CEO takes office have tended to award higher CEO compensation.[32]

## Collegiality and Team Spirit

The directors who negotiate with the CEO over compensation also work closely with the CEO, who is generally a fellow member of the board and often its chair. Whether or not a particular director was appointed during the CEO's reign, that director is likely to develop a personal relationship with the CEO as well as with other directors who may be even closer to the CEO.

In addition, except perhaps in times of crisis, the members of the board are expected to act collegially toward one another. According to a director who has served on the boards of several public companies, including Marriott Corporation, "It is hard to explain to a person who is not a director. It is in many ways a club."[33] While each board may have slightly different social rules, these norms tend to foster board cohesion. As Rakesh Khurana observed in his study of CEO hiring, there is on boards "a strong emphasis on politeness and courtesy and an avoidance of direct conflict and confrontation."[34]

Perhaps once or twice a year, members of the compensation committee must take off their hats as colleagues of the CEO and put on their hats as arm's-length bargainers with the CEO over his or her compensation. This switch is likely to be difficult even for well-meaning directors attempting to represent shareholders' interests in these negotiations. Evidence indicates that individuals working within a group feel pressure to placate group members, often at the expense of interests not directly represented at the table.[35] There is no reason to believe that the members of the compensation committee are immune to such pressure.

## Authority

The CEO is not merely a colleague of the directors. The CEO is the most important figure in the corporation—the leader whose decisions and vision have the most influence on the future direction of the firm. Thus, directors naturally tend to treat the CEO with respect. They accept the CEO's authority on many corporate matters and may even look up to the CEO.

Furthermore, on many decisions for the company, board members tend to defer to the CEO even when they have a different view. On many issues, the directors' role is to provide strategic advice and serve as a sounding board but not to overrule the CEO or make decisions for the company. As long as the directors wish the CEO to remain, it makes sense not to force their views on the CEO but rather to let the CEO be in the driver's seat. And when some directors cannot in good faith continue to support a CEO who has the support of the rest of the board, they are expected to step down.[36]

Again, switching hats to bargain with the CEO over compensation is difficult. Directors who otherwise tend to treat the CEO with respect and deference will find it difficult to assume a true arm's-length bargaining posture when negotiating the CEO's pay.

## Cognitive Dissonance

In staffing compensation committees, companies have made substantial use of executives and former executives. In 2002, 41 percent of the directors on compensation committees were active executives, with about half of them active CEOs. Furthermore, another 26 percent of the members of compensation committees were individuals who had retired from their primary employment, and these retirees were for the most part former executives.[37]

The compensation decisions of directors who are or were executives themselves are likely to be affected by cognitive dissonance.[38] Individuals are known to develop beliefs that support positions consistent with their self-interest. These beliefs enable individuals to avoid the discomfort of enjoying benefits that they believe to be undeserved.

An executive or former executive who has benefited from generous and favorable pay arrangements is thus likely to have formed a belief that such arrangements are desirable and serve shareholders. For example, an executive who has benefited from, say, a conventional option plan is likely to support the view that such plans are an efficient form of compensation. Similarly, an executive who has or had a compensation agreement with generous severance provisions is unlikely to support the view that such provisions are undesirable or even counterproductive. Thus, the presence on the compensation committee of well-paid executives is likely to lead to higher pay. Indeed, Brian Main, Charles O'Reilly, and James Wade find a significant association between the compensation level of outsiders who serve on the compensation committee and CEO pay.[39]

Finally, cognitive dissonance might lead even independent directors who are not executives themselves to hold beliefs that are conducive to granting generous executive compensation. Directors will tend to err on the positive side in assessing how well the company is doing relative to its industry peers, how capable their CEO is relative to the CEO's peers, and so forth. To be sure, cognitive dissonance may also impair the thinking of individuals who are the sole owners of their own firms. But such owners will bear significant personal costs if they let themselves be overly influenced by cognitive dissonance. In contrast, for most independent directors of public companies, the personal cost of favoring executives is rather small.

## The Small Cost of Favoring Executives

Economic incentives and psychological and social factors, we have seen, all lead independent directors to favor executives. The question, then, is whether there are countervailing forces that make favoring executives prohibitively costly for directors. Unfortunately, the potential costs to most directors of favoring executives are rather small. These costs can take two forms: (1) reduction in the value of any shares that the directors own in the corporation and (2) reputational costs to the directors.

### *Reduction in the Value of Directors' Holdings*

Although stock-based compensation for independent directors has become the norm,[40] the fraction of the company's shares held by independent directors is commonly insignificant.[41] John Core, Robert Holthausen, and David Larcker found that half of the directors in their study owned 0.005 percent or less of the companies on whose boards they sat.[42] While these amounts might go up in the future,[43] most directors are likely to remain holding only a tiny fraction of the company's shares.[44]

As a result, directors commonly bear only a negligible fraction of the cost imposed by flawed compensation arrangements. Consider, for example, a director who owns 0.005 percent of the company's shares. And suppose that the director is contemplating whether to approve a compensation arrangement requested by the CEO that would reduce shareholder value by $10 million. Given the director's fraction of total shares, the reduction in the value of the director's holdings that would result from approval of the CEO's request would be only $500. Such a cost, or even one several times larger, is highly unlikely to overcome the various factors exerting pressure on the director to support the CEO's request.

Of course, although the cost of favoring executives is negligible for most independent directors, it might not be so trivial for independent directors who own (or are appointed by those owning) a large block of shares. Such directors will bear more of the cost associated with distorted compensation arrangements and will be more likely to oppose them. This fact probably accounts for the evidence that CEO pay is lower, and the sensitivity of CEO pay to firm performance is higher, when compensation committee members hold a large amount of stock.[45]

## Reputational Costs

In theory, directors who approve compensation arrangements that benefit managers at the expense of shareholders could suffer a reputational cost. Prominent financial economists Eugene Fama and Michael Jensen have argued that independent directors have an incentive to safeguard shareholder interests in order to preserve and enhance their reputations as expert decisionmakers.[46] Fama and Jensen apparently have in mind those independent directors who are CEOs or hold other decision-making positions. For such directors, the value of their human capital would depend on their decision-management reputation. According to the Fama-Jensen view, by being effective guardians of shareholder value, independent directors can signal their expertise in decision control and boost the value of their human capital in their primary careers. Furthermore, it can be argued that developing a reputation as an effective guardian of shareholder interests will improve a director's chances of landing directorships in other companies.

We agree that directors' reputations and human capital, both in their primary positions and in the market for directors, could suffer should the board approve compensation arrangements that are subsequently regarded as egregious. For example, following the Enron scandal, outrage was directed against members of the Enron board.[47] There were calls for Dr. John Mendelsohn, one former Enron director, to step down from his position as head of the M. D. Anderson Cancer Center. There was also opposition to the reelection of another former Enron board member, Frank Savage, to the boards of Lockheed Martin and Qualcomm. In the end, Mendelsohn remained head of the M. D. Anderson Cancer Center, and Savage was reelected to both boards, although he eventually resigned from Qualcomm's. Perhaps anticipating similar battles, former Enron directors Wendy Gramm, Robert Jaedicke, and Herbert Winokur Jr. simply resigned from other board positions after the scandal broke.[48]

Although concerns about reputational costs arising from egregious compensation might place some limits on how far directors will be willing to go, these limits are hardly tight. As long as the pay arrangements approved by the board are within the range of what is considered conventional and acceptable, directors are unlikely to bear reputational costs. Consider a director who also is a CEO or executive of another firm. The compensation decisions of the board on which the director serves are unlikely to influence, or even be noticed by, those who might in the future seek to appoint the director to an executive position. Prospective employers are unlikely to have much information about the contribution of a particular independent director to a company's compensation arrangements. More important, prospective employers would likely focus on directors' performance in their primary, full-time executive positions rather than on their performance in an independent directorship.

The performance of an individual independent director would probably be of most interest to those considering appointing the director to the board of another corporation. Here, however, earning a reputation for challenging CEO compensation has been unlikely to help, and if anything has been likely to hurt the director's prospects of securing appointments to other boards. Recall that the key to a board seat is being included on the company's slate, which is put together by the board and its nominating committee. A reputation for challenging CEO compensation is likely to be viewed as a minus, not as a plus, by other firms' nominating committees.

The absence of reputational incentives to guard shareholder interests in the compensation context is thus a product of the director-selection process. In chapter 16, we suggest reforms that would give shareholders meaningful opportunities to select directors. Such reforms could create incentives for directors to develop a reputation for serving shareholders rather than executives. For now, however, we cannot count on the reputational mechanism to counter directors' economic incentives and natural inclinations to side with executives.

## Insufficient Time and Information

Even independent directors who for some reason wished to serve shareholders' interests in bargaining over the CEO's pay have usually lacked the time and information to do so.[49] Most independent directors have their own full-time careers. Independent directors have typically spent little time focusing on the performance of the corporations on whose boards they sit. Surveys of board practices prior to the wave of corporate scandals that began erupting in late 2001 indicated that independent directors devoted only about 100 hours a year to each board.[50] Indeed, as Rakesh Khurana documents in his book on CEO hiring, boards have spent surprisingly little time even on the critical task of selecting a new CEO.[51]

In the last several years, the time that independent directors devote to their directorships has been increasing significantly. According to one estimate, in 2002 directors at Fortune 1000 companies spent about 190 hours on board service,[52] and the number of hours is expected to rise further. But one should keep in mind that the Sarbanes-Oxley Act and the increased formalization of board processes have also created additional demands on directors' time. Part-time independent directors will still be expected to spend a rather limited amount of time on the design and approval of complex compensation arrangements. A "best practices calendar" for corporate boards that one prominent law firm issued recently to its clients suggested that the compensation committee meet three days during the year, two days in January and one day in November.[53]

In addition to facing time constraints, many directors do not have the knowledge and expertise needed to properly evaluate the compensation arrangements they are asked to approve. Jeffrey Sonnenfeld, associate dean of Yale's School of Management, observed: "I work with several compensation committees, and I know that a lot of the time board members don't understand the complexity of the documents they're reviewing. People don't want to look foolish by asking how some of the instruments work."[54]

In reaching compensation decisions, independent directors have generally had to rely on information and advice provided by the firm's human resources department and by compensation consultants hired by the department; this reliance has further tilted matters in favor of executives.[55]

## Compensation Consultants

Directors have economic incentives and psychological tendencies that would probably produce outcomes favorable to executives even if the information and advice provided to the directors came from individuals focusing solely on shareholder interests. But the providers of information and advice themselves have their own incentives to favor executives. This has been true not only for firms' human resources departments, which are subordinate to the CEO, but also for compensation consultants. Compensation consultants have faced strong incentives to please, or at least not to anger, the CEO. As Warren Buffet remarked, compensation consultants "had no trouble perceiving who buttered their bread."[56]

Typically, consultants have been hired through a firm's human resources department, and CEOs have often been involved in the selection process.[57] Even if the CEO has not been involved, the chosen consultant has understood that a recommendation that displeases the CEO may preempt the consultant's future employment. Moreover, executive pay consultants have usually worked for consulting firms that derived most of their income from other services to firms' human resources departments. The consulting firms often had, or at least could expect to get in the future, other assignments with the hiring company. One compensation consultant commented: "There are two classes of clients you don't want to offend—actual and potential."[58]

Finally, because their incomes have not been linked to shareholder value, compensation consultants have not borne any of the costs that favoring managers has imposed on shareholders; consultants could only benefit from using their discretion to favor the CEO. Two directors interviewed by *Fortune* under conditions of anonymity described the overall incentive structure of consultants in a rather blunt way:

> I would say that it is unusual to find a consultant who does not end up, at the least, being a prostitute. The consultants are hired by management. They're going to be rehired by management.

> Any other kind of consultant you can think of is brought in to try to cut costs. [However], the basic goal of compensation consultants is to justify whatever it is the CEO wants to make. After all, who's going to recommend these consultants to other CEOs?[59]

Compensation consultants' incentives are important because they have substantial discretion in performing their tasks. Consultants provide the data that underlie directors' compensation decisions. They also frame the issues and present the menu of choices. The limited time that directors have to devote to compensation decisions, and their lack of information and expertise, lead them to rely heavily on consultants' input. Thus, a tilt in favor of executives on the part of compensation consultants could produce outcomes favorable to executives even if directors themselves did not have any incentives and tendencies to favor executives.

Among other things, consultants can favor the CEO by generating a mass of compensation data that "objectively" justifies the desired pay plan. For example, they have tended to design surveys to focus on comparative data that help make the case for higher pay.[60] When a firm did well, consultants pushed for high compensation, arguing that pay should reflect performance, and should therefore be higher than the industry average and certainly higher than the pay of CEOs who are doing poorly. When a firm did poorly, the consultants looked not to performance but rather to peer group pay norms to argue that the salary of the CEO should be higher to reflect prevailing compensation levels.[61]

In the future, compensation consultants may well be hired formally by compensation committees rather than by human resources departments. The NYSE's new listing requirements require that the charter of the compensation committee provide it with the sole authority to retain the compensation consultant assisting it in evaluating executive compensation.[62] However, the human resources department may be a source of recommendations for such a consultant. And given that consultants make most of their money providing services to human resources departments, they will continue to have strong incentives to make a favorable impression on the human resources department and to avoid annoying the CEO. Thus the reforms might reduce, but not eliminate, the additional tilt produced by compensation consultants.

In any event, giving the compensation committee sole authority to hire the compensation consultant can at most make consultants pay attention to the wishes of the committee and not to those of the executives. The compensation consultants cannot be expected to have direct incentives to focus on the interests of shareholders. Thus, to the extent that directors continue to have incentives and tendencies to favor executives, consultants can be expected to assist them in doing so.

## Newly Hired CEOs

Boards approve CEO compensation both when the CEO is hired and during the CEO's tenure. In a critique of our earlier work, Kevin Murphy claimed that incoming CEOs are unlikely to have much power over the board when they negotiate their first pay package. Even if there is no arm's-length bargaining between boards and continuing CEOs, Murphy argued, such bargaining takes place when CEOs are first hired, especially when they are hired from outside the company.[63] In our view, although negotiations with outside CEO candidates may have been closer to the arm's-length model than negotiations with incumbent CEOs, they still have deviated substantially from that model.

To be sure, some of the social and psychological factors leading directors to favor incumbent executives are absent when directors negotiate compensation arrangements with prospective outside hires. The CEO candidate was not involved in appointing any of these directors to the board. Therefore, the directors will not feel the sense of obligation and loyalty that they would feel to a CEO who supported their appointment to the board. In addition, the familiarity and collegiality that come with serving together on a board will not yet have developed.

It is nevertheless likely that bargaining over the compensation of outside CEO candidates has commonly been far from arm's length. Given that the CEO candidate will be the next CEO if the negotiations are successful, directors still have considerable incentive to please the candidate. The incoming CEO will have influence over the directors' reelection prospects and over the level of director compensation. The CEO will also be in a position to reward the directors.

Further, some of the social and psychological factors that cause directors to favor incumbent CEOs are equally present in compensation negotiations with an incoming CEO. Since directors will anticipate working closely and collegially with the incoming CEO, they will naturally want to get things off to a pleasant start. The self-serving cognitive biases that lead directors who themselves are well-paid executives to be generous with CEOs will apply equally in the case of a newly hired CEO. And, because directors typically own only a small fraction of the firm's stock, the financial cost to them of being generous to their new colleague and leader remains extremely low.

Finally, the time and information constraints that limit the abilities even of well-intentioned directors to bargain with incumbent CEOs have applied equally to board negotiations with outsiders. As Rakesh Khurana documents, directors are far from thorough even when selecting a new CEO.[64] The choice of CEO is often a more important factor for the future performance of the firm than is the particular pay arrangement with which the CEO starts. If directors put little effort into choosing the new CEO, they are unlikely to put much effort into bargaining over the CEO's compensation.

Furthermore, as in the case of incumbent CEOs, time constraints force directors considering a new CEO's pay to rely on the information and advice provided by the firm's human resources department and compensation consultants. Members of the department know that the person for whom they are designing the plan soon will be their boss. Compensation consultants have known that the incoming CEO would influence the decision of whether to continue using their services. Thus, both human resources departments and consultants have had an incentive to use their discretion to favor the new CEO.

Lastly, given the negative scrutiny that will be applied to the board if it fails to hire a replacement CEO in a timely fashion, it is in directors' interests to sacrifice hard bargaining to expedience. Acceding to the candidate's compensation demands minimizes the risk of offending the candidate or creating the impression that the board will be a tough taskmaster, thereby increasing the chances that the candidate will accept the offer. The board will not want to appear to have bungled the search by "losing" the person it thought was best suited for the job. In addition, directors will wish to complete the search process as quickly as possible to reduce the burden on them. At the same time, the cost to directors of giving in to a CEO candidate's extravagant compensation demands is trivial given their tiny stakes in the firm. Thus, directors personally have little to gain and much to lose from being a tough bargainer. In contrast, CEO candidates have every incentive to hold out for higher and less performance-sensitive pay in order to ensure that they will be well paid even when their own performance is poor. The combination of these factors operates to the benefit of newly hired CEOs.

## The (Infrequent) Firing of CEOs

The incidence of board firing of CEOs in the 1990s was somewhat higher than in earlier decades. This change has been attributed to the increased role of independent directors.[65] The willingness of some boards to fire poorly performing CEOs has received a fair amount of attention and has been regarded as a sign of improved corporate governance.[66]

Critics of our earlier work, such as Wall Street Journal columnist Holman Jenkins, have suggested that the increased willingness of boards to fire CEOs provides evidence that boards do in fact deal with CEOs at arm's length.[67] If boards are willing to go as far as firing CEOs, it is argued, surely they are capable of negotiating at arm's length over compensation. But the phenomenon of forced CEO resignations fails to demonstrate the existence of an arm's-length relationship between managers and boards.

It is important to keep in mind that the incidence of firing is still extremely low. A study of more than 1,000 companies found that between 1993 and 1999, fewer than 1 percent of all CEOs resigned or were forced out each year because of poor performance.[68] Another study reports that the turnover of CEOs of public firms is significantly less sensitive to performance than the turnover of CEOs of corporate subsidiaries.[69] CEOs of public firms usually have to perform dismally or abuse their power in order to be fired. For the board to take such a step, there must usually be substantial outside pressure of the kind produced by a highly significant and visible managerial failure or unethical behavior.

Moreover, in the rare cases where CEOs are asked to resign, the board often provides them with gratuitous goodbye payments—payments and benefits on top of those required by the CEO's contract—to sweeten the departure. We discuss these gratuitous payments in detail in chapter 7. Whether these gratuitous payments are necessary to overcome some directors' resistance to do anything that would hurt the CEO, or whether they serve to alleviate the board's discomfort with forcing out the CEO, their frequent use in cases where CEOs are asked to leave suggests that directors are not dealing with the CEO at arm's length.

Even if some boards can make detached decisions to fire CEOs in "crisis" situations, this hardly implies that boards regularly make detached decisions about "business as usual" matters, such as pay arrangements. When a corporation performs dismally, there may be substantial outside pressure on directors to solve the problem. Directors may fear that doing nothing would be such a clear and visible dereliction of duty that it would invite embarrassing public criticism or perhaps even a proxy contest. When the personal stakes are that high, the incentives to fire the CEO can overcome the social, collegial, and psychological factors that normally make directors reluctant to displease the CEO. There is, however, little risk of such outrage when the board is asked to approve compensation that is not visibly excessive.

## Better and Worse Pay-Setting Processes

Although the pay-setting process has departed from arm's-length bargaining in most widely held public companies, this process has likely worked better in some companies than in others. The myriad factors impeding arm's-length bargaining—managers' influence over director appointment, managers' ability to reward cooperative directors, the social and psychological forces leading directors to favor managers, the limited costs to directors of favoring executives, and directors' lack of sufficient time and information—vary from company to company. The stronger these factors are in aggregate, the larger will be the departure from arm's-length bargaining. In chapter 6, we discuss evidence that CEO pay is higher and less sensitive to performance when the CEO has relatively more influence over directors.

In the same way that the magnitude of departures may vary among companies, it may also change over time. The factors impeding arm's-length contracting are in part a product of legal rules and corporate practices. With the rules and practices that we have had to date, directors have been subject to a myriad of incentives and forces that have prevented them from bargaining at arm's length with the CEO over pay.

The future, of course, may differ from the past. Indeed, some take the view that, even though the pay-setting process until now has not been characterized by arm's-length negotiation, the 2003 stock exchange listing requirements regarding independent directors will move this process sufficiently close to the arm's-length ideal. As we have seen, however, the modifications of stock exchange listing requirements will weaken but fail to eliminate the various factors that have until now led directors to favor executives at the expense of shareholders.

Notwithstanding the changes in the listing requirements, independent directors will still find avoiding conflict with the CEO to be the safest strategy for being reelected to the board and otherwise rewarded by the CEO through the various channels that remain at the CEO's disposal. The social and psychological factors of friendship, collegiality, loyalty, team spirit, and natural deference to the firm's leader will continue to operate on many directors. And there will be little to counter these incentives and tendencies, given the small personal cost that favoring executives imposes on most directors.

Corporate governance experts writing in the late 1990s suggested that the increased dominance of independent directors during that decade had already made boards effective in overseeing CEO performance.[70] As we have seen, however, substantial deviations from arm's-length contracting have remained. Current predictions that the new stock exchange requirement will restore arm's-length bargaining, we believe, are also unwarranted. In chapters 15 and 16, we propose reforms that could considerably reduce CEOs' power over their boards. For now, however, we conclude that the executive compensation landscape has been very much shaped, and without additional reforms will continue to be significantly affected, by CEOs' influence over corporate directors.

# 3

## Shareholders' Limited Power to Intervene

Directors have the power, authority, and wide discretion to make decisions on executive compensation.

Delaware Supreme Court in
*Brehm v. Eisner*, 2000

HAVING SEEN THAT boards have not been bargaining at arm's length with executives, we now turn to the question of whether other constraints nevertheless compel boards and executives to adopt the same kind of pay contracts that arm's-length negotiations should theoretically produce.

In particular, shareholders have sought to constrain executive compensation arrangements in three ways—by (1) suing the board, (2) voting against employee stock option plans, and (3) putting forward shareholder resolutions. As we explain below, none of these methods has imposed significant constraints on executive pay.

### Litigation

We do not believe that the problems of executive compensation can be addressed by judicial intervention. Courts are simply ill equipped to judge the desirability of compensation packages and policies. To understand the contemporary compensation landscape, however, one must realize that courts in fact have avoided involvement in the design of compensation arrangements and that the option to seek protection from courts has not in practice been available to shareholders.

In theory, shareholders can challenge inefficient executive compensation packages in court as violations of the directors' and officers' fiduciary duties to the shareholders. If such a case were initiated, however, a court would be highly unlikely to review the substantive merits of the specific compensation arrangement. As a practical matter, judicial review has failed to impose any meaningful constraint on executive pay. In fact, a 1992 study found that courts in almost all cases since 1900 have refused to overturn compensation decisions made by the boards of publicly traded firms.[1]

Under the well-established business judgment rule, courts defer to and refuse to review the substantive merits of board decisions as long as these decisions satisfy certain process requirements. In the case of executive compensation, if nominally independent and informed directors approve the arrangement, their decision receives the protection of the business judgment rule. Furthermore, courts have not been particularly demanding when determining whether directors' decision making in fact satisfied the process requirements. Courts have generally allowed business judgment protection whenever a package has been considered and approved by a compensation committee composed of independent directors who received some materials or heard presentations from inside or outside compensation experts.

As long as a decision satisfies these undemanding process requirements, courts will generally cite the business judgment rule and refuse to consider arguments that the approved package was unreasonable. The only argument that courts would be willing to hear is that a given compensation package is so irrational that no reasonable person could approve it and that it therefore constitutes "waste."[2] As noted by the Delaware Supreme Court, this standard is an "extreme test, [that is] rarely satisfied by a shareholder plaintiff."[3] Indeed, a well-known judge stated that cases in which it is possible to demonstrate "waste" are—like the Loch Ness Monster—so rare as to be possibly nonexistent.[4]

Because some arguments can be made even in defense of plans that are highly undesirable, the standard for judicial intervention is extremely difficult to meet. In fact, a study by Mark Loewenstein reports that there have been almost no appellate court decisions involving a publicly traded company that affirm an order to reduce managerial compensation on the theory of waste.[5]

For the sake of completeness, we should note that shareholders who wish to challenge an executive compensation arrangement also face procedural barriers that make it extremely difficult even to get their substantive claims heard. Excessive compensation does not hurt shareholders directly; it hurts them indirectly, through their equity interests in the firm. Under corporate law, shareholders in such cases generally must file what is called a "derivative suit"—a suit brought on behalf of the corporation.

Because the board, not shareholders, generally makes decisions on behalf of the corporation—including decisions to initiate a lawsuit—the courts have severely restricted shareholders' ability to proceed with a derivative suit.

A major procedural restriction is the "demand requirement," which forces shareholders to demand formally that the board investigate and address the given problem before they initiate a lawsuit. If such a "demand" is not made, the board can usually have the case dismissed.[6]

If shareholders demand that the board pursue the litigation, however, the board then takes control of the lawsuit and can decide not to proceed with it. If the board appears to have acted independently and to have conducted a reasonable investigation of the allegations, the court will respect the board's decision to terminate the litigation, thus ending the legal challenge to the board's original compensation decision. As a result, the only way that shareholders can proceed with litigation is by circumventing the demand requirement. To do this, they must convince the court that making the demand is "futile."

To establish demand futility, the plaintiff must present "particularized facts" that create a reasonable doubt that the directors are disinterested and independent. This requirement is difficult to satisfy, especially given that at this stage the plaintiff has not had the opportunity to conduct "discovery," that is, to obtain relevant documents and take depositions from the defendants.

Finally, even when shareholders satisfy the demand futility requirement, the board can still appoint a "special litigation committee" of independent directors to consider whether continuation of the suit is in the "best interest" of the firm. If the committee recommends termination, the court will likely defer to this decision and dismiss the suit. All in all, there are many procedural hurdles to overcome before a court will hear a claim involving executive compensation, and even then the shareholders will still have to win on the merits—a daunting task given courts' deference to the business judgment of directors.

Recent litigation in the Delaware courts involving the Disney company has received a great deal of attention and has been viewed by some as signaling a change in the judicial attitude toward compensation arrangements.[7] The case involves Michael Ovitz, who left Disney after serving as president for less than a year. Although his performance was widely regarded as a failure, he walked out with a package valued at more than $100 million thanks to a counterproductive no-fault termination clause.

Under this clause, as long as Ovitz's behavior did not amount to "malfeasance," termination following poor performance still entitled him to receive as much compensation as if he had served his full contract.

The Delaware Supreme Court upheld the decision of the lower court not to hear arguments that the package was undesirable because of the perverse incentives it provided to Ovitz. But the high court did give plaintiffs an opportunity to submit to the lower court an amended complaint based on flaws in the compensation-setting process. When plaintiffs then unearthed evidence about the egregiously careless way in which the compensation committee approved the package, the lower court decided to permit the case to proceed, and the case is now being litigated. That this case was allowed to proceed, rather than dismissed at the outset, has been viewed as a great victory for the shareholder plaintiffs.

Although this litigation may recover some value for Disney's shareholders, it in fact highlights the considerable limits to judicial involvement in this area. The case does not signal any willingness on the part of courts to review the substantive merits of compensation arrangements. Rather, the case was permitted to proceed only because of unique circumstances that suggested shocking director carelessness. The Disney plaintiffs unearthed evidence suggesting that the compensation committee approved the arrangement after spending a small fraction of a one-hour meeting on it, without receiving any materials in advance or any recommendations from an expert, and without even seeing a draft of the agreement. In the future, boards can easily ensure that such circumstances do not arise.

Thus, the Disney case suggests only that courts may be willing to hear suits against directors who lack a paper record showing even a minimal level of deliberation and seriousness. As long as the compensation committee receives relevant materials and spends some time examining them, however, courts have not shown any indication of abandoning their longstanding (and understandable) reluctance to constrain directors' discretion in shaping compensation packages.

## Voting on Option Plans

In 2003, the SEC approved revisions to stock exchange rules that will require a shareholder vote on most stock option plans. At least in theory, then, public shareholders now have an opportunity to influence executive compensation when they vote on stock option plans.

Even before shareholder voting on option plans became mandatory, however, shareholders were already voting on most stock option plans.[8] In many cases, shareholders had the right under state corporate law or stock exchange rules to approve or reject equity-based compensation plans. Shareholders of firms incorporated in New York, for example, have the right to vote on all stock option plans. The corporate statutes of all states require shareholder approval of amendments to the corporate charter, and the implementation of some stock option plans has required increasing the number of shares authorized in the charter. Finally, the stock exchanges had preexisting rules requiring shareholder approval of stock option plans that were not broadly based.

Even when firms were not required to put option plans to shareholder vote, they often chose to do so. Section 162(m) of the Internal Revenue Code disallows deductions of compensation exceeding $1 million per year unless the compensation is "performance-based," and one of the requirements for a performance-based option plan is that it receive shareholder approval. Thus, boards seeking to preserve the deductibility of executive compensation often have allowed shareholders to vote on option plans even when such a vote was not required by corporate statute or stock exchange rules. Finally, boards often sought shareholder ratification of option plans to provide enhanced protection from fiduciary duty suits relating to the firm's use of employee options.[9]

Unfortunately, shareholder voting on option plans has not provided a strong impediment to deviations from arm's-length bargaining. For starters, the plans on which shareholders vote generally do not specify the design of a particular executive's compensation. Instead, they set out general parameters for the use of stock options, such as the total number of options that can be issued under the plan. Shareholders cannot reject or approve a particular executive's pay package.

To be sure, shareholders have been able to reject an option plan to protest inappropriate CEO compensation. But they could have hardly relied on such rejection to make themselves better off. When shareholder ratification of a plan is essential to executive retention, vetoing the plan might well lead to a management crisis. In addition, failure to ratify might prompt the board to provide executives with additional compensation in ways likely to be even more inefficient and costly for shareholders. A board can switch to arrangements that are similar to options but that do not require the issuance of actual securities, such as share appreciation rights. These rights promise executives future cash payments based on the appreciation of the company's stock price. Perhaps worse, the board can offer compensation that is not equity based at all, such as large cash bonus plans. As we will discuss in chapter 10, such plans are often quite insensitive to performance.

Furthermore, in cases in which shareholder approval was needed primarily to enable the firm to obtain a tax deduction, shareholders would have shot themselves in the foot had they rejected the option plan. The board would still have been able to grant the options, and the firm would simply have lost the tax deduction. Indeed, proxy materials distributed in connection with such votes have generally put shareholders on notice that the board may grant options without shareholder approval, and institutional investors have generally assumed that the board was prepared to do so.[10] Now that shareholder approval is required for most option plans, firms will not be able to threaten to grant options without shareholder approval. However, shareholders will likely remain concerned about the possibility that the board will instead offer executives generous plans not based on stock options that could be worse for shareholders in terms of after-tax cost or the provision of incentives.

It is also worth noting that current voting processes in publicly traded companies have built-in biases toward management-sponsored proposals. Given the difficulty of collective action, it is rarely worthwhile for any given shareholder to expend significant resources to campaign against a proposed option plan. In contrast, the firm covers whatever expenses are incurred in soliciting proxies for the board's proposals.

Furthermore, managers have been able to count on certain votes beyond their own. Many firms have an employee stock ownership plan (ESOP), and the management-appointed trustee who controls the voting of those shares can generally be expected to vote for management-sponsored proposals. In addition, as is now widely recognized, the votes of some institutional investors have been biased in favor of management.[11] Many such investors, including insurance companies, mutual funds, and banks, have or hope to have business dealings with the firm, such as managing the firm's employee retirement accounts. Thus, such funds have an interest in being on good terms with management. Indeed, there is evidence that the tighter the business ties between a firm and its institutional shareholders, the higher its CEO's compensation.[12]

Given that a particular money manager's vote is unlikely to be pivotal, and that whatever benefits may arise from voting for efficient compensation will largely be captured by other investors, the money manager's other business interests may substantially influence voting decisions. This problem received great media attention in connection with the HP-Compaq merger in 2002. In that case, accusations arose that Deutsche Bank cast its portfolio votes in favor of management because of its business with the company.[13] Because executive compensation is a matter especially dear to management's heart, and voting against an option plan provides at most a limited benefit to shareholders, institutional investors are unlikely to oppose a management-backed stock option plan.

Until 2003, managers could also count on broker support in votes on certain option plans—those that did not involve more than 5 percent of the firm's outstanding shares.[14] The stock exchanges permitted brokers to vote customers' shares in connection with such plans and other "routine" management proposals whenever the customers did not provide specific voting instructions. As a result, brokers typically voted 10–15 percent of outstanding shares and almost uniformly voted with management.[15] Two researchers studying broker voting estimated that brokers provided the swing vote in about 12 percent of routine stock option plan proposals.[16] In 2003, the SEC approved changes to stock exchange rules on broker voting that effectively prohibit broker voting on all major stock exchanges in connection with equity compensation plans.[17] Thus, managers will still be able to look to the ESOP trustee and institutional investors for support on management stock option proposals, but not to brokers.

Consistent with the above analysis, only 1 percent of option plans put to a vote in the past have failed to obtain shareholder approval.[18] Thus, shareholder voting on option plans has been a weak constraint on compensation arrangements. And although recent stock exchange requirements will strengthen this constraint somewhat, it is still unlikely that shareholder voting will eliminate substantial departures from arm's-length arrangements.

## Voting on Precatory Resolutions

In addition to voting on some option plans, shareholders have also been able to initiate and put to a shareholder vote "precatory" resolutions on various corporate matters. (The resolutions are called "precatory" because they are not binding on the board even if they garner support from a majority of the voting shareholders.) Many of these resolutions have focused on executive compensation. A study by the proxy soliciting firm

Georgeson Shareholder reports that 40 percent of the 427 shareholder-initiated governance resolutions brought to a vote in 2003 dealt with compensation-related issues.[19]

Until recently, most of the precatory resolutions on executive compensation were offered by social or labor activists. A substantial fraction proposed drastic measures, such as low ceilings on executive pay or the elimination of options. Given that institutional investors have not favored such measures, it is not surprising that executive compensation resolutions have, on average, received little support.[20] In recent years, however, an increasing number of precatory resolutions have called for changes that institutional investors favor, such as expensing stock options, and these proposals have received significant support.[21]

Even when unsuccessful in attracting a majority of votes, shareholder resolutions on executive compensation have put some pressure on boards by focusing shareholder and media attention on managers' pay. These proposals strengthen the "outrage constraint" that may limit departures from efficient arm's-length arrangements. Resolutions with strong shareholder backing have naturally put more pressure on boards.

But voting on such resolutions, as well as on option plans, cannot effectively prevent departures from arm's-length contracting. The basic problem is that such resolutions can provide only a limited constraint on board discretion as long as they are merely advisory. Indeed, boards commonly decline to implement precatory resolutions that obtain support from a majority of the shareholders.[22] Shareholder proposals would become a more meaningful constraint only if shareholders could adopt resolutions that are binding on the board, a reform that we advocate in chapter 16.

# 4

## The Limits of Market Forces

Incentives present in existing markets generally induce managers to act in investors' interests.

Judge (and former University of Chicago Law School professor) Frank Easterbrook, 1984

**W**E SAW THAT boards have not been bargaining at arm's length and that shareholders have lacked the power to make boards adopt arm's-length arrangements. We now examine whether market forces can exert sufficient pressure on firms to compel such an outcome. An important school of thought maintains that markets—for managerial labor, corporate control, capital, and products—effectively align the interests of managers and shareholders. This "Chicago School" view is associated with the work of such legal academics as Frank Easterbrook and Daniel Fischel and such financial economists as Eugene Fama.[1] We agree that market forces place constraints on executive compensation. These constraints, however, are far from tight enough to ensure that compensation arrangements do not substantially deviate from what arm's-length contracting would produce.

In earlier work, one of us has shown that market forces can correct agency problems with respect to some but not all types of managerial decisions. In particular, market mechanisms cannot deter managers from exploiting opportunities to take "significantly redistributive" actions—actions that transfer to managers value that is not much smaller than the resulting loss to shareholders.[2] In such cases, the benefit a manager reaps by taking the action is likely to exceed the penalty that markets might impose on him or her for the resulting share price decline.

Extracting higher executive compensation is a prime example of a significantly redistributive action. The personal gains to the executive are direct and can be quite large. Obtaining favorable compensation arrangements is thus the type of action that market forces cannot be expected to eliminate. We examine below each of the market forces and explain why they are unlikely to impose tight constraints on executive pay.

## Managerial Labor Markets

The behavior of employees—senior executives are, after all, employees—is usually affected by the labor market. Good performance by employees may be rewarded by promotion within the firm or by an attractive offer to join another firm. Poor performance may lead to dismissal.

For the CEO, however, internal promotion is impossible. There is always a chance of external promotion—becoming the head of a larger or more prestigious firm—but most CEO positions are filled internally.[3] A large majority of CEOs do not become CEOs of other firms.[4]

In any event, the likelihood of outside promotion depends on a CEO's overall performance, not on the CEO's pay package. The possibility of being hired elsewhere is unlikely to deter a CEO from seeking higher pay, and pay that is less performance sensitive, at least as long as the pay package does not visibly fall outside the range of what is conventional and acceptable. Indeed, when CEOs do get new jobs, the initial hiring grants from their new firms are highly correlated with the value of the unvested options and restricted stock the CEOs leave behind.[5] If anything, the prospect of being hired by another firm increases rather than decreases executives' incentive to obtain favorable pay arrangements.

Fear of dismissal also does not deter CEOs from seeking favorable pay arrangements. CEO dismissal is quite rare, and the risk of being fired depends mostly on overall firm performance, not on the type of pay package sought by the CEO.

Finally, one aspect of the labor market that is thought to discourage managers from actions that decrease shareholder value is executive compensation itself. Any reduction in shareholder value decreases the value of shares and options granted as part of the CEO's executive compensation. Equity-based compensation might indeed discourage managers from taking actions that result in personal gains that are small relative to corporate losses. The direct benefits that managers reap from increasing their pay, however, might well be larger that any resulting reduction in the value of their shares.

Studies indicate that the shares and options owned by the average CEO increase the CEO's personal wealth by approximately 1 percent of any increase in the stock market capitalization of the firm's equity.[6] Consider an "average" CEO who is contemplating whether to seek an extra $10 million in compensation, which, because of the poor incentives generated by the arrangement, will reduce firm value by $100 million. The arrangement would provide an extra $10 million in compensation while reducing the value of the CEO's existing shares and options by $1 million, leaving a net gain of $9 million. As this example illustrates, managers' holdings of shares and options have been unlikely to dissuade CEOs from seeking higher—and potentially inefficient—compensation arrangements.

## Market for Corporate Control

The market for corporate control is often viewed as an important mechanism for aligning the interests of managers and shareholders.[7] In theory, a company whose share price sags should become more vulnerable to a hostile takeover, which might lead to the replacement of the CEO and the entire board. Alternatively, the incumbents could be ousted through a proxy contest. The fear of a hostile takeover or proxy contest, runs the argument, should compel executives and directors to craft pay arrangements that maximize shareholder value.

In fact, the fear of a control contest has been unlikely to discourage managers from seeking greater compensation because existing rules and arrangements have provided incumbents with substantial protection from removal. As noted earlier, outsider challenges via proxy contests have been extremely rare. Hostile takeover bids have been more common but have confronted strong defenses.

The most significant of these defenses is the staggered board, an arrangement that prevents a hostile acquirer from gaining control for at least a year. According to a study by John Coates, Guhan Subramanian, and one of us, staggered boards are in place at a majority of publicly traded companies, and they often enable incumbent managers to completely block hostile bids that shareholders find attractive.[8] The study finds that during the second half of the 1990s, only about 1 percent of publicly traded companies received a hostile bid. Furthermore, most of the targets receiving a hostile offer remained independent or were acquired by a friendly bidder. To overcome incumbent opposition, successful hostile bidders had to pay an average premium of 40 percent. The market for corporate control has thus left managers with considerable autonomy.

Furthermore, in the rare event of a successful hostile bid, ousted incumbents do not fare too badly. As will be discussed in chapter 7, successful bids often trigger generous golden parachutes and other benefits for the target's executives.[9] Such cushioned landings have further weakened the disciplinary force of takeovers.

Furthermore, even if a takeover is a real and very costly possibility, the benefits to a CEO from favorable pay arrangements may well exceed the cost of any resulting increase in the likelihood of a control challenge. Consider an attempt by executives of a $10 billion company to increase the present value of their compensation by $100 million, and suppose that the increase would also distort incentives and thereby reduce firm value by a total of $250 million. Obviously, the $100 million direct benefit to the executives would be very large. In contrast, the increase in takeover risk resulting from a 2.5 percent reduction in firm value would probably be quite limited. Indeed, a study by Anup Agrawal and Ralph Walking reports that firms whose executives are relatively overpaid compared with their peers in the industry are not more likely to become takeover targets.[10]

To be sure, the market for control may impose some costs on managers whose pay packages are viewed as especially detrimental to shareholders. At a certain point, shareholders may become sufficiently outraged to support outside challengers in a control contest. Indeed, as we will discuss in chapter 6, CEOs of firms with weaker takeover protection get pay packages that are both smaller and more performance sensitive than those received by CEOs of firms with stronger protection. Thus, the threat of a takeover has had some effect on executive compensation. The important point, however, is that the market for corporate control, as currently operating, cannot impose substantial constraints on executive compensation and permits substantial deviations from arm's-length contracting.

## Market for Additional Capital

Another potential source of discipline arises from the possibility that the firm will need to raise additional capital in the equity market. The prospect of selling additional shares to the public might force boards and managers to exercise self-discipline and to adopt compensation arrangements that do not depart significantly from those that arm's-length contracting would yield. Most firms, however, return to the equity markets to raise capital very rarely, if at all. The chief source of capital for publicly traded firms is retained earnings, debt comes second, and equity is a distant third.[11]

Even if a situation arose in which equity markets were the only available source of financing, the absence of arm's-length contracting over compensation would not limit a firm's access to those markets. Excessive executive compensation does not make equity unavailable, it only raises the cost of equity financing: inefficient compensation arrangements reduce firm value and thus cause investors to pay less for the firm's shares in a secondary offering than they would otherwise. Firms will have to issue more shares to raise a given amount of capital but will not be denied access to equity financing.

Admittedly, a reduction in the price at which new shares would be issued would decrease the wealth of all existing shareholders, including executives. As we have noted, however, executives typically hold only a small fraction of the firm's shares and thus bear only a small part of the reduction in existing shareholders' wealth. The cost that the executives themselves would have to bear would likely to be too small to discourage them from seeking the direct benefits of favorable compensation arrangements.[12]

## Product Markets

Finally, let us consider whether product market competition places an effective constraint on executive compensation. In a competitive product market, runs the argument, excessive pay and managerial slack would produce competitive disadvantage. Such inefficiencies could cause shrinking profits, business contraction, and even failure.[13]

In fact, the redistribution of firm profits from shareholders to executives may have no significant effect on the company's operations that produce these profits. The diversion of profits to managers might not alter the cost and quality of a company's products and therefore might not interfere with the firm's ability to compete in product markets. To the extent that executive compensation arrangements distort managers' business decisions, they may reduce operational efficiency, but product markets are not usually perfectly competitive: large companies often operate in markets characterized by oligopolistic or monopolistic competition.[14] Because these firms have market power, they are able to generate considerable profits that provide additional resiliency. In such markets, distorted pay arrangements are unlikely to threaten company survival.

Even if distorted pay arrangements do seriously harm company performance, the increased likelihood of failure will not deter managers from seeking these arrangements. The direct benefit of higher compensation to executives is substantial, while its effect on the likelihood of business failure is typically small. Furthermore, the "golden goodbye" payments given to departing managers—including those who have performed quite poorly—commonly cushion executives from the effects of their own failure.

Take, for example, a bank whose CEO obtains an excessive and inefficient pay package that induces the CEO to keep unprofitable operations. The return to equity will suffer and shareholder value will be adversely affected, but the bank is unlikely to fail completely. Even if the situation becomes sufficiently serious for the bank to be forced to seek an acquirer, that transaction may not happen until after the CEO's retirement. And if it happens before, the incompetent CEO may well profit handsomely, despite having performed poorly, given the practice of rewarding executives when their firms are acquired.

## Overall Force

Even in the aggregate, then, market forces are unlikely to impose tight constraints on executive compensation. They may impose some constraints and deter managers from deviating extremely far from arm's-length contracting arrangements, but overall they permit substantial departures from that benchmark.

The conclusion that market forces do not impose stringent constraints on executive compensation is supported by the studies we will discuss in chapter 6. These studies examine the extent to which nonmarket factors—including the CEO's power vis-à-vis the board, the firm's shareholders, and potential acquirers—affect CEO pay. The evidence indicates that such nonmarket factors are in fact an important determinant of CEO compensation. That these factors make a difference implies that market forces are not sufficiently strong to dictate outcomes.

# Part II

## Power and Pay

# 5

## The Managerial
## Power Perspective

What it amounts to is that there's no one representing
shareholders. It's like having labor negotiations where one
side doesn't care.

A *Fortune* 500 CEO, 2001

THE ARM'S-LENGTH contracting model, we have shown, is insufficient
to provide an adequate account of executive compensation. One must
also consider the role of managerial power. We introduce in this chapter
some conceptual building blocks of the managerial power perspective,
concepts that will be useful for examining the executive-compensation
landscape.

We will first look at the relationship between managerial power and
rents. Managers use their power to secure rents—that is, extra value beyond what they would obtain under arm's-length bargaining. Because
managers and directors might have to bear market penalties and social
costs if they adopt pay arrangements that are perceived as egregious,
"outrage" costs and constraints place some limits on deviations from
arm's-length contracting. To avoid outrage, compensation designers attempt to hide, obscure, and justify—in other words, to "camouflage"—
the amount and form of executive pay. We conclude by addressing alternative explanations of why executive compensation arrangements may
deviate from arm's-length outcomes.

### Power and Rents

Like the arm's-length contracting view, the managerial power analysis
begins by recognizing the agency problem inherent in the manager-
shareholder relationship. The managerial power approach, however, does
not view executive compensation primarily as a remedy for this agency

61

problem; on the contrary, the pay-setting process is itself seen as a major part of the problem. And, in contrast with the arm's-length contracting approach, the managerial power approach does not assume that the board focuses solely on shareholders' interests when negotiating executive pay arrangements.

Our analysis in the preceding chapters identified a myriad of factors that enable managers to have considerable power and influence over directors and, in turn, over the managers' own pay. We can expect managers to use this power to obtain compensation more favorable than they would get under arm's-length bargaining. Their power enables them to extract rents.

Economists use the term "rents" to refer to extra returns that firms or individuals obtain due to their positional advantages. We will use the term to refer to the additional value that managers obtain beyond what they would get in arm's-length bargaining with a board that had both the inclination to maximize shareholder value and the necessary time and information to perform that task properly.

It is important to emphasize that the power on which we focus is different from whatever "bargaining power" executives might have in a true arm's length negotiation because of their personal capabilities and characteristics. For example, a particular executive might enjoy bargaining power vis-à-vis the company by bringing to the table a unique set of management skills. The bargaining power provided by such unique skills would enable the executive to obtain higher pay even if the company had a sole owner and the sole owner were conducting the bargaining over the executive's compensation. Similarly, such bargaining power would also help the executive in negotiations with a board solely dedicated to shareholder interests. Accordingly, the presence and use of such bargaining power are not inconsistent with arm's-length bargaining. In contrast, our focus is on the power that executives have over their boards that enables the executives to obtain value beyond what they would receive in arm's-length negotiations, given whatever bargaining position they have vis-à-vis the company by virtue of their skills.

The rents captured by managers with power come in different forms. Managers, like most people, generally prefer to have more money rather than less, so we can expect executives to use their power to obtain higher pay than they would receive under arm's-length contracting. It is important to recognize, however, that compensation arrangements may also favor managers in other ways. For a given amount of compensation, managers prefer to bear less risk and feel less pressure to generate shareholder value. Managers wish to enjoy as much slack as possible. A primary objective of efficient compensation arrangements is to reduce slack, that is, to discourage managers from pursuing strategies, such as corporate empire building, that serve their interests but not shareholders' interests. When they can get away with it, managers like to have their cake and eat it, too; they prefer to receive a given amount of monetary compensation without cutting managerial slack.

Given a certain amount of expected compensation, managers would prefer to have that compensation decoupled from performance. The more their compensation depends upon their performance, the more risk managers must bear, the more effort they must exert, and the more they must forgo self-serving strategies such as empire building.

Consider the following two pay arrangements. In the first, a CEO is guaranteed to receive $5 million regardless of company performance. In the second, a performance-dependent arrangement, the manager receives $5 million only if the firm meets certain performance targets. Suppose the performance-dependent arrangement will induce the manager to meet the performance target (and thus earn $5 million) by taking steps that are personally costly, such as trimming the size of the firm, abandoning a pet project, firing an unproductive crony, and so forth. Though the CEO can expect to earn $5 million under both packages, the first package is more favorable because it does not require acting against the executive's private interests.

Note that if the CEO uses influence to acquire the first arrangement, the personal benefit of the resulting managerial slack may well be smaller than the slack's cost to shareholders. Suppose that in the above example, the benefit of the slack to the manager is $2 million and its cost to shareholders is $20 million. If the manager secures the performance-independent arrangement, the resulting $2 million rent comes at a tenfold cost to shareholders. The important point here is that managers may use their influence not only to obtain more pay but also to structure that compensation in forms that are less performance sensitive. And, to the extent that deviations from arm's-length contracting lead to compensation arrangements that dilute or distort incentives and thus create efficiency costs, shareholder losses will be larger than managerial gains.

Because of the association between managerial influence and rents, the managerial power approach predicts a correlation between power and rents. All executives have some power and therefore all can secure some rents, but the amount of managerial power varies across firms depending on each firm's ownership and governance structures. The greater the CEO's power, the managerial power approach predicts, the larger the CEO's rents will tend to be.[1] As we will discuss in chapter 6, empirical evidence confirms this prediction.

## The CEO and Other Top Executives

Who receives rents under the managerial power model? The CEO, of course. But sometimes other top executives receive rents as well. Although the CEO is likely to have the most power and influence, in many cases other top executives also have some influence on board decision making.[2] When executives other than the CEO serve on the board, for example, some of the factors that provide the CEO with influence on other directors also benefit the other executives. All the executives over the board, for example, gain from the forces of collegiality, team spirit, and respect for those leading the firm. And, as members of the board, they may also have some influence on future nominations and director compensation.

Even when the only executive with influence on the board is the CEO, rents are likely to spill over to other executives. When other senior executives are friends or protégés, the CEO may use influence to obtain favorable pay arrangements for them. Increasing the pay of other top executives can also benefit the CEO by obscuring the CEO's own rent extraction. In fact, James Wade, Charles O'Reilly, and Timothy Pollock find that in firms where the CEO is highly paid (relative to similarly situated CEOs), executives at all four levels below the CEO also tend to be overpaid.[3] These spillover rents will come largely at the expense of shareholders.[4]

In sum, the CEO's compensation will almost always reflect managerial power, and in many companies the same will be true for other top executives. Thus, our analysis applies to the compensation of such top executives and not only to CEO compensation.

## "Outrage" Costs and Constraints

Managers' potential rents are not unlimited. Although market forces, the need for board approval, and social sanctions do not altogether prevent deviations from arm's-length contracting, they do place some constraints on compensation arrangements.

In the face of these constraints, how far firms will go in favoring managers will depend not only on how much contemplated arrangements will actually favor executives but also on how these arrangements will be perceived by outsiders. Whether directors and managers will be deterred from adopting a given compensation arrangement depends on the extent to which it will be viewed by relevant outsiders as unjustified or even abusive or egregious. We will broadly refer to negative reactions by outsiders as "outrage," even though some of them may amount to criticism not reaching the level of outrage, and to the costs that such reactions impose on managers and directors as "outrage costs." The more widespread and strong these negative reactions are—that is, the greater the outrage—the larger the costs to directors and managers. When the potential outrage costs are large enough, they will deter the adoption of arrangements that managers would otherwise favor. We shall refer to arrangements that are deterred in this way as ones that violate the "outrage constraint."

Why should perceptions—and, in particular, outrage—matter? To begin with, the extent to which markets penalize managers and directors for the adoption of particular arrangements will depend on how these arrangements are perceived. Consider the market for corporate control. This market may penalize the adoption of arrangements highly favorable to managers by increasing the vulnerability of managers and directors to a control contest. Such a penalty is likely to be significant only if the firm adopts compensation arrangements that appear sufficiently outrageous. Institutional investors may view such arrangements as a strong signal that the executives or directors are relatively insensitive to shareholder interests. These investors may become less likely to support the incumbents should a hostile takeover or a proxy fight occur. In this manner, through the operation of the market for corporate control, outrage over compensation can impose a penalty on managers and directors.

Consider also the labor market and the reputation of managers and directors in this market. Reputational damage might have an adverse effect on the future career prospects of managers and directors. It might also affect their current business dealings with others outside the firm. Indeed, some outside directors join boards partly for the prestige and connections that the posts provide, and gaining a bad reputation could take away these benefits and impose costs instead. Reputational losses to managers and directors will likely be significant, however, only if their firms adopt compensation arrangements that generate sufficiently negative reactions—that is, sufficient outrage. An arrangement that fails to serve shareholders would be unlikely to impose such costs as long as it falls within the range of what is perceived as conventional and legitimate.

Indeed, we believe that arrangements that are perceived as abusive or outrageous impose on executives greater costs than an analysis based solely on the above market incentives suggests. That is, we believe that constraints on rent extraction are somewhat tighter than suggested by an analysis of the (limited) market penalties that outrageous compensation arrangements involve. In chapter 2, we explained that directors are affected not only by "narrow" interests of a *homo economicus* but also by various social and psychological factors (such as collegiality, loyalty, and so forth) that pull them in the direction of favoring executives. Similarly, there are social and psychological factors that increase the costs that managers and directors incur from adopting arrangements that are viewed by outsiders as sufficiently outrageous.

Managers and directors are likely to care about the extent to which relevant social and professional groups view them with approval and esteem. Directors are likely to prefer to avoid criticism or ridicule from the social or professional groups whose opinions they value—even if such criticism or ridicule does not involve any economic losses for them.[5] As a result, even if the economic incentives provided by the markets for corporate control and managerial labor would be insufficient to deter managers from seeking certain outrageous compensation, fear of embarrassment or criticism could discourage managers from doing so. When former General Electric CEO Jack Welch made headlines by giving up much of the retirement perks to which he was contractually entitled— including the free use of a corporate jet and a New York apartment—he was undoubtedly seeking to protect the approval and esteem he had earlier enjoyed at the expense of his narrow economic interests.[6]

Clearly, for outrage to impose significant costs, it must be sufficiently widespread among a relevant group of observers. It is not enough for a small group of researchers or arbitrageurs to identify a compensation scheme as egregiously bad for shareholders. For executives or directors to be adversely affected in a material way by market penalties or social costs, the outrage must be shared by those outsiders whose views matter most to them: the institutional investor community, the business media, and social and professional groups to which directors and managers belong.

## Camouflage

The main costs to directors and managers of adopting compensation arrangements that favor managers, then, depend mainly not on how costly the arrangements actually are to shareholders, but on how costly the arrangements are *perceived* to be by important outsiders. Perceptions matter. This brings us to another concept that is critical for understanding the compensation landscape: camouflage.

Because perceptions are so important, the designers of compensation plans can limit outside criticism and outrage by dressing, packaging, or hiding—in short, camouflaging—rent extraction. The more reasonable and defensible a package appears, the more rents managers can enjoy without facing significant outrage. Accordingly, under the managerial power approach, managers will prefer compensation practices that obscure the total amount of compensation, that appear to be more performance based than they actually are, and that package pay in ways that make it easier to justify and defend.

The greater the ability of plan designers to engage in camouflage, the more they can be expected do so. Before 1992, the SEC required firms to report executive compensation to the public but allowed them to do so in the format of their choosing. Not surprisingly, firms took full advantage of their discretion to obscure the amount and form of their pay. An SEC official describes the pre-1992 state of affairs as follows:

> The information [in the executive compensation section] was wholly unintelligible. . . . The typical compensation disclosure ran ten to fourteen pages. Depending on the company's attitude toward disclosure, you might get reference to a $3,500,081 pay package spelled out rather than in numbers. That gives you an idea of the nature of the disclosures: it was legalistic, turgid, and opaque; the numbers were buried somewhere in the fourteen pages. Someone once gave a series of institutional investor analysts a proxy statement and asked them to compute the compensation received by the executives covered in the proxy statement. No two analysts came up with the same number. The numbers that were calculated varied widely.[7]

In 1992, the SEC tightened its disclosure rules by providing standards for how information about executive pay must be presented. The standardized compensation tables that firms now must use have made camouflage more difficult. As we describe in subsequent chapters, however, the 1992 disclosure requirements have hardly brought an end to firms' ability to camouflage the amount and form of executive pay.

One might reasonably ask how, if rent extraction is camouflaged, any observer (including this book's authors) can determine that executives are enjoying rents. In theory, rent extraction could be camouflaged so well that it becomes absolutely undetectable. In fact, however, camouflage is successful as long as the rent extraction is not apparent to those outside observers whose outrage would be particularly costly for directors and managers, even if other observers are aware that the executives are enjoying large rents.

Thus, the notion of camouflage is consistent with the possibility that an outsider might identify the hidden rents of a compensation arrangement. Such a conclusion would simply reflect the observer's judgment, not yet widely shared, that the compensation program is distorted in favor of managers. In time, of course, such conclusions might become widely accepted, in which case the rent extraction will no longer be camouflaged. But a given form of rent extraction might continue to be camouflaged long after it has been recognized by some observers.

## Outrage and Camouflage at Work

Some critics of our earlier work argued that the idea of outrage costs, and the related idea of camouflage, are not empirically testable.[8] But this is not the case. There is evidence that directors and executives are indeed influenced—in compensation and other types of decisions—by strong outside criticism and outrage. And there is evidence that they engage in camouflage.

To begin with, there is evidence that shareholder precatory resolutions that criticize managers' high compensation have an impact. Although such resolutions are nonbinding and generally fail to pass anyway, their appearance may shine a critical light on problematic aspects of the firm's executive compensation policies and make them less opaque. Indeed, a study by Randall Thomas and Kenneth Martin examined the effect of pay-related precatory resolutions during the mid-1990s and found that they had a moderating influence on subsequent compensation decisions.[9] The study found that during the two-year period following the passage of shareholder resolutions criticizing executive pay in particular firms, total compensation (adjusted for industry) in those firms declined by a statistically significant average of $2.7 million. In a subsequent study, the researchers also found that higher negative votes on management-sponsored proposals to ratify an option plan slowed the increase in CEO compensation in subsequent years.[10]

Another study, by Alexander Dyck and Luigi Zingales, documents the effects of media scrutiny on corporate decisions in general. The authors found that such attention leads firms to adopt more environmentally friendly policies, for example. As for issues of corporate governance, they also found that media attention reduces the amount of value that controlling shareholders siphon off.[11]

A well-known example of how outside criticism affects governance decisions involves the campaign of shareholder activist Robert Monks against the directors of Sears. During the late 1980s and early 1990s, Monks urged the Sears board to adopt various proposals to improve the firm's dismal performance. In April 1992, having been repeatedly ignored by the board, Monks took out an advertisement in the *Wall Street Journal* titled "The Non-performing Assets of Sears" and identified the directors by name. The presumably embarrassed directors then adopted many of Monks's proposals, generating an abnormal stock price return (the change in stock price adjusted for overall stock market movements) of almost 10 percent when the changes were announced.[12]

Another example is the California State Pension Fund for Public Employees' (CalPERS) practice of identifying poorly run companies. For some years, CalPERS put poorly performing firms on what it called its "focus list" and suggested various ways to improve their corporate governance practices, such as making compensation and nominating committees fully independent. In many cases, firms placed on the list implemented some of the requested changes. Then, in 1991, after several CEOs told CalPERS that being less antagonistic would be even more effective, CalPERS decided to adopt a "kinder, gentler" approach that did not involve public shaming. Absent the threat of adverse publicity, however, firms approached by CalPERS were actually much less cooperative. The then-CEO of CalPERS, Dale Hanson, said at the time, "It has shown us that a number of companies won't move unless they have to deal with the problem because it's in the public eye." In 1992, CalPERS reinstated its policy of publicly shaming uncooperative firms.[13]

In fact, CalPERS' policy of shaming has had a measurable effect on targeted corporations. YiLin Wu found that firms put on CalPERS' poor governance focus list were subsequently more likely to reduce the number of inside directors on their boards. These firms were also more likely to experience CEO turnover.[14] Shaming also appears to have adversely affected the careers of inside directors who left the targeted firms' boards. They were much less likely than inside directors departing nontargeted firms to land other board positions. As this study makes clear, negative publicity—or outrage—does impose costs.

Finally, and perhaps most importantly, there is substantial evidence of camouflage activities. A testable implication of the camouflage idea is that when compensation arrangements deviate from arm's-length bargains, they should do so in a way that makes the amount of pay or the insensitivity of pay to performance less visible. This prediction is borne out by actual compensation practices. As we shall describe in subsequent chapters, many common compensation practices—such as retirement pay, deferred-compensation arrangements, company loans, and the structure of conventional options—provide camouflage benefits.

## The Role of Compensation Consultants

Public companies in the United States typically employ outside consultants to provide input on the executive compensation process.[15] From the arm's-length contracting perspective, the use of consultants can be justified on the grounds that they provide expert assistance in the design of pay packages: the consultants are privy to pay data that are not shared directly among companies. Firms participate in consultants' compensation surveys with the understanding that individual company data will be kept confidential. The consultants then use the data to improve the design of their clients' compensation arrangements.

Although we agree that compensation consultants can and sometimes do play a useful role, it is important to understand how they are also used to camouflage rents. The fact that directors adopt a pay package recommended by a compensation consultant—rather than developing their own—provides legitimacy. When challenged, the directors can justify their compensation decision as being based on the outside expert's recommendation.

Courts, in fact, have generally given greater deference to board decisions that relied on advice by outside experts. Compensation consultants can similarly add legitimacy to board compensation decisions in the eyes of other outsiders. In fact, James Wade, Joseph Porac, and Timothy Pollock provide evidence that pay consultants are used strategically to justify executive compensation to outsiders. Their study finds that firms that have more concentrated and active outside shareholders, which are more inclined to monitor and scrutinize pay arrangements, are more likely to rely on consultants in justifying compensation decisions.[16]

Unfortunately, the mere fact that a CEO pay's package is recommended by a compensation consultant does not mean that it is indeed well chosen. Indeed, in their study, Porac, Wade, and Pollock examined the choice of peer firms against whose performance each firm was benchmarked. They found that when a firm performed poorly relative to the industry, or the CEO was highly paid compared with other CEOs in the industry, the definition of "peer firms" was expanded beyond industry boundaries.[17] Kevin Murphy found that "two-thirds of the largest 1,000 corporations reported beating the performance of their industry peers over the last five fiscal years."[18] Such inconsistent assessments were facilitated by the co-operation of pay consultants.

## Ratcheting

The combined efforts of consultants, who have incentives to help the CEO, and boards, which are similarly inclined, have led to an escalation of pay levels over the years. John Bizjak, Michael Lemmon, and Lalitha Naveen reviewed the 1997 compensation committee reports of 100 firms in the S&P 500 index. They reported that the "vast majority" of firms that use peer groups set compensation at or above the fiftieth percentile of the peer group.[19] Such generous benchmarking is likely to boost ex-ecutive compensation over time even if managerial performance does not improve.

To investigate this phenomenon, Bizjak and his coauthors examined the actual compensation decisions of approximately 1,500 publicly traded firms during the period 1992–1998. They found that CEOs who were initially paid below the median amount received larger than average pay increases, in both percentage and absolute terms, even when their firms had worse accounting and stock price performance. Such practices lead inevitably to ever-increasing compensation.[20]

Kim Clark, Dean of Harvard Business School, recently described the process of ratcheting as follows: "The use of consultants . . . creates . . . 'the Lake Wobegon effect.' You recall that in Lake Wobegon everybody is above average. And in a lot of companies the way the system works is most CEOs want to be at the 75th percentile of the distribution of compensation. . . . You get a ratcheting-up effect as that information pervades the market, and we get serious distortions in CEO compensation."[21]

## Managerial Power and the Past Decade

Kevin Murphy and Brian Hall have criticized our earlier work on the connection between power and pay, suggesting that our approach cannot explain the large increases in executive compensation during the 1990s.[22] *Wall Street Journal* columnist Holman Jenkins challenged our work on similar grounds.[23] These critics argue that CEO power declined during the 1990s as boards added more independent directors. If the managerial power approach is correct, they claim, pay ought to have also declined rather than increased during this period.

However, it is not at all clear that CEO influence declined during the 1990s. Although the composition of boards might have improved, take-over defenses were also strengthened. Thus, boards and executives were much less concerned about the threat of a hostile takeover during the 1990s than they had been during the preceding decade.

Our critics also observed that the increase in compensation during the 1990s took place after the adoption in 1992 of the enhanced disclosure requirements.[24] If managerial power plays an important role in the setting of executive compensation, they argue, increased transparency should have lead to a reduction, not an increase, in pay.

Everything else being equal, we believe, increased transparency should operate to constrain pay. However, there were other changes taking place in the 1990s that tended to boost pay and, we believe, more than offset the effect of better disclosure. In our view, executive pay increases during the 1990s resulted from developments in the compensation environment—such as shareholders' increased interest in linking pay to performance and the broader stock market boom—that managers were able to use to their advantage.

In the early 1990s, institutional investors and federal regulators, with the support of financial economists, pressed for greater use of performance-based compensation. The enactment in 1992 of Section 162(m) of the Internal Revenue Code, which denies firms a deduction for compensation paid to an executive in excess of $1 million a year unless the excess compensation is "performance-based," was intended to encourage the use of such compensation.

Executives took advantage of this surge of enthusiasm. They used their influence over directors to obtain substantial additional option pay without having to bear a corresponding downward adjustment in cash compensation. In an arm's-length world, an employer is often able to trade an increase in one part of a compensation package for an offsetting reduction in another part of the package. But in the real world of manager-influenced compensation, boards and executives responded to the calls for equity-based compensation by adding more such compensation to existing arrangements rather than substituting it for performance-insensitive compensation.

Furthermore, executives used their influence to make the design of option plans advantageous to them. As we explain later, conventional option plans do not link pay tightly to managers' own performance; rather, they enable managers to reap windfalls from stock price increases that are due solely to market and sector forces beyond managerial control. As a result, managers capture much larger gains than more cost-effective option plans would have provided.

In view of the huge increases in pay during the past decade, critics of our approach might ask why risk-averse managers did not use their influence to get higher cash salaries rather than more options. Holding the value of compensation constant, managers would certainly prefer to get it in cash rather than in options. But managers seeking to increase their pay during the 1990s were not offered a choice between additional cash compensation and additional option compensation with the same expected value. Instead, outsiders' enthusiasm for equity-based compensation created an opportunity for managers to obtain additional option compensation without offsetting reductions in their cash compensation.

In addition, because option compensation offers the possibility of improved incentives, the use of options made more defensible compensation amounts that would have triggered prohibitive outrage had they been solely in cash. In 2001, Apple CEO Steve Jobs was able to obtain an option package worth more than half a billion dollars, albeit with some outcry.[25] Cash compensation of this magnitude is still inconceivable. As we discuss in detail in chapter 11, firms could have used better designed option plans that would have provided the same incentives for significantly less cost. But the large windfall elements of the option plans that firms did use were not sufficiently clear and transparent to make these plans blatantly unjustifiable. In short, managers were able to use shareholders' general interest in increasing the performance sensitivity of pay—and the fact that option pay is easier to defend and legitimize even if the pay is based on flawed schemes—to get unprecedented amounts of compensation that were to a substantial degree unrelated to their own performance.

The stock market boom is a second important factor that worked to managers' advantage in the 1990s. Executive compensation has historically been and still is correlated with a firm's market capitalization. Executives of companies with larger market capitalization tend to receive higher compensation.[26] Thus the rising stock market of the 1990s, which buoyed many poorly performing companies, provided most firms with a convenient justification for substantial pay increases.

Furthermore, investors and other outsiders are generally less bothered by excessive and distorted pay arrangements when markets are rising rapidly. The bull market of the 1990s—the biggest bull market since the Depression—weakened the outrage constraint, giving managers and boards more latitude to boost executive pay. The stock market boom thus played a role in the upward trend of executive compensation during this period. Conversely, shareholders who have seen the value of their investments decline precipitously are more prone to scrutinize managerial behavior and less likely to be forgiving of what they perceive (correctly or incorrectly) to be managerial overreaching. It is no coincidence that large stock market declines are often followed by new laws that seek to curb what is viewed as insider overreaching.[27] Thus, the fact that pay has not continued to escalate rapidly since 2000 is in part due to some tightening of the outrage constraint.

## Alternative Explanations for Inefficient Contracts

In the coming chapters, we will describe various compensation practices that appear to be inefficient and thus inconsistent with arm's-length contracting. They are, however, consistent with managerial influence at work. Before proceeding, however, we wish to discuss briefly two alternative explanations for inefficient compensation practices, and how their predictions differ from those of the managerial power approach.

### Norms and Conventions

The desire to conform to prevailing norms and conventions influences individuals' behavior in many contexts. In recent years, a number of legal scholars have studied the role of norms in the context of corporate law and corporate governance.[28] It is natural to ask whether norms play a role in executive compensation. Inefficient arrangements may arise and persist, it might be argued, simply because boards have a tendency to conform to the practices of other firms, whether or not those practices serve shareholder interests.

We agree that the tendency to conform likely plays a significant role in board decisions about executive compensation. Directors will be more willing to approve pay arrangements that are similar to those of other firms. Following the herd requires less explanation, less justification, and less confidence in one's own judgment than does carving out a new path. Thus, compensation committees and boards have a natural desire to conform to "the norm," or at least to be perceived as conforming to the norm.

The desire to conform makes any change in the status quo—any move from one "equilibrium" to another—slower than it would otherwise be. The evolution of compensation arrangements is slowed down or made "sticky" by compensation committees' preference for adhering to conventions and their reluctance to deviate substantially from established pay practices.

However, the desire to conform cannot explain the ways in which compensation arrangements have evolved. Nor can it predict the direction in which compensation arrangements will evolve in the future. The stickiness arising from the tendency to conform implies only that movement from one equilibrium to another will be gradual and slow. It can neither explain why we reached a particular equilibrium nor what the next equilibrium is likely to be.

Patterns of executive compensation do change substantially over time. Some of the practices to be discussed in coming chapters either have emerged or have become much more important in just the past decade. The stickiness arising from the desire to conform cannot tell us much about why arrangements evolved in one direction rather than another.

To provide a full account of executive compensation, norms and conventions must be combined with another theory, such as arm's-length contracting or managerial power. A theory combining norms with the arm's-length contracting approach would predict that the evolution of executive compensation arrangements, although slowed by the tendency to conform, is shaped by market forces. In this model, as changing circumstances make an existing equilibrium inefficient, market pressures induce boards to adopt arrangements that are efficient in the new circumstances. Although the desire to conform prevents instantaneous adjustment, market forces move arrangements in the direction of efficiency and, ultimately, the efficiency gap created by the new circumstances may well be eliminated.

In contrast, a theory combining norms with the managerial power approach would predict that the evolution of executive compensation will be shaped, at least in part, by executives' desire to secure rents. When changing circumstances create an opportunity to enjoy more rents or to better camouflage their rents, managers will try to take advantage of the opportunity. The stickiness due to the desire to conform will slow the pace of these changes, but the changes will tend to be in directions favorable to managers and to reflect their ability to influence their own pay.

The landscape of executive compensation, we should emphasize, is hardly static. Many talented professionals—from compensation consultants to tax attorneys—are hard at work developing, adjusting, and implementing new executive pay arrangements. In the following chapters, we will discuss a variety of potentially inefficient but executive-friendly compensation practices that have developed and quickly spread during the last decade or two. We will also discuss some potentially efficient improvements in compensation practices that, during the same period, have been often discussed but have failed to take root.

Why have companies easily adopted innovations favored by executives but not innovations resisted by them? The stickiness caused by the desire to conform, combined with arm's-length contracting, should not systematically yield outcomes that are favorable to managers. The tendency of changes to favor executives, however, is consistent with such stickiness combined with the operation of managerial influence.

## Mistakes and Misperceptions

There is another natural explanation for inefficient compensation contracts: human error. Even in an economic context where arm's-length bargainers have incentives to reach efficient outcomes, they can make mistakes. They misperceive, miscalculate, misestimate, and suffer from a variety of cognitive biases. These human imperfections may lead to the adoption of inefficient compensation contracts. One observer has referred to this explanation for inefficient compensation packages as "honest stupidity."[29]

To assess this mistakes-based explanation, it is first necessary to specify the identities of those making the errors. Under one version of this explanation, all those involved in the pay-setting process—including executives, their advisers, and compensation consultants—make mistakes. But this is a highly implausible explanation for the persistence of the inefficient practices we will be discussing.

The problems we will discuss are hardly complex. It is highly unlikely that they have so long escaped the attention of managers and their sophisticated, well-paid advisers. Furthermore, this version of the explanation cannot account for the fact that apparent departures from arm's-length contracting systematically favor managers. "Honest stupidity" should occasion both departures favorable to managers and departures unfavorable to managers.

A more plausible version of the "honest mistakes" explanation focuses on independent directors, who have little at stake in compensation decisions and devote little time to them. One might argue that they may have failed to grasp some of the flaws in compensation practices we will be discussing. In a response by Kevin Murphy to our earlier study, and in a subsequent paper by Murphy and Brian Hall, these authors have advanced such an explanation—which they label "the perceived cost view"—for the prevalence of seemingly inefficient option plans.[30]

As we will discuss in chapter 11, it is puzzling from the perspective of arm's-length contracting that conventional option plans make little effort to filter out stock price increases that are due to general market or sector movements. Hall and Murphy argue that boards have used conventional option plans because they have failed to perceive the true economic cost to shareholders of such options. Because conventional options can be granted without any cash outlay and have not required an accounting charge, Hall and Murphy suggest, boards have perceived them as rather inexpensive and have therefore been overly willing to grant them. Options that filter out windfalls in fact cost less, but boards have erroneously viewed them as more expensive because reduced-windfall options do require an accounting charge.

We are skeptical that directors have failed to recognize that conventional options involve substantial costs for shareholders, whose holdings are diluted by the option grants. We likewise doubt that directors have been unaware that the cost of conventional options to shareholders exceeds the cost of options that filter out stock price increases not due to the executives' own efforts. But for the sake of argument, let us suppose that, when appointed to boards, directors—many of whom are executives or prominent figures in the business world—have been oblivious to the true cost of conventional options. Let us suppose further that—once these directors are on the board—compensation consultants have failed to educate them about these costs. If so, the possibility of misperceptions by these directors is best seen not as an alternative to the managerial power explanation but rather as additional evidence that supports it.

As discussed earlier, there are several reasons why boards have failed to negotiate compensation arrangements that best serve shareholders. Directors tend to have financial and nonfinancial incentives to please or at least not to displease the CEO; even absent such incentives, a host of social and psychological factors are likely to lead directors to favor managers. In addition, directors have lacked adequate time and information for the investigation of alternative, efficient compensation arrangements with executives. Directors' misperception of the cost of options is but one example of the last problem.

For many purposes, it does not matter whether managers' influence over their own compensation has come from the pliability of the board or from directors' naïveté. Whether the problem is conscious favoritism, honest stupidity, or a combination of both, the important fact is that directors have been at least to some extent willing to approve option arrangements that favor managers at the expense of shareholders.

For some other purposes, however—such as for improving compensation arrangements—it might well matter whether inefficient contracts arise from conscious favoritism or from honest stupidity. If misperceptions were the only source of past departures from arm's-length contracting, for example, outside observers could simply correct the misperceptions—by educating directors or by providing them with more accurate information—to achieve arrangements much closer to the efficient, arm's-length ideal.

Therefore, it is worth noting briefly that there is evidence that managers' influence over their own pay is due not only to directors' "honest stupidity" but also at least partially to directors' willingness to favor managers. For one thing, even if the failure of firms to filter out windfalls results from directors misperceiving the costs of conventional options, managers have also been favored in other ways that cannot be explained away so easily. Misapprehensions cannot explain, for example, why firms have been using retirement plans and executive loans in ways that seem designed to make compensation less noticeable.

Furthermore, if managers could not influence their own pay and were simply benefiting from directors' misperceptions, one would not expect executive pay to correlate with executives' power. As we explain in the following chapter, however, considerable evidence indicates the existence of such a correlation. This pattern indicates that directors' willingness to favor the CEO, not merely directors' misperceptions, has played a significant role in shaping compensation arrangements.

## 6

# The Relationship between Power and Pay

We find that CEO compensation is higher when . . . the outside directors are appointed by the CEO.
From a 1999 empirical study of executive pay by John Core, Robert Holthausen, and David Larcker

IN COMPANIES WITH dispersed ownership and no controlling shareholder, executives will commonly have enough power to enjoy more compensation and managerial slack than they would under an arm's-length arrangement. The extent of managerial power, however, is not uniform across all such companies. The managerial power approach predicts that compensation packages will be more favorable to managers—that is, that pay will be higher and/or less sensitive to performance—in firms in which managers have relatively more power. Other things being equal, managers will tend to have more power when (1) the board is relatively weak or ineffectual, (2) there is no large outside shareholder, (3) there are fewer institutional shareholders, and (4) managers are protected by antitakeover arrangements. The empirical evidence indicates that each of these factors does indeed affect executive compensation in the way predicted by a managerial power analysis.

## Strength and Independence of Boards

Although CEOs generally influence the board, the degree of influence differs from company to company depending on the relative strength of the board. The evidence indicates that CEOs obtain more favorable pay arrangements when they are more powerful vis-à-vis the board.

A CEO is likely to be relatively more powerful as the size of the board increases. Larger boards tend to be less cohesive because individual directors may feel less "responsible" and therefore may focus less on the firm's affairs in general and on management pay in particular. Members of large boards also are less likely to be constrained in their decisions by the threat of public outrage; the larger the board, the harder it is for outside observers to direct their outrage at any one member. Additionally, directors interested in challenging the CEO on compensation or otherwise will find it more difficult to convince a majority of a large board to join them. For all these reasons, managers with a larger board will tend to have more power and can be expected to obtain more favorable pay arrangements. Indeed, John Core, Robert Holthausen, and David Larcker find that CEO compensation is higher when the board is larger.[1] Similarly, a study conducted by David Yermack finds that pay-performance sensitivity decreases as the size of the board increases.[2]

The presence of directors who serve on multiple boards—and are therefore less focused on the affairs of any one company—is also likely to increase the relative power of the CEO.[3] Accordingly, pay arrangements can be expected to be more favorable to the CEO when outside directors sit on multiple boards. The Core, Holthausen, and Larcker study provides evidence consistent with this prediction. It indicates that CEO compensation increases, all else being equal, with the number of outside directors serving on three or more other boards.[4]

A CEO who also serves as chair of the board is likely to be more powerful. The board chair runs board meetings and sets their agendas. It is thus hardly surprising that CEOs occupying that position are less likely to be fired by the board for poor performance.[5] A CEO who is also chair of the board therefore can be expected to obtain more favorable pay arrangements. Indeed, numerous studies conclude that compensation tends to be higher when the CEO serves in this additional role.[6]

The presence of directors who have ties to or feel an obligation to the CEO is also likely to increase the latter's power. Studies indicate that pay is higher, and the CEO is more likely to get a "golden parachute," when more of the outside directors have been appointed under—and thus may feel a greater sense of gratitude or obligation to—the current CEO.[7] Similarly, the longer the CEO's term—and thus the more likely it is that directors were appointed under the CEO—the less sensitive is the CEO's pay to firm performance.[8]

Interlocking directorships may also increase the CEO's ability to influence the board. CEO-interlocking directorships—where the CEO of Firm A sits on Firm B's board and the CEO of Firm B sits on Firm A's board—

are likely to increase the influence that both CEOs have over their respective boards. As the managerial power approach predicts, CEO pay increases when a board contains interlocking directors.[9]

Turning from the board to its compensation committee, the makeup of that committee itself also affects the structure of CEO pay in the way suggested by the managerial power perspective. First, a CEO's pay is higher when the chair of the compensation committee has been appointed during the term of that CEO.[10] Second, when at least one member of the compensation committee is an insider and therefore subordinate to the CEO, the sensitivity of pay to performance is lower.[11] Finally, compensation committee members who own significant amounts of stock will tend to be more involved in company affairs and more attentive to shareholder value. Indeed, a study confirms that CEO pay is negatively related to the share ownership of the board's compensation committee.[12]

## Presence of Outside Blockholders

The presence of outside shareholders that own large blocks of stock will also affect managerial power. A large shareholder has more incentive than dispersed shareholders to monitor management and invest effort in reducing managerial opportunism.[13] Thus, the managerial power approach predicts that the presence of a large shareholder, even one who does not have a controlling or dominant stake, will weaken managers' ability to obtain favorable compensation arrangements.

This prediction is borne out by a study that finds a negative relationship between the equity ownership of a firm's largest shareholder and the amount of CEO compensation. It concludes that the presence of a shareholder with a stake larger than the CEO's ownership interest reduces CEO compensation by an average of 5 percent.[14] Two other studies have looked at the effect of a 5 percent or larger blockholder (other than the CEO) on CEO compensation. They find that the existence of such a 5 percent blockholder reduces CEO compensation.[15]

As might be expected, these studies also find that pay is less sensitive to performance in companies that do not have a 5 percent external shareholder.[16] The arm's-length contracting view would not predict such a relationship. Agency problems are likely to be more severe absent an outside blockholder. The arm's-length contracting model would therefore predict that, if anything, boards would make pay-performance sensitivity higher in such cases, in order to counteract these more pronounced agency problems.

A creative empirical study by Marianne Bertrand and Sendhil Mullain-athan provides additional evidence that managers' pay is less performance sensitive in the absence of a large external shareholder.[17] The study examines whether the presence of a 5 percent (or larger) shareholder affects how managers are compensated for "luck"—that is, for changes in company performance beyond their control. The study finds that CEOs in firms lacking large external shareholders tend to receive more "luck-based" pay. Another study by the same authors finds that CEOs in firms without large shareholders experience smaller reductions in cash compensation when options-based compensation is increased.[18]

The significance of outside shareholders as a check on managerial power may depend not only on the presence of a large shareholder but also on the percentage of shares held by institutional investors. Although institutional investors are often reluctant to fight management about pay issues, they are generally more vigilant than are individual investors, who have little at stake in any given firm.

In a study of S&P firms during the 1990s, Jay Hartzell and Laura Starks found that a higher concentration of institutional ownership leads not only to lower executive compensation but also to pay that is more performance-sensitive.[19] This evidence indicates that the presence of institutions serves to reduce both excess pay and managerial slack.

Another study, by Parthiban David, Rahul Kochar, and Edward Levitas, divides institutional shareholders into two categories. One category includes those that have no other business relationship with the firm and are thus concerned only with its share value ("pressure-resistant" institutions). The second category includes those institutions that have other business relationships with the firm (such as managing a pension fund) and are thus vulnerable to management pressure ("pressure-sensitive" institutions). As the managerial power approach predicts, CEO pay turns out to be negatively correlated with the presence of pressure-resistant institutional investors and positively correlated with the presence of pressure-sensitive ones.[20]

## Antitakeover Protection

The market for corporate control—the threat of a hostile takeover—does not exert sufficient force to prevent substantial departures from arm's-length contracting. It does, however, provide some constraint on managers' desire and ability to obtain favorable pay arrangements. Accordingly, the more protected incumbents are from a takeover, the higher and less performance sensitive their compensation is likely to be.

One study, by Kenneth Borokhovich, Kelly Brunarski, and Robert Parrino, reports that CEO compensation increases significantly after antitakeover provisions are adopted—that is, after CEOs have become less vulnerable to a hostile takeover.[21] This cannot be readily explained by arm's-length contracting; if managers' jobs are more secure, shareholders should be able to pay managers less because managers' risk-bearing costs are lower.[22]

Another study finds that CEOs of firms that become protected by antitakeover legislation reduce their holdings of shares, apparently because the shares are less necessary for maintaining control.[23] This finding, again, is difficult to explain from the perspective of arm's-length contracting. Arm's-length contracting might, in fact, predict the opposite—that a CEO protected by antitakeover legislation would, if anything, be required by a shareholder-oriented board to *increase* equity holdings to maintain adequate incentives to enhance shareholder value.

It is worth noting that managers who are less vulnerable to a hostile takeover take advantage of their power in other ways as well. Several studies report that when protected from takeovers by strong antitakeover laws or antitakeover charter provisions, managers generate less value for shareholders.[24] One study indicates that when managers have fewer reasons to fear a hostile takeover, they tend to operate their firms less efficiently, producing narrower profit margins and slower sales growth.[25] This study further reports that insulation from takeover threats results in greater consumption of private benefits by managers and a greater tendency to engage in empire building.

## The New CEOs Objection

In a critique of our earlier work, Kevin Murphy presents a finding that, he argues, is inconsistent with the predictions of the managerial power approach.[26] Murphy found that CEOs hired from the outside received, in their first year, almost twice the total compensation received by CEOs promoted from within. Outside CEOs do not yet have power to influence their pay, Murphy argues; their higher compensation therefore must be inconsistent with the managerial power hypothesis.

However, as we explained in chapter 2, boards cannot be expected to bargain at arm's length even with outside CEO candidates. Among other things, directors negotiating with a new CEO anticipate that, once hired, the CEO will have influence over their renomination to the board and their compensation. In addition, directors recognize that the person whose compensation they are structuring will soon become the firm's leader and one of their colleagues—that the incoming CEO is, in short, a person with whom they would like to have collegial relations. This further reduces directors' incentives to engage in true arm's-length bargaining with the would-be CEO.

We agree with Murphy, however, that outside CEO candidates should have less power and influence over their prospective pay than inside candidates. And the managerial approach suggests that, all else being equal, managers with less power should obtain less favorable arrangements. However, in Murphy's comparison between outside and inside CEO candidates, all else is not equal. The managerial power approach does not suggest that managerial power is the sole determinant of managerial pay. Other characteristics, such as managers' abilities and their bargaining positions, will also affect executive compensation. Outside candidates, as a group, are likely to differ from internal candidates along these dimensions.

Companies generally have an incentive to hire inside the firm if they can find a suitable candidate. Insiders are preferred because of their familiarity with the firm and perhaps also because of their existing ties to the board. As a result, 75 to 80 percent of CEOs are hired internally.[27] Because of most boards' reluctance to extend the search beyond a firm's ranks, a board will hire an outsider only if the outsider is significantly stronger than internal candidates. As a result, outside hires are likely to be, on average, a stronger group.

Furthermore, outside hires are often already CEOs of other firms, while inside candidates, by definition, are not. Outside candidates who are already CEOs are using their current positions to extract rents, and firms hoping to hire such candidates must match these rents. In contrast, inside candidates need not be paid for giving up the rents associated with a CEO position. The higher pay received by outside CEO hires is therefore hardly inconsistent with the managerial power approach.

## The Pattern

A clear pattern emerges from the many empirical studies described in this chapter. The evidence indicates that there is a link between managerial power and pay. The more power managers have, the more favorable their compensation arrangements are.

Unlike most financial economists studying executive compensation, some of the researchers conducting these studies concluded that rent extraction might occur where managers are especially powerful. Bertrand and Mullainathan, for example, concluded that some "skimming" occurs in companies without a 5 percent shareholder.[28] These researchers appear to believe, however, that rent extraction does not occur in companies lacking such a shareholder.

In contrast, in our view, once the connection between power and rents is recognized, there is reason to believe that significant rent extraction is taking place even in companies with a 5 percent shareholder. To be sure, managers in such companies may have somewhat less power, and thus less ability to extract rents, than managers in companies without a large outside shareholder. However, these managers still have considerable influence.

Consider cases in which a 5 percent or even a 10 percent external shareholder is present. Such a shareholder may well have some influence, but probably not enough to oust management, given the power that managers have to defend against hostile takeovers and to control the proxy machinery. Executives in such cases are still likely to wield a substantial amount of power—and thus to be in a position to extract considerable rents.

Indeed, the compensation practices we discuss in subsequent chapters—practices that reflect both power and camouflage—are not limited to companies without a 5 percent shareholder. These practices are common also at companies that have a significant blockholder or a substantial presence of institutional investors. This pattern indicates that rent extraction may well take place, even if to a reduced extent, in companies where the presence of blockholders or institutional investors makes managers relatively less powerful.

# 7

## Managerial Influence on the Way Out

It's quite normal for a board to want the departing CEO to be a friend, not an adversary.

Corporate lawyer interviewed by
*Fortune* magazine, 2000

CEOS LEAVING A company commonly receive substantial payments. While some of these departure-related payments are mandated by the CEO's employment contract, our focus in this chapter is on gratuitous departure payments—that is, payments not mandated under the CEO's contract at the time the executive decides (or is asked) to leave. These payments are made at the board's discretion, over and above anything required by the executive's contract. As we discuss below, such gratuitous payments have often been made (1) when CEOs are fired, (2) when they agree to have their companies acquired, and (3) when they retire.

Gratuitous payments and benefits have taken a number of forms. These include forgiveness of loans, accelerated vesting of options and restricted stock, increases in pension benefits (for example, by "crediting" CEOs with additional years of service), awards of lump-sum cash payments, and promises of consulting contracts that will provide the departing CEO with generous annual compensation for little or no work.

Most employees who retire or are let go receive whatever benefits or payments they are contractually entitled to and little else. An employer in an arm's-length relationship with these employees is very unlikely to give them large, uncontracted payments upon termination of employment. The gratuitous departure payments received by CEOs thus provide evidence that directors do not deal at arm's length with CEOs, even in those rare cases where they push the CEO out the door.

## When CEOs Are Fired

As we noted earlier, boards rarely compel CEOs to resign. Because many directors—even nominally independent directors—are likely to be influenced by or loyal to the head of the company, boards have generally been reluctant to fire CEOs whose performance is passable. When the CEO performs quite poorly and the need for a replacement becomes obvious, however, directors may succumb to the pressure for change at the top.

When a board replaces a CEO, it often grants various benefits to ease the executive's exit. For example, when Mattel CEO Jill Barad was forced out by her board, she had a $4.2 million loan forgiven and received an additional $3.3 million in cash to cover the tax liability arising from the forgiveness of another loan. In addition, her unvested options were allowed to vest automatically and to remain exercisable until the end of their original terms. These gratuitous benefits accompanied the severance package already guaranteed under her contract, which included a termination payment of $26.4 million, annual retirement benefits of more than $700,000, and other benefits.[1]

Another example is the departure arrangement for Webvan CEO George Shaheen. Shaheen resigned shortly before Webvan declared bankruptcy, saying that he felt there was a need for "a different kind of an executive to lead the company." He had a $6.7 million loan forgiven in exchange for $150,000 of Webvan stock, a benefit to which he had not been contractually entitled.[2]

Likewise, when Bank One CEO John McCoy was pushed out in 1999 for poor performance, he met with his friends on the board to hammer out a separation agreement. The package included a $10.3 million cash payment (in addition to $7.5 million in "special recognition" awards for 1997 and 1998), plus a pension of $3 million annually beginning in 2001.[3] Presumably, this arrangement made it easier for his friends on the board to go along with other board members' desire to end his service.

It is difficult to reconcile such gratuitous payments with arm's-length contracting. A board has authority to fire a CEO, paying only the severance benefits required by contract. There appears to be no need to "bribe" a poorly performing CEO to step down. In addition, the signal sent by a gratuitous departure payment will, if anything, only weaken the next CEO's incentive to perform.

On the other hand, such payments can readily be explained by the existence of managerial power over the board. First, at least some directors may be reluctant to fire a CEO, even for poor performance. To coax them to acquiesce, it may be necessary to induce the CEO to resign voluntarily or at least to offer very generous terms. When such directors constitute a majority of the board, the CEO cannot be replaced without a gratuitous departure payment. Even when the CEO's allies constitute a minority, they can make the replacement process contentious and un-pleasant for their colleagues. The other directors may wish to avoid the acrimony by being generous to the departing CEO. In either case, the gratuitous payment acts as a "bribe" to secure the cooperation, or reduce the resistance, of the CEO's allies on the board.

Second, even directors who are willing to replace their CEO may prefer to sweeten their action with a gift. They may wish to alleviate the general discomfort or even guilt they feel for pushing out their colleague and leader, to please or console the CEO, to express their gratitude or friend-ship, or to make themselves more attractive, or at least less threatening, to the CEOs of other companies who might consider appointing them to their boards.

Underlying all of these explanations is a relationship between the di-rectors and the CEO that differs substantially from what is assumed to exist in the arm's-length model. The fact that the gratuitous goodbye payment is paid with shareholders' money, at very little cost to the di-rectors personally, makes it easier for directors to act on their preference to be nice to the CEO.

It is important to note that, taking managerial power as given, gratu-itous payments to fired CEOs may sometimes benefit shareholders. Given the loyalty of many directors to the CEO, providing such a sweetener may be necessary to obtain a board majority in favor of replacing a poor performer. In such a case, the gratuitous departure payments benefit shareholders as long as the CEO's departure increases shareholder value by more than the cost of the payment. For our purposes, however, what is important is that the practice of gratuitous goodbye payments reflects managers' influence over directors.

## When Companies Are Acquired

Managers of firms that are being acquired often receive acquisition-related benefits beyond those required by their employment contracts. These gratuitous acquisition payments can take a variety of forms, such as special cash payments or increases in the value of previously negotiated golden parachutes. For example, the U.S. West board voted to boost CEO Sol Trujillo's golden parachute by an estimated $46 million shortly before the firm was acquired by Qwest Communications.[4] A study by Jay Hartzell, Eli Ofek, and David Yermack reports that in 27 percent of acquisitions, the target board gives the CEO a special cash payment at the time it approves the merger. Furthermore, in 12 percent of the cases where the target CEO has a golden parachute, the target board increases the golden parachute payout at the time it approves the merger.[5]

The two types of possible explanations for gratuitous acquisition-related payments parallel the explanations for gratuitous departure payments. First, some directors may vote in favor of an acquisition that is good for shareholders only if the CEO supports the deal or is at least treated generously in the transition. When such directors constitute a majority, sweetening the acquisition for the CEO may be necessary for the deal's success. And even when such directors are in the minority, the desire to avoid a confrontation may be sufficient to induce the majority to sugarcoat the CEO's acquisition-related departure with a gratuitous payment.

Second, even if the entire board is willing to approve the acquisition without special treatment for the CEO, the directors may still prefer to give the CEO a golden goodbye. They may wish to favor a CEO who is about to be displaced in a takeover for the same reasons they may confer benefits on a CEO who is being forced out by the board. They may be swayed by loyalty, gratitude, or friendship. They may seek to alleviate their own unease as they take control away from the CEO. And because the directors personally bear only a negligible fraction of the cost of such a payment, they see little reason not to make one.

It is worth noting that, when companies are acquired, the outrage constraint is likely to be relatively loose, enabling the CEO and board of the target company to get away with larger gratuitous payments than might be possible in other contexts. Target shareholders are usually paid a substantial premium over the preoffer market price, reducing their inclination to scrutinize and criticize the firm's pay arrangements. In addition, when the firm is being acquired and the end of its independent existence is near, the directors have less reason to be concerned about shareholder reactions because they will all be stepping down anyway. In an acquisition, then, there is likely to be less outrage generated by a gratuitous payment to the CEO, and any such outrage is likely to impose a lower cost on the CEO and the board.

Again, we wish to make clear that, taking managerial power as given, providing the target CEO with a gratuitous payment may benefit shareholders. When such sweetening is necessary to obtain board approval for a beneficial acquisition, shareholders are likely to be better off with both the gratuitous payment and the acquisition than with neither. Thus, accepting the reality of managers' power and influence over the board, prohibiting such payments is unlikely to be desirable. Again, though, for our purposes, the critical point is that these payments indicate the existence of managerial power over directors.

## Acquirer-Paid Sweeteners

In addition to benefits received from their own boards, target firm managers often receive substantial benefits from acquiring firms. An acquirer, of course, is not contractually obligated to give anything to the CEO of the firm being acquired, but such payments are often made. The reason is simple: compensating these managers allows the acquirer either to proceed with the acquisition or to complete the deal on more favorable terms.

For example, when MCI was negotiating to be acquired by British Telecommunications (BT) in 1996, MCI's president, Timothy F. Price, arranged for a $170 million "retention pool" for himself and other key employees as part of his company's deal with BT.[6] The retention pool's existence did not depend on the deal closing on the original agreed terms. So when BT reduced its offer by 20 percent, Price acquiesced, telling shareholders that the lower price was "a win-win arrangement for both companies." In the end, WorldCom outbid BT and acquired MCI, but only after it, too, agreed to pay retention bonuses to MCI's top executives.

A prominent mergers and acquisitions lawyer interviewed in the *New York Times* made the following observation: "I have had a number of situations where we've gone to management looking to do a deal and been stopped at the door until a compensation arrangement was signed, sealed, and delivered." Another lawyer described it this way: "Publicly, we have to call these things retention bonuses. Privately, sometimes it's the only way we would have got the deal done. It's a kickback. And sometimes it's my job to negotiate the kickback."[7]

Hartzell, Ofek, and Yermack investigate the practice of acquirer-paid sweeteners more systematically. Examining 311 large-firm mergers completed between 1995 and 1997, they found that target CEOs accept lower acquisition premiums when the acquirer promises them a high-ranking managerial post after the acquisition.[8] Another study, by Julie Wulf, found that in 40 merger negotiations between equal-sized companies during the 1990s, CEOs were willing to trade higher acquisition premiums for better managerial positions in the merged firm.[9]

The willingness of acquirers to pay off target executives provides further evidence of managerial power. Because CEOs can exert influence over their boards, they can prevent the acceptance of offers that are attractive to shareholders but harmful to the CEOs themselves. Conversely, they can convince their boards to accept acquisition offers that are in the CEOs' interests, even if they are not in the best interests of the shareholders. Given this managerial power, treating CEOs of target firms generously has often been in acquirers' interests.

## When CEOs Retire

Boards have often conferred large gratuitous benefits on CEOs who choose to retire for age or other personal reasons, even when substantial retirement payments are already provided contractually. For example, in 1999, when the market was rising but Eastman Kodak's stock price had fallen, Kodak gave its retiring CEO a $2.5 million parting gift in recognition of the company's financial performance.[10] In 2000, GE's CEO, Jack Welch, received a retirement gift of 3 million stock options with a value of approximately $20 million.[11]

Golden retirement goodbyes sometimes have taken subtler forms. One way to provide substantial additional value to retiring CEOs is to make last-minute alterations to their retirement plans. For example, when CEO Terrence Murray retired, FleetBoston Financial Corporation modified his retirement plan to more than double the annual payouts. The pension formula had previously been based on his average annual salary and bonus over the five years preceding his retirement. The formula was changed to one based on his average annual taxable compensation over the three years he received the most such compensation. "Taxable compensation" was defined to include not only salary and bonus, but also option-exercise gains, the proceeds of sales of vested restricted shares, and the payout before retirement of some of Murray's deferred compensation. The change boosted Murray's annual pension from an estimated $2.7 million to an estimated $5.8 million.[12] Reacting to this change, a Prudential Securities banking analyst noted that FleetBoston's shares "underperformed the average bank for a decade" and wondered: "What happened to [just] getting a gold watch?"[13]

From the perspectives of the board and the retiring CEO, an important advantage of boosting postretirement benefits is that such benefits are much less salient than cash payments of the same value. As we will discuss in chapter 8, even though companies must disclose in their SEC filings the formulas used to calculate postretirement benefits, they need not place a dollar value on these benefits. More important, the benefits' value is omitted from the compensation tables that present executive compensation figures, greatly reducing the salience of the benefits to the media and other outside observers. In the case of FleetBoston, for example, the bank did not have to disclose (and in fact did not disclose) that the changes in Murray's retirement plan would add up to an annual cost to the company of $3.1 million. We know this figure only because a newspaper took the unusual step of retaining an actuary to calculate the amounts involved.

Executives' contracts generally provide them with substantial retirement benefits. The practice of gratuitously augmenting these hefty benefits when a CEO retires does not reflect arm's-length contracting. We will later question whether companies should even be in the business of providing retirement benefits for executives, rather than letting them save for retirement themselves. For now, however, we are focusing on gifts made to CEOs on the way out. One could argue that the prospect of a retirement gift might provide executives with an incentive to perform well during their tenure. It is hard to see, however, why well-designed option and bonus plans that reward excellent performance are not a better means of providing incentives than retirement gifts.

Large retirement gifts are easier to understand in light of the personal relationships that directors have with departing CEOs. Directors may wish to take this last opportunity to confer value on the CEO, to honor their collegial ties, or to express gratitude for what the CEO has done for them. According to one compensation consultant, the consulting contracts frequently given to retiring CEOs "often have more to do with favors for past deeds" than with future services.[14] And because the cost of these extra payments is mostly borne by public shareholders, there is little real cost to directors in making such personally satisfying gestures.

## It's Now or Never

In each of the contexts we discussed—when CEOs are fired, when the firm is acquired, or when CEOs retire—there is a common factor increasing both the eagerness of the CEO to request gratuitous payments and the willingness of the board to provide them. That factor is the endgame nature of the situation. In each case, the CEO leaves the company. And in one situation—acquisition of the firm—the directors are likely to leave the company as well. For this reason, they have little to lose.

As long as CEOs remain in their positions, they know they will be able to use their influence to get favorable treatment from their boards in the future. The directors also know that they will have additional opportunities to reward their CEOs. But the impending departure of the CEO—whether resulting from forced resignation, acquisition, or voluntary retirement—presents both CEOs and boards with a "now or never" choice. CEOs have every reason to extract rents aggressively, cashing in whatever friendship and loyalty chips they have accumulated with directors. Likewise, directors know that this is their CEO's last request and their last opportunity to confer substantial financial benefits on their CEO. When faced with the choice between now or never, many directors opt for now and agree to provide a departing CEO with a golden goodbye.

# 8

## Retirement Benefits

> One car a year from Ford with the option of buying several
> more at a discount. Financial planning assistance, executive
> office at headquarters with administrative assistant. Ford
> will . . . endow a scholarship in his name at the educational
> institution of his choice. Annual pension of $1.27 million.
>
> Ford CEO Jacques Nasser's retirement package,
> as reported in the *Wall Street Journal*, 2002

CAMOUFLAGE IS AN important aspect of the executive compensation
landscape. Compensation plan designers have an incentive to obscure or
make more opaque the total value of an executive's compensation
package, as well as to disguise the extent to which the form of compensation deviates from what best serves shareholders' interests.

As disclosure requirements for executive salaries, bonuses, and long-
term compensation have become stricter, firms have increasingly turned
to postretirement payments and benefits as ways to compensate managers. These methods enable firms to provide a substantial amount of
performance-insensitive value in a less transparent form than, say, salary.
Postretirement value has been provided to executives through four main
channels: retirement pensions, deferred compensation, postretirement
perks, and guaranteed consulting fees.

Before discussing each of the four channels, we should note two at-
tributes they all share. First, these arrangements differ substantially from
those that firms elect to provide to other employees. Although firms often
provide pensions and deferred compensation to lower-level employees,
they do so only to the extent that these arrangements receive a tax subsidy.
This pattern suggests that, absent such a subsidy, pensions and deferred
compensation are generally not efficient. Yet most of the arrangements
provided to executives do not enjoy similar tax advantages. Furthermore,

consistent with economists' belief that in-kind benefits are inefficient, firms do not generally provide retired employees with coverage for specified consumption expenses. Such benefits are, however, given to high-level executives. And although firms occasionally use retired employees as consultants when the need arises, they generally do not guarantee life-time consulting fees to any employees other than executives.

The second shared attribute of these various retirement payments is that they all make it possible to obscure large amounts of performance-decoupled compensation. As we shall see, firms do not have to disclose the value transferred to executives through these channels in the same way that other forms of compensation—such as salary, bonuses, and stock options—must be disclosed. Retirement payments hence offer what might be called "stealth compensation."[1] Indeed, the dollar figures used by the media in reporting compensation levels, and by financial economists in their studies, usually do not include the large value provided to executives through retirement benefits.

## Retirement Pensions

Many employees are covered by pension plans that provide payments to workers after retirement. At first glance, it seems only natural for firms to provide such benefits to their executives. A closer look, however, raises serious questions about whether the extensive use of executive pensions as a form of compensation reflects arm's-length bargaining.

### Differences from Regular Pensions

Most of the pension plans used for employees are designed to be "qualified" for favorable tax treatment. The firm gets a current deduction for contributing funds to a qualified plan for employees—the same deduction it would have received had it paid the amount of the contribution to workers in the form of salary. Workers, however, do not pay income taxes on the pension money until they retire and begin receiving payouts from the plan. In the meantime, the funds invested by the firm grow tax-free. Neither the firm nor the employees must pay any taxes while the plan's investments increase in value. Thus, the plans provide a tax benefit to employees at no cost to the firm.[2]

Given the opportunity, boards might well prefer to offer executives qualified retirement plans. A qualified pension plan, however, can use only about $200,000 of annual compensation as the basis for determining benefits under the plan. For example, a plan that promises to pay all retirees, annually, 50 percent of the compensation earned during their last year of service cannot pay a retired executive more than $100,000 annually, even if the executive earned $1 million of compensation during that final year. As a result, firms cannot use qualified plans to provide executives with pensions that are similar in size to their annual compensation. For this reason, most firms also provide executives with non-qualified "supplemental" executive retirement plans (known as "SERPs").[3]

SERPs differ from typical qualified pension plans in two critical ways. First, they do not receive the favorable tax treatment enjoyed by qualified plans; no investment income goes untaxed under a SERP. The company pays taxes on the income it must generate in order to pay the executive in retirement. If the money had been distributed as salary, on the other hand, the executive who invested the money for retirement would have had to pay taxes on any income generated. The effect of the SERP, therefore, is to shift some of the executive's tax burden to the firm.[4]

If the employee and the firm are subject to the same tax rate and are able to earn the same pretax rate of return on their investments, a SERP cannot reduce the total amount of taxes paid by the parties. For every dollar the employee's tax burden is reduced, the firm's tax burden is increased by one dollar. Unlike a qualified plan, the SERP would not reduce the parties' total tax burden.[5]

In reality, of course, the situation is more complicated.[6] In many cases, the total tax liability faced by the parties will be affected by whether the executive or the firm saves for the executive's retirement. Even if the firm and the executive are able to earn the same return on their investments, they may face different tax rates. Suppose, for example, that an executive investing personal funds for retirement in the stock market is subject to a long-term capital-gains tax rate of 15 percent, while the firm pays taxes on the income generated for the executive's retirement at a corporate tax rate of 35 percent. In such a case, using SERPs would be tax-inefficient and would *increase* the total amount of taxes paid by the two parties. On the other hand, if the firm had no taxable earnings and was not expected to pay taxes for a considerable amount of time, the reverse might be true: shifting retirement savings from the executive to the firm might be tax-efficient.[7]

Similarly, even if the firm and the executive face the same tax rate, the investment returns available to the firm may be higher than those available to the executive. For example, firms having difficulty raising capital may enjoy a higher expected rate of return on new investments than the market generally. (This is unlikely to be the case for companies with easy access to capital, as such companies are unlikely to have unutilized investments with returns much higher than the market.) If the firm has better investment opportunities, having it invest for the executive's retirement will be efficient for both parties, even if their tax rates are identical.

However, there is no reason to believe that, absent a tax subsidy, it is generally efficient to have the firm save for the executive. On the contrary, there are good reasons to think that it is *inefficient* for many firms to save for their executives' retirement, given individuals' low long-term capital-gains tax rate. It is telling that firms providing SERPs to executives do not offer nonqualified retirement plans to other employees. Consider the case where it is efficient for a firm to provide a SERP to its executives because the firm has better investment opportunities than they do. In such a case, it should also be efficient for the firm to provide nonqualified retirement to its nonexecutive employees who supplement their qualified pensions with personal retirement savings. However, firms rarely, if ever, do so. This fact suggests that, absent the tax subsidy provided to qualified plans, using nonqualified retirement benefits is commonly not an efficient way to compensate employees. Yet in 2002, more than 70 percent of firms provided nonqualified SERPs to their executives.[8]

The second important difference between executive SERPs and qualified pension plans for nonexecutive employees concerns the risk borne by the firm and by the participant. Qualified pension plans offered to new lower-level employees are usually based on a *defined contribution*. The firm commits to contribute a specified amount each year. The value available to an employee upon retirement depends on the performance of the plan's investments. The risk of poor investment performance falls entirely on the employee.

In contrast, SERPs offered to executives are *defined-benefit* plans, which guarantee fixed payments to the executive for life. All of the CEOs in the S&P ExecuComp database have defined-benefit plans.[9] These plans shift the risk of investment performance entirely to the firm and its shareholders. No matter how poorly the firm and its investments perform, the executive is guaranteed a specified lifelong stream of payments.

Given that arm's-length negotiations with most employees lead to defined-contribution arrangements, why should arm's-length bargaining with executives yield such a different result? If anything, there are reasons to believe that defined-benefit plans should be *more* valuable to regular employees than they are to executives. Unlike most executives, ordinary employees are unlikely to accumulate substantial wealth over their lifetimes. They are likely to be more dependent on their pensions to meet their financial needs in retirement and therefore less able to bear the investment risks associated with defined-contribution plans. In contrast, executives faced with defined-contribution plans could easily insure themselves against poor investment performance by using some of their already high salaries and option-based compensation to buy fixed annuities that would provide them with guaranteed payments. If only one of the two groups were to receive defined-benefit plans, arm's-length contracting would predict that group to be nonexecutive employees, not executives.

## Camouflage Benefits

Although the efficiency benefits of providing executives with defined-benefit SERPs are far from clear, such plans do considerably reduce the visibility of a substantial amount of performance-insensitive compensation.

SERP payments are usually based on years of service and preretirement cash compensation. The higher the executive's salary and the longer the period of employment, the higher the payout. SERP payments—like salary—are therefore largely decoupled from the executive's own performance. Many firms have also credited executives with years they did not actually serve, ratcheting up the final payout under the plan's formula.[10]

In their annual public filings, firms must publish compensation tables indicating the dollar value of different forms of compensation received by the current CEO and the four other most highly paid executives of the firm. The numbers in these tables are the most visible indicators of executive compensation in public firms. They are easily accessible to the media and others reading the public filings. Indeed, the standard databases of executive compensation, which are used by both financial economists and compensation consultants, are based on these numbers.

If an executive's pensions were structured as a defined contribution plan, the firm's annual contributions to the executive's account would be reported in the compensation tables. An important camouflage benefit of SERPs is that the annual increase in the present value of an executive's defined benefit plan—due to pay raises and the addition of another year of service—is largely hidden from view: firms are not required to include this increase in value in the compensation tables. A person examining the compensation tables would not see the steady buildup in value of an executive's SERP.

Furthermore, and importantly, disclosure requirements require firms to include in their annual compensation tables only amounts paid to their current executives. Because the executives are no longer employed by the firm when the pension payments begin, the payments need not be included in the published tables. Thus, the value of an executive's defined-benefit SERP never appears in the place where the media and researchers collect most of their information about executive compensation. And because the value of an executive's pension payouts is obscured, the performance insensitivity of such payments also gets little notice.

Consider a situation in which a CEO serves a company for ten years and then receives annually, for life, a payment that equals a large fraction of the salary earned during the last year of service. In such a case, the total value of the pension payments may in the end exceed the total value of the salary received during the CEO's actual tenure. Unlike the salary amounts, however, the value of the pension payments will never appear in the firm's published compensation tables.

For example, when IBM CEO Louis Gerstner retired after about nine years of service, he was entitled to a $1,140,000 annual pension beginning at age 60.[11] The actuarial value of this annuity was of a similar order of magnitude as the approximately $18 million in salary he received during his nine years as CEO. But IBM was not required to include the pension in the compensation tables or even place a dollar value on it.[12]

Not surprisingly, SERP plans are designed and marketed specifically as ways to increase compensation "off the radar screen of shareholders."[13] Indeed, according to media reports, some directors have voted to adopt SERPs only after being reassured that the amounts involved do not have to be reported to the public.[14]

To be sure, although neither the increase in value of the SERP plan before retirement nor the amount of payments after retirement appears in the compensation tables, the existence of SERPs, and the formulas under which payouts are made, must be disclosed in the firm's SEC filings.[15] But it is difficult for anyone without actuarial or financial training to estimate with precision the value—and thus the cost to the company—of these future payments.[16] As noted above, firms are not required to supply, and usually do not provide, any estimate of the dollar value of a particular executive's defined-benefit pension plan. The lack of easy access to the monetary values of these substantial benefits presumably explains their absence from the standard databases used for research on executive compensation.

Indeed, it is often difficult even to figure out the total SERP liability of a firm with respect to its executives as a group. A firm must report only one figure: the sum of the liabilities associated with all of its employee pension plans that are "unfunded" or "underfunded" (that is, plans for which the firm does not have assets set aside to cover the plans' liabilities fully).[17] The Financial Accounting Standards Board (FASB) does not require that liabilities associated with SERPs be itemized separately.[18] Thus, firms can simply report one number that represents all the liabilities associated with underfunded qualified plans and unfunded SERPs.

Although they are not required to do so, some firms do report the total obligations arising under SERPs. These figures can be staggering. In 2000, for example, GE reported a $1.13 billion pension liability for all of its executives.[19] Unfortunately, GE did not report what portion of this amount was due specifically to its CEO and other top executives. Most companies do not even break down pension liabilities into separate categories for executives and other employees.

It is worth noting at least one way in which executives' plans may not be as advantageous to their beneficiaries as the plans of lower-level employees. Firms using qualified plans are required, as a condition for favorable tax treatment, to set aside assets to ensure that they can pay their liabilities under the plans. Given that executives' SERP plans would not qualify for the favorable tax treatment even if they were so funded, firms do not bother funding SERP plans. Executives' retirement benefits are thus at greater risk of nonpayment than the benefits of ordinary workers—and Congress is considering legislation that would make it difficult for firms to shelter executives from this risk.[20]

In the past, however, firms facing financial problems have often purchased insurance policies that payment of executive retirement benefits, transferred guaranteed money to a designated trust, or taken other steps to guarantee the benefits against insolvency.[21] Delta Airlines, for example, set up an executive-protecting arrangement shortly after September 11, 2001, when the solvency of the airline industry appeared to be in danger.[22] Although putting the money beyond the reach of the firm's creditors triggers a tax liability for the executive, firms often "gross up" the payment to cover part or all of that liability.[23] It was reported in 1991 that approximately 50 major companies had set up fully guaranteed executive pension plans.[24] This practice may have been much more widespread; many firms, fearing criticism that they are insulating managers from the effects of their own failures, have failed to announce the existence of such guarantees.[25]

## Deferred Compensation

Deferred compensation is a second technique used to transfer large amounts of mostly performance-insensitive value to executives without attracting much shareholder attention. Many firms offer programs that permit executives, or sometimes even require them, to defer receipt of compensation until some future date. In the meantime, the deferred compensation "builds" according to a formula devised by the firm. Executives do not pay taxes on the original compensation or on the accumulated increase until they receive payment, which often occurs after they leave the company. At that time, the firm takes a tax deduction for the amount paid. Most large companies have plans of this kind.[26]

Deferred compensation plans can take different forms. Some firms require that managers receiving salary in excess of $1 million, which would otherwise be nondeductible under Section 162(m) of the Internal Revenue Code, defer the excess. Other firms have purely elective plans. Some arrangements permit deferral of salary only, while others also allow deferral of long-term incentive compensation and gains from the exercise of stock options or from the sale of restricted stock. Companies frequently provide matching contributions, with the amounts varying from firm to firm. At some companies, contributions are awarded at the board's discretion. At others, they are determined by formulas.[27]

Plans also differ in how the deferred compensation is "invested," that is, how the amount owed to the executive at the end of the deferral period is determined. Many companies provide a guaranteed rate of return (or a guaranteed minimum rate) on the funds.[28] Firms have often granted extra benefits to executives by providing rates of return that are higher than the market rate. For example, in 2001, at a time when one-year Treasury bills offered returns of 3.39 percent to 4.63 percent, both GE and Enron guaranteed executives a 12 percent rate of return. Other firms have offered a market return plus a premium. For example, Lucent has offered the return on the ten-year Treasury bill plus 5 percent.[29] Congress is now considering legislation aimed at preventing firms from providing executives with above-market returns in their deferred-compensation plans. Although the adoption of such legislation would eliminate this particular benefit to managers, deferred compensation plans would still provide executives with significant other financial and camouflage advantages as we discuss below.

## Differences from 401(k) Plans

Deferred-compensation arrangements appear analogous to the familiar 401(k) plans used by many employees. But, just as SERPs differ from the qualified retirement plans offered to lower-level employees, there are some important differences between executives' deferred compensation and 401(k) plans.

To begin with, 401(k) plans give workers an opportunity to put money in designated investment instruments; whatever the investments, employees get the same pretax returns they would receive by investing in similar instruments outside the 401(k) plan. In contrast, executives' deferred-compensation arrangements have often provided higher returns than those available in the market.

In addition, 401(k) plans are given a tax subsidy, while executive deferred-compensation plans are not. Under a 401(k) plan, a fraction of the employee's salary is placed in a tax-deferred account. The firm may also make a separate contribution to the account. As in a qualified retirement arrangement, the funds are invested and grow tax-free. Neither the firm nor the employee pays taxes on the income and capital gain generated in the account. Employees do not pay taxes on the contributions or the increase until they withdraw the funds. The employer, on the other hand, gets a deduction for both its contribution and the employee's contribution to the 401(k) plan. By placing current compensation in a 401(k) account, the employee gains the benefit of tax deferral without the employer's loss of a tax deduction.[30]

Firms could provide deferred compensation to executives through 401(k) plans. However, there are limits on how much money can be contributed annually to a 401(k) account. For the tax year 2004, employees covered by such a plan ordinarily cannot defer more than $13,000 of compensation.[31] In order to provide executives with amounts exceeding this limit, firms implement deferred-compensation arrangements outside the tax-advantaged framework of 401(k) plans. Executives' deferred compensation is therefore not based solely, or even primarily, on 401(k) plans.

Rather than contribute a portion of the executive's compensation to an account where the investment grows tax-free, the firm simply with-holds part of the executive's pay and credits the executive each year with a prespecified return on the money, allowing it to "grow" over time. The withheld compensation, along with the appreciation credited to it by the firm, is paid to the executive at a later date.

The company pays taxes on the income it must generate in order to pay the executive the promised buildup of the deferred compensation. If, on the other hand, the deferred compensation had been distributed when it was originally owed the executive, the executive would have invested the money and paid taxes on any income or capital gains subsequently generated. Thus, as in the case of a SERP, the effect of executive deferred compensation is to shift some of the executive's tax burden to the firm.[32]

If the employee and the firm are subject to the same tax rate and are able to earn the same pretax rate of return on their investments, executive deferred compensation, like a SERP, cannot reduce the parties' joint tax burden. While every dollar of deferred compensation lowers the execu-tive's taxes, it boosts the firm's taxes by one dollar. Like a SERP, and unlike qualified 401(k) and retirement plans, deferred-compensation plans for executives provide no tax-efficiency benefit when the firm and the executive share the same tax rate and investment opportunities.[33]

As in the case of SERPs, of course, there will be many cases in which deferred compensation outside 401(k) plans can increase or reduce the total amount of value available to the executive and the firm.[34] The firm and the executive may face different tax rates. Even if the firm and the executive face the same tax rate, the investment returns available to the firm may be higher than those available to the executive (although, as we noted in our discussion of SERPs, this is unlikely to be the case for companies with easy access to capital). However, there is no reason to believe that, absent the tax subsidy provided by qualified plans, there is generally a benefit to the parties when the firm defers the executive's compensation. In many cases, the tax burden on the firm is greater than the tax benefit to the executive, increasing the total tax that the two parties pay to the government.

Consider, for example, the case in which an executive of a profitable company is promised a return that is linked to a stock index. If the executive invests the money in shares of a stock index fund, the gains will be taxed at the long-term federal capital-gains rate, which in the highest bracket is 15 percent (as of 2004).[35] If, instead, the firm invests the money—in those shares, other investments, or its own business—the gains could be taxed at the marginal corporate rate of 35 percent.[36]

Thus, it is puzzling that over 90 percent of firms offer deferred-compensation programs to their executives.[37] As in the case of SERPs, there are good reasons to think that, in many firms, such programs are not an efficient form of compensation. It is curious that firms offering nonqualified deferred-compensation arrangements to executives do not offer such nonqualified plans to other employees. After all, if nonqualified deferred compensation is an efficient form of compensation for the executives of certain firms—say, because the firms have better investment opportunities than their executives—nonqualified deferred compensation should also be an efficient form of compensation for the nonexecutive employees of these firms. But firms rarely, if ever, provide nonexecutive employees with the option of nonqualified deferred-compensation arrangements in addition to their 401(k) plans. This pattern suggests that, in most cases, offering nonqualified deferred compensation to an executive does not increase the joint wealth of the executive and the firm.

## Camouflage Benefits

While it is far from clear that deferred-compensation arrangements provide efficiency benefits, their camouflage value is substantial. The compensation being deferred must be reported in the compensation tables in the year in which it would otherwise have been received. However, the substantial benefits that have been conferred by the deferred-compensation plan—the tax-free (and sometimes above-market) buildup over time—are not evident to outsiders.

Even assuming that the nominal rate of return used by a deferred-compensation arrangement is no higher than the market rate, the effective interest rate earned by executives is higher than it appears because of the substantial tax benefits. Executives must pay taxes on investment income earned outside deferred-compensation arrangements, but investing *within* such plans provides them—at the expense of the firm—with a tax-free buildup. Thus, as long as the rate of return in deferred-compensation arrangements is above the executive's after-tax rate of return, the executive makes substantial gains that do not show up in the compensation tables. The *New York Times* reported, for example, that CEO Roberto Goizueta of Coca-Cola was able to defer taxes on $1 billion of compensation and investment gains over a 17-year period.[38] Coca-Cola picked up the tab, paying taxes on the earnings needed to cover the returns credited to Goizueta's deferred-compensation account.[39]

Furthermore, while 401(k) plans offer lower-level workers returns equivalent to those available in the bond or stock markets, many deferred-compensation arrangements have provided executives with substantially higher returns. These executives have thus received investment income that was not only tax-free for them (at the expense of the firm) but also above-market. The benefits from these above-market returns have also been hidden to a significant extent.

The SEC requires firms to include in the compensation table for each executive the above-market interest earned that year on deferred compensation. In the case of a guaranteed interest rate, "above-market" interest is defined as returns in excess of 120 percent of the applicable federal rate (AFR) used by the Internal Revenue Service (IRS) at the time the guaranteed interest rate is set, multiplied by the amount of deferred compensation. By exploiting the SEC's definition of "above-market rate," firms have sometimes been able to provide executives with rates of return that are higher than those they could get on their own, without including this benefit in the compensation tables.

The SFC's definition of "above market" long-term interest rates is especially generous because boards can reset interest rates whenever doing so benefits executives. If market interest rates and the AFR rise so that the current guaranteed rate is not especially attractive, the firm can simply adopt a new, higher, guaranteed rate. As long as the reset rate is lower than 120 percent of the new, higher AFR, the additional interest accruals need not be reported in the compensation tables. If, however, market interest rates and the AFR fall, the firm can continue to pay at the old guaranteed rate, which is now above market. And because the AFR used for the disclosure threshold is that prevailing when the guaranteed interest rate was initially set, no matter how low market rates drop, the above-market interest paid to the executive never appears in the compensation tables.

Finally, even benefits that have come from rates of return exceeding the SEC's threshold are unlikely to be fully reflected in the compensation tables. The reporting requirement ends when the executive retires, but the executive often has had the option to continue enjoying the above-market rates after retirement. Such a stream of postretirement benefits—which could be quite substantial in value—would never appear in the firm's publicly filed compensation tables.

As in the case of SERPs, deferred-compensation plans could expose executives to the risk of firm bankruptcy. While 401(k) plans must be backed by their assets, which cannot be seized by the firm's creditors, deferred-compensation arrangements are simply a promise by the firm to pay compensation in the future. The executives owed this compensation are unsecured creditors who may not be paid in full if the firm becomes insolvent. As in the case of SERPs, Congress is considering legislation which would make it difficult for firms to shield executives from this possibility. To date, however, firms have often taken steps to insulate executives from insolvency risk. Many firms have used "security devices," such as trusts, to ensure that deferred compensation will be available to the executives. In addition, firms have usually permitted executives to withdraw deferred compensation at any time—such as when inside information suggests that a firm is about to fail. Shortly before Enron filed for bankruptcy, for example, its executives withdrew millions of dollars of deferred compensation.

For executives and their friends on the board, SERPs and deferred compensation have been very useful. They have provided a means for channeling large amounts of performance-insensitive compensation in a way that, under current disclosure regulations, has not been highly visible to outsiders. As one compensation analyst pointed out: "The disclosure of the myriad executive compensation plans—pension, supplemental executive retirement plans, deferred compensation, split-dollar life insurance—is not adequate in answering a fundamental question: What is the projected value of these plans to the executive upon his retirement?"[40]

## Perks in Retirement

Many compensation contracts promise executives a substantial stream of perks after retirement. For example, many executives receive a certain number of hours of corporate aircraft use annually for themselves, and sometimes for their families and guests as well. Some executives have even received unlimited lifetime use of corporate aircraft.[41] Other perks that often follow the executive into retirement include chauffeured cars, personal assistants, financial planning, home-security systems, club memberships, sports tickets, office space, secretarial help, and cell phone service.[42] Outgoing IBM CEO Louis Gerstner, for example, was given access to apartments, planes, cars, home-security services, and financial planning. Terrence Murray, former CEO of FleetBoston, received 150 hours of company aircraft use, a chauffeured car, an office, office assistants, financial planning, and a home-security system.

Another common benefit is giving contributions to charities designated by the retiring executive. FleetBoston gave retiring CEO Murray the ability to direct $3.5 million of the firm's charitable contributions to Murray's favorite institutions.[43] And Ford promised retiring CEO Jacques Nasser to endow a scholarship in his name at the educational institution of his choice (in addition to providing Nasser with a new car each year, financial-planning assistance, an office, and an assistant).[44]

Most of these perks cost the company more than may be apparent at first glance. Consider retiree use of corporate jets, now a common perk. Although the marginal cost of allowing a retired executive to use the company jet may appear limited,[45] it can run quite high. Consider the use of a company plane for a flight from New York to California and then back several days later. Because the New York–based aircraft and flight crew will return to the East Coast after dropping the retired executive off, the actual charge to the company is two round trips: a total of eight takeoffs and landings and approximately 20 hours of flying time, most likely costing—for fuel, maintenance, landing fees, extra pilot and crew fees and incidentals, and depreciation (an aircraft's operating life is reduced for every hour it flies and, more important, for every takeoff and landing)—at least $50,000.[46] Henry R. Silverman, CEO of Cendant, was promised lifetime use of the corporate aircraft or, if the plane was in use, an equivalent chartered plane at a direct cost of thousands of dollars per hour.[47]

Firms usually do not provide postretirement perks to nonexecutive employees. There is good economic logic to avoiding such in-kind compensation. Promising a retiring employee $10,000 a year for certain travel expenses is less efficient than providing $10,000 in cash. The reason is straightforward. If the retiree views travel as the best way to spend $10,000, the cash and the travel coverage will have identical utility. However, cash is superior if there are any possible circumstances in which the retiree would prefer spending some or all of the money on goods or services other than travel, because the retiree will receive greater utility at the same cost to the firm.

A retiree's needs and preferences are likely to change over time. Thus, economic logic suggests that if in-kind retirement benefits are provided, they should not be provided for long periods. Yet such long-term, in-kind benefits are often provided to retired CEOs: for example, Louis Gerstner of IBM received use of a plane, cars, offices, and financial planning services for ten years.

Although postretirement perks are unlikely to be an efficient form of compensation, they offer an effective means of camouflaging compensation. The value of postretirement perks is not reported when they are agreed to, and the firm incurs costs only after the executive has left, at which point any value provided is no longer included in the salient compensation tables. Postretirement perks thus offer yet another way of providing additional value to executives without ever having to include the benefits in compensation tables or even place a dollar value on them.

## Consulting Contracts

Like perks, consulting contracts provide substantial value to retired executives. They usually offer the retiring CEO an annual fee for "being available" to advise the new CEO for a specified amount of time per year. Approximately 25 percent of CEOs negotiate a postretirement "consulting" relationship with their old firm.[48]

For example, AOL Time Warner is paying retired CEO Gerald M. Levin $1 million a year to serve as an adviser for up to five days a month.[49] In 2000, retiring Carter-Wallace CEO Henry Hoyt was promised annual payments of $831,000 for a similar monthly obligation.[50] Verizon co-CEO Charles Lee negotiated a $6 million consulting contract for the first two years of his retirement. Delta Airlines CEO Ronald Allen's 1997 retirement package provided him with a seven-year, $3.5 million consulting deal under which, according to Delta's public filings, he was "required to perform his consulting services at such times, and in such places, and for such periods as will result in the least inconvenience to him."[51] Allen or his heirs will be entitled to the annual fee of $500,000 even if he is totally disabled or dies.[52]

These consulting arrangements provide flat, guaranteed fees for the retired executive's "being available" rather than payment for work actually done, and for a good reason: companies generally make little use of the availability for which they pay generously. For better or worse, new CEOs are usually not inclined to seek advice from their predecessors.[53] Allen, for example, reportedly "rarely talks" with the new Delta chief executive, Leo Mullin. Even compensation consultants acknowledge that retired executives add little if any value to the firm under these arrangements. According to Frank Glassner, CEO of Compensation Design Group, most of these consulting contracts are merely a way of increasing the severance payment to the departing executive. According to another executive compensation expert, Alan Johnson, "Most former CEOs are doing very little for what they're getting paid. . . . Usually, the demands [from new management] are minuscule."

Like postretirement perks, the consulting payments to retired executives never find their way into the compensation tables because they are provided when the executive is no longer an officer. However, in contrast to postretirement benefits, these contracts enable boards to provide retired executives with cash rather than in-kind benefits.[54] Retirement consulting fees are essentially a cash severance payment, turned over in installments, disguised as compensation for postretirement work.

If these fees are just a form of cash severance, what is the advantage of packaging them as consulting agreements? Besides ensuring that the payments are kept out of the compensation tables, dressing them up as consulting fees obscures their nature as severance payments that essentially increase the total compensation received by executives for their pre-retirement work. Some observers might believe that the outgoing CEO will in fact provide valuable advice to new management, and therefore they view the payments as legitimate consideration for postretirement services. Needless to say, these consulting agreements do not tie the retired executive's pay to any personal contribution to shareholder value either before or after retirement.

### Decoupling Pay from Performance

Although the following chapters will discuss at length the insufficient correlation between pay and performance under current compensation practices, it is worth noting here that the retirement payments reviewed in this chapter are largely insensitive to performance. SERPs typically provide executives with some additional multiple of their cash compensation that is largely independent of performance. Deferred compensation provides value to executives through tax-free income buildup at favorable rates that are usually not affected by managers' performance. Likewise, postretirement perks and consulting fees are generally fixed in advance, rather than made contingent on future performance.

It could be argued that these retirement benefits reflect arm's-length contracting because they provide performance-insensitive compensation in a more tax-efficient way than increasing cash salary. Recall that Section 162(m) of the Internal Revenue Code limits firms to deducting each year, with respect to a particular executive, no more than $1 million in pay that is not performance-based. Firms can circumvent this limitation on deductibility by paying performance-decoupled compensation *after* the executive retires, when the rule does not apply. If, for some reason, it were efficient to provide executives with large amounts of performance-insensitive compensation, there would indeed be tax advantages to doing so through retirement benefits rather than through additional cash salary. The channeling of value through retirement benefits keeps the compensation not only out of shareholders' sight but also beyond the reach of Section 162(m).

Clearly, given a fixed, large amount of performance-decoupled compensation, shareholders are better off if the firm is able to deduct it. Everything else being equal, shareholders might therefore prefer much of the executive's non-performance-based compensation to be paid after retirement, when Section 162(m) no longer limits deductibility. But the important question is whether executives should receive so much pay that is decoupled from performance. Because of the camouflaging of retirement benefits, not only managers' total compensation is higher than it appears from the compensation tables but also the fraction of total compensation that is decoupled from performance is larger than an examination of these tables would suggest.

# 9

## Executive Loans

As of December 31, 1998, the outstanding principal balances of the . . . loans to [officers and directors] . . . which are guaranteed by Conseco were as follows: Mr Hilbert, $106,982,175; Ms Cuneo, $29,362,942; Mr Dick, $51,259,296; Mr Coss, $7,872, 996; Dr Decatur, $17,539,752; Mr Gongaware, $24,871,750. . . .

Conseco's 1999 Proxy Statement

ALTHOUGH PUBLIC COMPANIES are now prohibited from extending loans to executives, firms' past practices in this area offer a nice illustration of camouflage. Executive loans have been widely used to provide managers with a substantial amount of performance-independent pay in a way that escaped outsider attention.

### The Use of Loans

In the past, firms often granted loans, or guaranteed third-party loans, to the CEO and other top managers.[1] Most of these loans were unsecured or secured only by the firm's stock. In addition, most of the loans carried below-market interest, and a substantial number were interest-free. Many of these loans were ultimately forgiven.

When WorldCom, Kmart, and other firms that had made large loans to executives filed for bankruptcy in 2002, the loans received a significant amount of negative public attention. This led Congress to include in the Sarbanes-Oxley Act of 2002 a prohibition against company loans to directors and officers with very narrow exceptions.[2] Existing loans, however, were exempted from the prohibition. As a result, directors and executives continue to reap the benefits from billions of dollars in existing loans.[3] Although new executive loans have been taken off the compensation menu for now, we can learn from their former ubiquity about the tendency of boards and managers to select from among available compensation devices those that provide significant camouflage.

Among the most notorious executive loans are those that were granted to WorldCom CEO Bernard Ebbers.[4] Between September 2000 and the beginning of 2002, WorldCom directly or indirectly extended hundreds of millions of dollars—approximately 20 percent of the cash on the firm's balance sheet—in unsecured loans to Ebbers to help him pay off margin debt in his personal brokerage account. In exchange, Ebbers promised not to sell his WorldCom shares. The loans were made at floating interest rates that hovered between 2.15 percent and 2.35 percent. These rates were well below the prevailing rates for large-margin accounts—Charles Schwab was charging 5.75 percent on large-margin loans—even though, unlike margin loans, the loans made to Ebbers were unsecured.

When Ebbers left WorldCom, he still owed the firm $408 million. He promised to satisfy these remaining obligations and, under the terms of his severance arrangement, he had until 2008 to do so. However, much of that $408 million will probably never be recovered. After WorldCom entered bankruptcy, the company shares that Ebbers agreed to hold became almost worthless, and Ebbers failed to make payments due under the terms of the arrangement.[5] Had Ebbers taken out a regular, higher interest margin loan from a broker, the lender would not have suffered such a fate. The shares serving as collateral for the margin loan would have been seized and sold to cover the loan when the stock price was still high enough to make this possible.

Other firms have extended or guaranteed large loans to executives. For example, in 1999, Conseco guaranteed loans of $175 million to its CEO and $375 million to other executives to buy company stock. When the stock later lost most of its value,[6] Conseco lent the executives millions of dollars to pay interest on the loans.[7] The total amount of the loans exceeded Conseco's 1997 net earnings of $567 million.[8] Hundreds of millions of dollars of these loans had not been paid back as of mid-2004.[9] Similarly, Comdisco guaranteed more than $100 million to its executives to buy Comdisco shares, whose price subsequently plummeted.[10] Tyco lent its CEO $62 million for "relocation costs."

Although most executive loans have been smaller than those granted by WorldCom, Conseco, Comdisco, and Tyco, the practice has been widespread. According to a study by The Corporate Library, an independent research firm, more than 30 percent of the 1,500 largest U.S. firms disclosed cash loans to executives in their 2002 regulatory filings.[11] The average size of the cash loans was about $11 million. The total amount of insider indebtedness under the loans was $4.5 billion. Although many cash loans were stock-purchase related, many were for home improvements, investments, or other purposes apparently unrelated to employment. More than 25 percent of the firms reporting executive loans did not bother to report their purpose.[12]

## Arm's-Length Contracting?

Most employees who need loans turn to banks, not to their employers. Clearly, if it were more efficient for firms to act as their employees' banks, they would do so across the board, not only for executives. Presumably, firms do not regularly operate as their employees' banks because they lack a comparative advantage over outside banks in providing banking services. Indeed, Kathleen Kahle and Kuldeep Shastri have concluded that most firms that lend to executives have higher lending costs than do conventional lenders.[13] Because executives have at least as much access to banks as other employees, one would not expect firms that are acting at arm's length to extend loans to executives but not to other employees.

Approximately 40 percent of loans are provided to enable executives to purchase more stock in their firms.[14] It is often argued that lending money to executives at favorable rates for that purpose benefits shareholders by aligning executives' interests with their own. However, even if it were desirable to give managers a financial incentive to borrow money to purchase shares, the loan does not have to be extended by the firm.

Suppose, for example, that a firm wishes to encourage an executive to take out a $1 million loan to purchase shares. It may do so by offering to lend him or her money directly at a rate that is, say, 2 percent below market. Alternatively, however, the firm can let the executive take out a bank loan at the market rate and simply commit to pay him or her 2 percent of the outstanding balance each year until the loan is repaid. The latter method offers the executive the same economic subsidy but does not require the firm to engage in lending.

Interestingly, firms extending loans to executives to buy company stock take few if any steps to prevent managers from simultaneously selling shares they already own. As a result, the Kahle and Shastri study finds that loans enabling managers to buy 100 shares of company stock increase managerial ownership by an average of only 8 shares.[15] This pattern makes it difficult to justify loans as an efficient device for increasing executive share ownership.

## Camouflaging Subsidized Rates

The favorable interest rates often carried by executive loans provide executives with additional compensation. An executive who borrows money on an arm's-length basis from a bank is required to pay the market interest rate on the loan. But about 50 percent of companies granting executive loans charge no interest, and the remaining companies charge rates that are on average significantly below market rates. The difference between the market interest rate and the reduced rate charged by the firm represents ongoing compensation to the executive, and a corresponding cost to the company, for as long as the loan remains outstanding.

But such compensation often does not fully appear in the published compensation tables on which many outsiders focus. Firms are required to disclose the difference between the actual interest paid on executive loans and the market rate in the "other annual compensation" column of the compensation table. But the SEC has not clearly defined the term "market rate," and firms have often used the ambiguity to exclude the interest subsidy—in whole or in part—from the compensation tables.

WorldCom, for example, excluded from its compensation tables the implicit income given to Ebbers via the loans extended to him, despite the fact that the rates were far below the prevailing rates on margin loans. WorldCom later explained that it had (conveniently) interpreted the low floating loan rates to be market rates because these were the rates at which WorldCom was borrowing under one of its credit facilities. This trick enabled the company to exclude from its compensation tables a benefit to Ebbers worth millions of dollars each year.

Note that, for tax purposes, executives have to report and pay taxes on the implicit income in below-market interest rate loans. The Internal Revenue Service (IRS) treats as taxable income the difference between the rate the executives are charged by the company and the Internal Revenue Service's specified applicable federal rate for the loan. Unfortunately, however, the SEC has not followed the IRS in clearly defining the market rate. As a result, firms have been able to exploit this ambiguity to exclude from their compensation tables the implicit income from interest rate subsidies that executives must report as income on their own tax returns.

To be sure, the existence and terms of loans to executives have usually been reported by firms as part of their disclosure of related-party transactions in SEC filings. However, firms have been able to avoid including the value of these favorable loans to executives in the compensation tables—or anywhere else in their public filings.

## Loan Forgiveness

The practice of loan forgiveness has further enhanced the camouflage benefits of executive loans.[16] An executive who borrowed money from a bank would be required to repay the money with interest or face the prospect of the bank seizing the executive's property. Not surprisingly, firms that lent money to their own executives were much more lenient. More than 25 percent of the firms whose public filings revealed whether repayment was required indicated that they had forgiven or were forgiving loans.[17] It has been estimated that as much as $1 billion of the loans extended before the Sarbanes-Oxley Act will eventually be forgiven, either while the executives are still at their companies or when they leave.[18] When loans are forgiven, firms often "gross them up": they make a large cash payment to the executive to cover income taxes arising from the forgiveness, as well as the additional tax liability associated with the cash payment.[19]

In many cases, the firm explicitly committed at the outset to full or partial loan forgiveness if certain conditions were met, such as the executive remaining employed for a specified period. The value provided by these "retention loans" was almost completely performance insensitive; all the executive had to do was remain at the firm. In addition, these loans offered camouflage benefits. The large amount of cash provided was not reported in the compensation tables when given to the executive. Rather, the firm was required to report executive income only later on, when the loan was formally forgiven (which often was in the last year of the executive's service). In addition, the firm reported the income not as "salary," which is transparently performance insensitive, but rather included it in the much more vague category of "other annual compensation."

When loans have been made for the purpose of purchasing stock, there may well have been an implicit understanding that the firm would forgive the loan if the price of the stock fell substantially (or at least that the firm would not demand repayment while the price remained low). Such an arrangement would have been similar to, but often less tax efficient than, granting the executive an option to buy shares at an aggregate exercise price equal to the amount owed on the loan. From a camouflage perspective, however, an important difference was that an option grant had to be reported in the executive compensation tables, while a loan to buy stock did not. Thus, the firm could provide the executive with something economically similar to options without including its value in the highly visible compensation tables.

Down the road, if the stock price went up, the executive repaid the loan, and any profit made on the shares did not have to be reported as compensation. If the stock price remained below the amount owed and the loan was actually forgiven, the amount forgiven was reported in the compensation tables only in the year the forgiveness took place. Because such forgiveness often took place when the executive left the company, the inclusion in the compensation tables occurred at a time when the executive was probably much less concerned about shareholder outrage.

## Camouflaging the Sale of Shares

Yet another way in which loans facilitated camouflage was by hiding from investors the magnitude of managers' stock sales. Each year, hundreds of executives used to make swaps under which loans were repaid with company stock.[20]

Before the Sarbanes-Oxley Act of 2002 took effect, executives selling stock on the open market had to report the sale by the tenth day of the following month. But when executives gave stock to the company to repay loans—essentially selling the stock to the company—they had to report such transactions only within 45 days after the end of the fiscal year in which the transaction occurred. Thus, the loans enabled insiders to hide their stock sales for up to a year.[21] In one notorious case, for example, Tyco's CEO, Dennis Kozlowski, returned $70 million worth of stock to the company, partly to repay loans, even as he continued to say publicly that he rarely sold his Tyco shares.[22] The transaction was publicly disclosed only much later after the stock price had fallen substantially.

# Part III

## Decoupling Pay from Performance

# 10

## Non-Equity-Based Compensation

Eighty percent of success is showing up.

Woody Allen

MANAGERS' INFLUENCE OVER their own pay has enabled them to obtain a larger amount of compensation than they would receive under arm's-length bargaining. Perhaps more important, managers have used their power to secure pay without performance—arrangements that weaken the link between compensation and performance and that sometimes even create counterproductive incentives. The failure of compensation arrangements to provide desirable incentives is the focus of this part of the book.

Arm's-length bargaining might conceivably yield sizable compensation packages for executives, but such arrangements would be expected to provide strong incentives to enhance shareholder value.[1] Indeed, the large increase in compensation levels has been defended, and indeed positively portrayed, as necessary to align managers' and shareholders' interests. The problem, however, is that the high price shareholders have been paying for executive compensation has bought too little incentive. Much of both equity-based and non-equity-based compensation is substantially disconnected from, or only weakly linked to, managerial performance.

In subsequent chapters, we will show that executives' stock- and option-based compensation has been much less performance sensitive than widely believed. We begin, however, with the large part of compensation that is not equity based—that is, not tied to changes in stock price. Although the equity-based fraction of managers' compensation has increased considerably during the past decade and has therefore received the most critical attention, non-equity compensation continues to be substantial. In 2002, for example, CEOs of S&P 500 firms received on average more than $2 million in salary and bonus.[2]

As we discuss below, there are several reasons why much of the non-equity compensation that managers have been enjoying delivers weak performance incentives. Executives hired from outside the firm often receive hefty "golden hellos" even before they walk in the door. Once in office, they may enjoy increases in salary, and even bonuses, when the firm profits for reasons that have little or nothing to do with their own performance. Although bonuses' raison d'être is to reward good performance, they often have been given even to poorly performing managers.

In addition to performance-decoupled bonuses, managers have benefited from various hidden forms of compensation, such as retirement benefits and loans that are also largely decoupled from their own performance. Generous severance arrangements for fired managers have further boosted pay without performance. In sum, although tax rules make it more costly for firms to provide non-performance-based compensation in excess of $1 million per year, companies have found ample ways to circumvent the spirit of this limitation. With the tax rules failing to produce an effective $1 million per year cap on nonperformance pay, its levels are higher than is commonly recognized.

## Windfalls in Salary and Bonus

From the perspective of efficient incentives, it is desirable to reward executives for good performance. To determine whether managers have performed well, however, we must assess the managers' performance against that of their peers. There is no incentive value in rewarding managers for increases in stock price or accounting earnings that have nothing to do with their efforts or decision making, but rather reflect general market or sector changes, or other forms of pure luck.

If salary and bonuses are to create desirable incentives, their amounts must depend on the executive's own performance. Salary increases should correlate strongly with executive performance relative to that of other managers in the industry during the preceding period. Likewise, bonus plans should be designed to reward an executive only for the executive's own contribution to the firm's bottom line.

But empirical work has failed to find any strong, persistent correlation between cash compensation—salary and bonuses—and managers' performance relative to their respective industries. Although some correlation may have existed during the 1980s, there was none in the 1970s or 1990s.[3] These findings indicate that managers' cash compensation has been at most weakly tied to their own performance.

While connecting pay to executives' relative performance can provide good incentives, tying pay to stock price or earning increases that are unrelated to executives' effort does not. But such a link might be expected from a system shaped by managerial influence. Executives with influence over the board can use unrelated gains as a pretext for increasing compensation. When the firm's stock price goes up or its earnings increase, the board has a convenient excuse to increase executive compensation. Additionally, the rise in the stock price makes shareholders less inclined to resent or even notice the pay hike. Indeed, the evidence indicates that CEO cash compensation is strongly correlated with market-wide stock price increases.[4]

In addition, two studies show that cash compensation increases in response to sector-wide and firm-specific windfalls. The first study, by Olivier Jean Blanchard, Florencio Lopez-de-Silanes, and Andrei Shleifer,[5] examines what 11 firms did with recoveries they received in connection with settled or victorious lawsuits. Most of the suits had nothing to do with the firms' current business activities, and the recoveries were largely unrelated to the efforts of current executives. The study found that, on average, 16 percent of the net award was used to increase the compensation given to the top three executives in each firm during the three years following the award. These "windfalls" boosted median cash compensation to these executives by 84 percent.

The second study, by Marianne Bertrand and Sendhil Mullainathan, found that managers are rewarded for sector-related "luck."[6] The authors examined the compensation of managers when their respective sectors did exceptionally well for reasons beyond their control. They studied three such situations: (1) when oil price increases boosted the performance of the oil industry; (2) when a change in exchange rates benefited import-affected industries; and (3) when, for some other reason, all other firms in the industry performed well. They found that, in all three situations, managers were paid the same for a "lucky" dollar as for a "general" dollar (a dollar that does not appear to be generated by such "luck").

Arm's-length contracting would be unlikely to produce a correlation between pay and luck. Rewarding managers for good developments that are beyond their control imposes risk-bearing costs without providing any useful incentives. In a system shaped by managerial influence, however, managers can be expected to take advantage of windfalls to increase their pay.

## Do Bonus Plans Reward Performance?

We now take a closer look at the structure of bonuses. The term "bonus" suggests a payment for particularly good performance. It may, then, come as a surprise that the total salary and bonus paid to executives do not correlate strongly with executives' performance compared with that of their peers. A close look at how bonus plans have been designed, however, makes this finding much less surprising. Bonus design commonly provides executives with value even when their relative performance is not particularly good.

Firms use both objective and subjective criteria for determining an executive's bonus eligibility and amount. The objective measures are goals whose attainment can readily be determined. When such measures are used, the ostensible link to performance allows the firm to deduct the bonus under Section 162 of the tax code. In truth, however, these measures are often designed to enable the executive to benefit even after mediocre performance.

In some cases, for example, bonuses are tied to whether the executive meets a budget. Attainment of this goal, however, is hardly a clear indication that the executive has increased shareholder value. In other cases, bonuses are awarded when profits exceed those of the preceding year. This use of past accounting results enables some executives to "earn" bonuses even when they perform poorly, because a firm's profits can be the worst in the industry and still beat the prior year's numbers. A firm whose profits fluctuate around a low level will still beat the prior year's profits half of the time. Interestingly, but in our view not surprisingly, a large majority of companies with bonus plans based on objective measures do not base bonuses on the firm's performance relative to its peer group.[7]

Awarding the CEO for surpassing the preceding year's performance may not only fail to provide beneficial incentives; it may also distort managers' existing incentives. Such a scheme reduces the penalty for performing poorly: doing badly in any given year negatively affects that year's bonus but positively affects the next year's bonus. The same scheme also lessens the reward for performing well: improving performance in any given year, though perhaps increasing one's bonus that year, raises the bar and makes it harder to get a bonus the next year.

There are other ways in which firms provide performance-insensitive bonuses. For example, companies have based bonuses on accounting earnings that include the appreciation of pension fund investments, which generally depend on stock market performance and not on the efforts of the companies' executives. Bonuses are also based on earnings derived from restating the "expected return" of such investments. Adjusting the earning figures used in calculating bonuses to exclude pension fund income can be done without much difficulty.[8] And the difference between adjusted and unadjusted earnings can be significant.[9]

For example, in 2000 and 2001, General Electric reported as part of its accounting earnings pension income of $1.3 billion and $2.1 billion respectively, about 10 percent and 11 percent of its pretax earnings. The company used this pension income in the calculation of bonuses. In 2000 and 2001, IBM reported pension income of $1.2 billion and $904 million respectively, 10 percent and 13.2 percent of its pretax earnings for those years. Like GE, IBM considered the pension income in determining managers' compensation. In 2001, Verizon Communications reported a net income of $389 million and awarded its executives bonuses based on that amount. Net income would have been negative, however, had the company not included $1.8 billion of pension income. Thus, Verizon was able to use pension earnings to convert net income to profits, giving the firm cover to provide managers with higher bonuses.

It gets worse. It turns out that Verizon's pension funds did not generate any real income in 2001; they had negative investment returns, losing $3.1 billion in value. How, then, could Verizon report income of $1.8 billion from its pension assets? The company merely increased its projection of future returns on pension assets to 9.25 percent, a move allowed under the accounting rules then in effect.[10] Thus, the $1.8 billion in pension income used to move Verizon into the black did not even reflect actual returns generated by the pension funds. The pension income was simply the result of a change in the accounting assumptions. This certainly did not create any value for the firm or its shareholders.

To be sure, including pension fund results can sometimes reduce accounting earnings. Therefore, in theory, including pension results in earnings will sometimes reduce executive bonuses. But there were no such losses during most years of the bull market of the last two decades. Indeed, after the bull market ended and pension fund performance did reduce accounting earnings, General Electric, Verizon, and other firms rushed to remove pension effects from bonus calculations in order to boost executive compensation. In some cases, firms have presented these modifications as corporate-governance reforms.[11]

Bonus plan design thus appears to respond to managers' interest in being highly paid regardless of performance. One insider made this point bluntly in a media interview:

> They now use performance formulas—based, say, on return to equity—that determine the size of the bonus pool. Most of the formulas are b.s. When you've got a formula, you've got to have goals—and it's the people who are the recipients of the money who are setting these. It's in their interests to keep the goals low so that they will succeed in meeting them.[12]

In addition to objective measures—which, as we have seen, often fail to link bonus pay to managerial performance—many firms' bonus plans rely wholly or in part on subjective, discretionary measures. For example, boards consider factors such as strategic decisions and effective leadership. When subjective measures are used, observers often might reasonably disagree on whether the executive has met the goals. The decision to provide the bonus depends on the judgment of the board or its compensation committee.

Some economists justify the use of discretionary measures on the grounds that objective measures cannot fully reflect executive performance.[13] According to this view, the addition of subjective measures enables the board to base bonus pay on a more complete and accurate picture of the executive's performance. We agree that if a board is genuinely seeking to link pay tightly to performance, supplementing objective performance measures with subjective ones can serve this purpose. But the advantage of adding subjective measures to the menu critically depends on the assumption that the board will genuinely use them to tie pay more tightly to performance. Discretionary measures are unlikely to improve the link between pay and performance when the relationship between the board and the executive is not at arm's length. In the absence of an arm's-length relationship, such measures merely provide another way for the board to compensate poorly performing managers while still paying lip service to the importance of incentives and shareholder value. In fact, the use of subjective performance measures may well contribute to the *absence* of a strong correlation between cash compensation and performance.

Besides using objective yet undemanding targets and purely discretionary measures, boards engage in yet another practice that enables managers who perform poorly to obtain bonuses nonetheless. Boards often lower the goal posts when it appears that CEOs are unlikely to achieve their designated targets, or indeed have already missed them.

One recent illustration is Coca-Cola's lowering of a key target in its CEO's bonus plan.[14] When Douglas Daft became CEO in 2001, the board promised him a bonus increase if the firm's earnings increased by more than 15 percent annually over the five-year period beginning on January 1, 2001. The bonus was supposed to be between $30 million and $60 million, depending on the amount by which earnings growth exceeded the 15 percent threshold. In Coca-Cola's public filings, the compensation committee reported that "the award allows Mr. Daft to achieve significant wealth only in the presence of significant performance." In April 2001, the company cut its earnings expectations. In May 2001, just a few months after the board put the incentive plan into effect, the board cut the bonus threshold from an earnings growth rate of 15 percent annually to an earnings growth rate of 11 percent annually.

AT&T Wireless similarly reset its bonus targets in the middle of 2002, after it became clear that its managers' performance would fall short. This maneuver enabled the top five executives to collect $2.9 million in bonuses.[15] Other firms have set financial targets for bonuses while adding a caveat that executives who fail to meet the targets can still receive bonuses if that is in "the best interests" of the company.[16]

## Bonuses for Acquisitions

We have seen how contractually promised bonuses do not correlate with managerial performance as strongly as one would expect under the arm's-length contracting model. This delinking of pay and performance is also found in the practice of awarding "gratuitous" bonuses that are not required by existing contracts. A good example is the awarding of bonuses to executives whose firms have acquired other firms. During the last decade, in about 40 percent of large acquisitions, the CEO of the acquiring firm received a gratuitous multimillion-dollar bonus for completing the deal. In most cases, the award was in the form of cash.[17]

For example, in September 2000, the chairman of Chase Manhattan

Corporation, William Harrison, signed a deal to buy J. P. Morgan & Company for $30.9 billion.[18] As a "reward" for overseeing the acquisition, which took him three weeks to negotiate, the board paid Harrison a bonus worth $20 million (half in restricted stock), to be spread over 2001 and 2002. Harrison's three lieutenants, including Geoffrey T. Boisi, a vice chairman who had joined Chase only four months earlier, received special bonuses of $10 million each, in addition to their regular salaries and bonuses. NationsBank paid its CEO, Hugh McColl Jr., almost $45 million in restricted stock after the firm bought Bank of America. William Wise, the chairman of El Paso Corporation, received more than $29 million for his company's acquisition of Sonat.[19] Edward Whiteacre, the CEO of SBC Communications, received a $3.3 million bonus for, among other things, completing a merger with Pacific Telesis Group and for his work in connection with the acquisition of another company.[20]

Even though acquisitions tend to benefit the shareholders of the target company considerably by providing them with substantial premiums over the current stock price, they typically do not provide similar benefits to the shareholders of the acquiring company.[21] Share prices of acquiring firms do not generally increase around the time an acquisition is announced.[22] A recent study estimates that between 1980 and 2001, public shareholders of acquiring firms lost a total of $218 billion from acquisitions.[23] A 2002 *BusinessWeek* study examining large acquisitions made in the spring of 1998 concluded that 61 percent of the buyers "destroyed their own shareholders' wealth" in the process by overpaying for their targets.[24]

Why do some managers engage in acquisitions that do not benefit their shareholders? One commonly offered explanation is that such executives wish to expand the size of their empire and thereby enhance their private benefits and prestige. Another explanation is managerial hubris: executives may be overconfident in believing that they can increase the value of the target firm.

In any event, there is no reason to expect managers to make fewer acquisitions than is desirable for shareholders. If anything, the concern is that executives may engage in too many acquisitions. Thus, there is little reason for an efficient contract to provide managers with additional rewards for acquiring other firms. Indeed, the promise—or even the expectation—of an acquisition bonus could exacerbate managers' excessive acquisition tendencies.

Interestingly, during the 18 months following Chase's acquisition of

J. P. Morgan, for which Chase executives received a gratuitous bonus of $50 million, Chase Manhattan stock lost more than 30 percent of its value. To be sure, this decline may have been due to other factors. But Chase was not an isolated case. A recent study by Yaniv Grinstein and Paul Hribar found that, on average, acquiring firm shareholders lost money in transactions where the CEO received a completion bonus. Moreover, the higher the acquisition bonus, the worse the deal tended to be for shareholders.[25]

Even if acquisitions tended to increase the value of the acquiring firm's shares, there would still be little reason, from the perspective of incentives, to make acquisitions occasions for special bonuses. After all, compensation packages already have a mechanism—large option grants—that provides incentives for executives to pursue opportunities that increase share value.[26] Because of managers' private interest in maintaining and building their empires, there might be a need to provide an additional award for value-increasing *downsizing*. But there certainly would be no need to give a special bonus for acquisitions. Indeed, special bonuses would only strengthen managers' personal incentives to make acquisitions rather than pursue other business strategies that might better serve shareholder interests.

As chapter 7 discussed, managers of target firms often receive large acquisition-related benefits. Some compensation consultants "blame" large payments to target firm managers for the practice of giving gratuitous bonuses to acquirer executives. Alan M. Johnson, president of a New York City compensation consulting firm, explained: "And then there's a bit of envy. The [acquirer] executives are going to be sitting two doors down from guys whose options just vested. They're asking: What happened to me?"[27] The reasons usually given for the large payments made to the executives of target companies, however, do not apply to acquirers' executives.

An acquisition causes target executives to lose much of the power and prestige associated with their former jobs, if not the jobs themselves. Payments may thus be required to induce target executives and their allies on the board to support the acquisition. In some cases, payments might be required to induce target managers to remain with the company during the transition. The acquirer's executives, however, do not face a loss of positions or benefits. On the contrary, they experience an expansion of empire that is likely to boost their pay, perks, and prestige. Thus, acquisition-related bonuses given to the acquirer's executives, unlike those given to the target's managers, are not necessary to facilitate a value-enhancing acquisition.

Although acquisition bonuses are difficult to explain under the arm's-length contracting view, they are hardly surprising from a managerial power perspective. Executives naturally wish to boost their compensation, and boards are often willing to accommodate them, as long as the increase can be packaged in a way that makes it seem justified or at least not patently unjustified. Arbitrarily paying $50 million bonuses to executives can create outrage. Because acquisitions occasionally increase value for acquirer shareholders, however, they provide a useful pretext for granting bonuses to acquirers' executives. Boards can take the position that they are merely rewarding managers for moves that are expected to boost shareholder value. In any given case, such a claim would be difficult to disprove.

Moreover, from a managerial power perspective, managers with more power can be expected to get bigger acquisition bonuses, all else being equal. Yaniv Grinstein and Paul Hribar indeed found that CEOs who chaired their boards or served on their boards' nominating committee received an additional $1.4 million for completing a deal. This is yet another example of the strong relationship between power and pay.

## Golden Hellos

The weak link between pay and performance often starts with a "golden hello"—a large initial payment on top of the annual compensation package. These golden hellos have become larger and more common in the last ten years. Among the more infamous examples from the late 1990s were the $45 million paid by Conseco when Gary Wendt joined the firm as CEO, and the $10 million-plus that Kmart promised to pay incoming CEO Thomas Conaway during his first five years in office.[28]

Although golden hellos often include some equity, almost all of them contain a substantial cash component. The cash takes a number of forms, such as signing bonuses, salary, guaranteed bonuses, and forgivable loans. Whatever its form, the cash component of a golden hello is completely detached from managerial performance, because a manager gets the full benefit even if performance in the new job is mediocre.

Gary Wendt's $45 million golden hello from Conseco, for example, was entirely in cash.[29] And Kmart's Conaway was offered a package whose cash component was $10 million to be paid over five years, plus a $5 million loan that would be forgiven if he stayed until July 31, 2003. The latter part of the golden hello turned into a golden goodbye: the loan was later gratuitously forgiven and "grossed up"—the company paid the taxes triggered by the loan forgiveness—even though Conaway did not stay until the specified date. In 1999, Global Crossing hired Robert Annunziata and paid him a signing bonus of $10 million. When he resigned about a year later, he was not required to return any of the bonus.[30] Robert Nardelli, who became CEO of Home Depot in 2001, received a $10 million loan, with 20 percent to be forgiven each year, including tax gross-up payments. In addition, he was guaranteed at least $4.5 million annually in salary and bonus.[31] Richard Roscitt of ADC Communications was offered $5.5 million over four years, plus a $1.5 million "hiring bonus." Aetna's John Rowe was granted a $2 million "signing bonus" and a $1.4 million "retention bonus."

Companies frequently justify golden hellos as necessary to attract star CEOs who are reluctant to forfeit the substantial income they expect to earn in their current positions. To attract such a CEO, it might be argued, a firm must offer a compensation package with an expected value exceeding the candidate's outside opportunities. Our focus here, however, is not on the magnitude of expected compensation but rather on its structure. Even very sizable golden hellos can be given in a form—say, in options—that makes the ultimate value obtained by the executive at least somewhat performance dependent. In addition to attracting the executive, such compensation would also provide incentives. Nevertheless, firms generally include substantial performance-insensitive components in their golden hellos. Thus, the practice of granting golden hellos contributes to weakening the overall link between compensation and performance.

## Split-Dollar Life Insurance Policies

In the past, many firms took out split-dollar life insurance policies for their executives, purchasing billions of dollars' worth of insurance. The adoption of the Sarbanes-Oxley Act has made firms reluctant to continue this practice because the act prohibits executive loans, and a split-dollar life insurance policy could be considered a loan to the covered executive.[32] Prior to the adoption of the act, however, the widespread use of such policies provided another source of performance-insensitive compensation for executives.

Under one common form of split-dollar life insurance, the executive owns the policy and the firm pays the premium. In some cases, the executive also pays part of the premium, but usually only a small fraction. A small part of the premium pays for the death benefit; the rest is invested tax-free to build up the "cash value" of the policy. The executive, meanwhile, assigns the employer a portion of the executive's interest in the proceeds of, or the cash surrender value of, the policy. This amount is used to repay the premiums paid by the employer. This split-dollar life insurance arrangement is equivalent to a transaction in which (1) the firm lends the executive, interest-free, the funds needed to make premium payments for the term of the policy; (2) the executive purchases an equivalent insurance policy for him or herself; and (3) the executive receives the cash value of the policy when it matures, using part of the money to repay the principal on the loan.

The accruing premium payments—the value transferred to executives—have often been quite substantial. Comcast paid nearly $20 million in executive split-dollar life insurance premiums during the years 1999–2001.[33] In 2000, Estee Lauder promised to pay $26 million in premiums over five years for its CEO, Frank Langhammer. Cendant made premium payments of a similar magnitude on a $100 million split-dollar policy for CEO Henry Silverman.[34]

It is possible to defend split-dollar life insurance policies as consistent with arm's-length contracting on tax grounds: a tax loophole, only recently closed by the IRS, enabled firms to use split-dollar policies to provide value to executives tax-free.[35] But because split-dollar policies involve a third party—the insurance company—they entail significant transaction costs, and these transaction costs could outweigh any tax benefits. Notably, firms have not offered such policies to nonexecutive employees, though one would expect them to do so if split-dollar policies were overall an efficient way to deliver compensation. Whether or not the tax benefits outweigh the transaction costs, however, the use of split-dollar policies has provided executives with a significant amount of pay without performance.

## Soft Landing in Cases of Utter Failure

The extent to which pay is tied to performance depends not only on how much managers are rewarded for relatively good performance, but also on how much they are "punished" for poor performance. Therefore, in examining the relationship between compensation and performance, we must consider the cost to executives of poor performance. Currently, most compensation contracts ensure that executives receive generous treatment even in cases of spectacular failure.

As discussed in chapter 7, in the unusual cases where executives are asked to leave because of poor performance, boards often provide large gratuitous goodbye payments. These payments, however, come on top of the already substantial severance payments that executives' contracts generally provide. Altogether, the large amounts paid to fired executives considerably reduce the cost of failure.

Among the better known soft landings in recent years is that of Mattel CEO Jill Barad. She received $50 million in severance pay after being employed for only two years, during which time Mattel's stock price fell by 50 percent, wiping out $2.5 billion in shareholder value. In another example, Conseco provided $49.3 million to departing CEO Stephen Hilbert, who left the company in a precarious financial situation.[36] The Conseco board then gave incoming CEO Gary Wendt a package that guaranteed more than $60 million in compensation, even if he failed. Procter & Gamble gave ousted CEO Durk Jaeger a $9.5 million bonus, even though he lasted only 17 months on the job and oversaw a 50 percent drop in the value of P&G stock, a loss of $70 billion in shareholder value.

Promises of such comfortable landings are not unusual. Henry Silverman, the CEO of Cendant, received a contract guaranteeing $140 million in cash if he were fired in 2003 or 2004 for any reason other than a small number of specified causes. Home Depot CEO Robert Nardelli was promised that if he quit or was fired under a broad range of circumstances during his first three-year contract, Home Depot would still pay the full compensation promised under the contract, forgive the balance of a $10 million loan, and provide $20 million in cash. Disney CEO Michael Eisner was guaranteed "post-termination annual bonuses" that would be paid if he were fired or quit except under a very narrow range of circumstances. The bonuses were to continue for two years after the expiration of the original contract and would pay at least $6 million annually.[37]

These generous severance packages are often guaranteed as long as the executives are not removed "for cause"—usually defined rather narrowly as felony, fraud, malfeasance, gross negligence, moral turpitude, and, in some cases, willful refusal to follow the direction of the board. As long as they are not clearly acting in bad faith or in a deliberately negligent way, then, CEOs are virtually guaranteed a "soft landing," no matter how dismal their performance may be.[38]

It might be argued that such provisions are necessary to provide risk-averse executives with insurance against termination for poor performance. We find this insurance rationale unpersuasive. For one thing, these packages typically provide the ousted CEO with severance equal to three or more years' total annual compensation.[39] Because the duration of the typical executive compensation contract is only three years, in many cases a CEO would not earn much less by getting fired than by completing the contract.

Moreover, severance arrangements designed with insurance in mind would cease providing value to the former CEO once the executive finds other employment. However, only 2 percent of firms in the S&P 500 would reduce any part of a severance package once the executive finds new work. In the vast majority of such firms, executives are under no obligation to seek further employment during the severance period, and if the executives do find such employment, their benefits will not be reduced.[40] Thus, severance arrangements not only insulate executives from the costs of termination, they may even make executives who take another job better off overall.

Finally, and perhaps most importantly, the insurance rationale is, if anything, more applicable to other employees. Nonexecutive employees are generally more likely to be terminated than executives, but they rarely receive severance provisions that insulate them from the costs of termination. Given executives' accumulated wealth and the generous retirement benefits they commonly receive after leaving the firm, they are likely to be, if anything, less risk-averse and better able to insure themselves than most other employees. In addition, executives' large compensation packages are commonly premised on the importance of providing them with incentives. Thus, we should expect executive pay to be more sensitive to performance, not less—and hence should expect executives to receive less protection, not more, in the event of dismal failure.

To be sure, one could argue that executives' severance payments are intended to protect them if they are forced out for reasons other than their own poor performance. However, given boards' reluctance to dismiss even mediocre CEOs, it is highly unlikely that a board will dump a CEO who is performing satisfactorily. For one thing, CEOs, unlike other employees, never face the risk that their position will be eliminated due to changes in the firm. Furthermore, even if dismissal for nonperformance reasons were a realistic possibility for executives, the specter of a substantial financial penalty would still improve incentives as long as termination is strongly correlated with poor performance.

In any event, it is possible (if desired) both (1) to deny large severance payments to an executive who has performed very poorly and (2) to protect an executive from the unlikely event of being fired by the board while performing adequately. Compensation contracts could specify that a departing CEO would receive no severance pay, or substantially curtailed pay, should the departure occur under certain objective conditions that reflect a high likelihood of extremely poor performance. For example, a contract could stipulate a reduction in departure benefits when the firm's performance (in terms of stock price or earnings) is sufficiently poor relative to that of its industry peers. Yet we do not find such provisions. Thus, the practice of providing generous severance packages, however weak the company's performance at the time of severance, contributes to the decoupling of pay from performance.

## The Myth of Limited Nonperformance Pay

During the 1990s, while executives received vast and ever-increasing levels of compensation, it was widely believed that this compensation was largely based on performance. The enactment of Section 162(m) of the Internal Revenue Code in 1992 reinforced this general perception. Because 162(m) limits the deductibility of non-performance-based pay to $1 million, one might believe that such pay had been capped and that compensation in excess of that amount must therefore be tightly linked to performance. This, however, has not been the case.

To begin with, managers in many companies have been paid salaries exceeding $1 million, even though the excess is not deductible.[41] In such cases, the use of nonperformance pay not only fails to produce desirable incentives but also imposes substantial tax costs. Interestingly, only 22 percent of corporations paying more than $1 million in nonperformance compensation defer some or all of that excess in order to preserve the deductibility of the compensation.[42]

In addition, although most bonus payments are regarded as performance based for purposes of Section 162(m), they often are only weakly tied to performance. As we have discussed, bonuses are often conditioned on easily attained performance targets that do not reflect good performance relative to peer firms. They also often reward executives for things—positive developments in the market or the sector as a whole, other types of luck, making acquisitions, and so forth—that clearly have nothing to do with managerial performance.

Furthermore, as discussed in the two preceding chapters, managers obtain substantial value from pensions, deferred compensation, post-retirement perks and consulting fees, and loan arrangements—value that is also largely decoupled from performance. Much of this income is never reported in the compensation tables filed with the SEC, and none of it appears in the pay statistics that financial economists use in their studies. This substantial "stealth" compensation further disconnects non-equity-based pay from performance.

In sum, the sizeable fraction of managerial compensation that is not based on options or restricted shares is linked only tenuously to performance. Firms continue to fail to harness this major element of executive compensation to increase performance incentives. Needless to say, the weak connection between non-equity-based pay and performance is not inevitable. Bonuses and salaries, for example, can easily be designed to reward managers for prior good performance relative to peers. Firms have decoupled non-equity-based compensation from performance because those who design pay arrangements have chosen to do so.

Defenders of compensation practices may try to downplay the significance of this pattern by arguing that the weak link between non-equity-based pay and performance is excusable because equity-based compensation is tightly tied to performance. As we shall see in the next several chapters, however, this is not the case. A significant amount of the stock and option compensation that executives receive is also decoupled from their own performance. As with non-equity-based compensation, equity-based compensation is more weakly linked with performance than many believe.

# 11

## Windfalls in Conventional Options

The huge gains from options for below-average performers should give pause to even the most ardent defender of current corporate pay systems.

Alfred Rappaport, *Harvard Business Review*, 1999

HISTORICALLY, MANAGERS' NON-EQUITY compensation has been only weakly linked to their performance. As a result, shareholders and policymakers have increasingly looked to equity-based compensation to strengthen the connection between pay and performance. Institutional investors and federal regulators, with the support of financial economists, began encouraging the use of such compensation in the early 1990s. Stock options became an increasingly important component of executive compensation during that decade.[1]

The use of equity-based compensation, however, has hardly lived up to its promise. Managers have been able to use their influence to grab the reins of the options bandwagon and steer it in a direction that serves their interests. As a result, they have obtained option plans that deviate substantially from those that arm's-length contracting would likely produce. These option plans have provided executives with ever-increasing amounts of compensation while failing to provide powerful incentives to generate shareholder value in an efficient, cost-effective manner.

### Option Plan Design: The Devil Is in the Details

We should emphasize at the outset our strong support for the general idea of equity-based compensation. There is considerable evidence that, at least within a certain range of ownership levels, managers who own more equity tend to generate more shareholder value.[2] Because option compensation increases equity ownership and thereby helps link pay to performance, option-based pay can provide managers with desirable incentives to serve shareholder interests.

However, the fact that equity ownership can provide executives with desirable incentives does not mean that throwing more shares and options at executives, regardless of their cost, is always good for shareholders. Like with many other things, the devil is in the details. Before one can conclude whether a particular equity-based plan is good for shareholders, one must verify that the incentives it produces are, in fact, overall beneficial and, if so, whether the features of that plan—the number and the terms of the shares or options—are designed to create cost-effective incentives. An option plan designed to make managers better off is unlikely to produce as much value for shareholders as a plan created with shareholders' interests in mind.

A recent empirical study provides evidence that option plans have not been well designed to serve shareholders. Michel Habib and Alexander Ljungqvist examined the effect on shareholders of option grants to CEOs of publicly traded U.S. firms between 1992 and 1997.[3] They found that boards give CEOs too many options: on the margin, the incentive benefit of the last option granted is less than the cost to shareholders. In other words, all else being equal, shareholder value would increase if the number of options held by CEOs were reduced. Consistent with Habib and Ljungqvist's results, a study by Salomon Smith Barney found that firms in the S&P 500 that heavily used options to compensate both executives and employees underperformed the index.[4]

In this and following chapters, we show that the option plans that have been used by the overwhelming majority of public firms are designed to favor executives. The option plans actually used by firms have delivered a considerable amount of pay without performance and packaged that pay so that it seems defensible and legitimate. These plans include several important features that are difficult to justify from an arm's-length contracting perspective. One of these features is the failure of option plans to filter out windfalls—substantial gains for managers that do not result from their own performance.

## The Benefits of Reducing Windfalls

From the perspective of incentives, it is desirable to base pay on the measure that is the most "informative"—that is, best reflects the manager's own actions.[5] Managerial actions are not directly observable and verifiable. Accounting results often fail to reflect the current value of growth opportunities. Therefore, the share price of a firm may seem a useful tool for evaluating executive performance.

Without significant adjustments, however, changes in share price are not a good indicator of a manager's own performance. A company's stock price can increase for reasons that have nothing to do with its managers' own efforts and decision making. Falling interest rates, for example, can cause stock prices to increase considerably without managers lifting a finger. Indeed, one study of U.S. stock prices over a recent ten-year period reported that only 30 percent of share price movement reflects corporate performance; the remaining 70 percent is driven by general market conditions.[6] If performance is measured by changes in share price, managers who perform poorly relative to their peers might still be rewarded when the market or sector rises as a whole.

Of course, when managerial compensation is linked to absolute changes in the share price, managers also incur losses unrelated to their own performance when the market or the firm's sector declines. But being exposed to both positive and negative "shocks" to market and sector levels is overall beneficial to managers. For one thing, because the market tends to increase over time, the expected value of future market changes is positive. Thus, over time, the exposure to market and sector changes is more likely to produce gains rather than losses.

Furthermore, even if upward and downward movements in market and sector levels were equally likely, the structure of options implies that negative moves will be unlikely to hurt managers as much as positive moves will benefit them. At worst, negative shocks would make the managers' options worthless. On the other hand, positive shocks can boost the value of options by an unlimited amount. Thus, the possibility of negative market or industry shocks reduces the value of the options—but not by as much as the possibility of positive shocks increases them. On average, market and sector volatility adds value to managers' conventional options.

From shareholders' perspective, an option plan should be designed either to maximize incentives for the dollars spent or to achieve a certain level of incentives at the lowest possible cost. When managers are rewarded for market- and sector-wide price movements unrelated to their efforts, shareholders' money is not well spent. A firm could either create the same incentives for less money or use the same amount of money to create even more powerful incentives.

Suppose, for example, that a firm gives its managers 1,000 options to buy stock at the current market price of $100. Some of the expected value of the options—and therefore some of the expected cost of the options to shareholders—comes from the fact that the stock price may increase independent of the managers' efforts. If industry- and market-wide effects boost the stock price, the managers will be "rewarded" for these increases. Shareholders will pay for this reward even though it has no effect on the managers' incentives for good performance.

Compensation would be more effectively targeted at generating incentives if changes in the stock price that are not due to managers' own efforts were excluded from the compensation calculus. Although identifying all these changes can be difficult, identifying those due to sector or general stock market trends is a more straightforward exercise. The effects of these changes on the company's stock price can be simply excluded by measuring the company's performance relative to these easily calculated benchmarks.

Removing or reducing the undeserved reward component of an option's value—that is, moving from conventional options to reduced-windfall options—could substantially reduce the expected cost of option compensation. One study, by James Angel and Douglas McCabe, estimates that the cost of providing conventional options to executives at the 100 largest NYSE-listed firms is 41 percent greater than the cost of providing options that screen out market effects.[7] The costs eliminated by using reduced-windfall options could be saved or used to provide managers with additional incentive-strengthening compensation.

## The Many Ways of Reducing Windfalls

A wide range of methods is available for reducing managers' windfalls from stock price increases that are unrelated to the managers' own performance. Some of these methods involve "indexing" or otherwise adjusting the exercise price of options. Others involve making the vesting of at least some options contingent on share price appreciation exceeding a certain benchmark (say, exceeding the appreciation of the shares of the bottom 20 percent of firms in the company's sector). Plan designers could create schemes that reduce windfalls in ways that are aggressive, moderate, or gentle, tailoring them to each situation. The broad range of possible designs makes the widespread failure to filter out *any* windfalls especially puzzling.

## Indexing

The most familiar way to reduce windfalls is by indexing the exercise price—having it rise and fall either with sector or broader market movements, thereby screening out the effects of those movements on a firm's stock price. Options that are indexed to the average performance of a particular industry screen out not only broad market effects but also effects associated with the firm's sector.[8] Alfred Rappaport argued for this approach in a well-known *Harvard Business Review* article, attracting much attention from management researchers and practitioners but little interest from boards.[9]

By tightening the link between compensation and performance, indexed options generate more incentive per dollar spent. A firm can therefore reduce costs without weakening incentives. Or, for the same cost, the firm can grant more options and thereby improve managers' incentives.

Take a firm that now grants managers 1,000 conventional options with an exercise price equal to the current market price of $100. Suppose that the firm could, at the same cost, provide managers with 1,500 options whose strike price is $100 multiplied by a market index. Under such a scheme, if the market has risen 30 percent since the options were granted, the exercise price would be $100 × (1.30), or $130. This alternative scheme would provide managers with more high-powered incentives, rewarding them by $1,500 rather than by $1,000 for each dollar increase in the stock price that is not due to general market movements.[10]

Standard indexing, either to the market average or to the average of a basket of peer firms, is not the only possibility. Suppose that one objects to indexing an executive's options to the average performance of peer firms because there is a substantial probability that the executive will not make any money on the options.[11] Someone with these concerns may prefer a more "moderate" form of indexing in which the exercise price is increased by a certain fraction of the increase in sector stock prices. Alternatively, the exercise price can be adjusted not by tying it to the average performance of firms but rather by linking it to the performance of the companies in, say, the bottom quartile or decile of the market or industry.

Note that indexing may result not only in increasing the exercise price but also, when the market or sector declines, in reducing this price. Although this involves a cost to the firm, it provides rewards for managers who outperform their peers during periods of declining markets. As we will discuss in the next chapter, firms with conventional option plans often react to market or sector declines that make existing options seemingly worthless by providing new options or by repricing existing ones. Indexing provides much of the needed adjustment automatically.

### Other Methods of Reducing Windfalls

Although tying the exercise price of options to market or sector indexes is the best-known way of reducing windfalls, other approaches can be used. One is performance-conditioned vesting. Under this approach, managers who do not meet certain performance targets forfeit their options. The exercise price is usually set to the grant-date market price. If performance targets are met, the executive may exercise the options and profit to the full extent of the stock's appreciation.

These performance targets may involve an index. For example, the executives may be permitted to exercise the options only if the company's stock beats the market or a basket of similar stocks over a certain period. The performance targets can also use benchmarks other than indexes. For example, vesting can be conditioned on the firm's earnings per share, return on capital, and/or cash generation.

Performance-conditioned options should be distinguished from another type of performance-based option, which might be called a "performance-accelerated" option. A performance-accelerated option enables executives to accelerate the vesting of their options if they meet specified performance targets. Arguably, performance-accelerated options provide stronger incentives than conventional options because they increase the rewards that managers receive for performance exceeding the specified targets. However, if the performance target is not met, performance-accelerated options provide the same payout as conventional options with the same exercise price and maturity. Thus, such options hardly eliminate the windfalls that executives enjoy from conventional options.

Although we have discussed various ways to reduce windfalls, our present intention is not to determine the most efficient form of reduced-windfall option. Indeed, it is highly unlikely that one size would fit all. The efficient design might well vary from industry to industry and perhaps even from firm to firm. Our main point is that using some form of windfall reduction is likely to be efficient for at least a significant fraction of companies, even if not for all companies.[12]

## The Puzzling Avoidance of Reduced-Windfall Options

Firms have in the past largely avoided any version, however moderate, of "reduced-windfall" options. This widespread failure to adopt mechanisms that filter out windfalls has led one prominent scholar of executive compensation to conclude that "the almost complete absence [of such mechanisms] seem[s] puzzling."[13] Only after the corporate scandals broke was there some slow movement—under pressure from shareholders—toward adoption of reduced-windfall arrangements.

Firms have not only generally failed to use standard indexing, that is, linking the exercise price to changes in market or sector averages, but have also even avoided using the partial or moderate forms of indexing we discussed above. Moreover, before the governance scandals, only a small number of firms attempted to partially filter out windfalls by conditioning the vesting of options on performance targets. For example, in the late 1990s Monsanto did not allow its CEO's options to vest unless the CEO generated shareholder returns of at least 10.5 percent a year over a five-year period.[14] These policies were widely praised by the business press and by well-respected market participants such as Warren Buffett, but the use of performance-conditioned vesting failed to spread.[15] In 2002, only 8.5 percent of large public firms issuing options to executives conditioned even a portion of the grant on performance.[16]

The overwhelming majority of executives have therefore been rewarded for absolute share price increases, even those that are purely a function of broad market or sector rises that lift all boats. Indeed, during the big market boom of the 1990s, even executives with subpar performance often reaped large gains from options. With conventional options, if the market goes up 300 percent, an executive whose firm lags the market by 50 percent will still make very large profits—larger profits, indeed, than an executive whose firm beats the market by 50 percent during a period when the market is flat. Remarking on the situation, Warren Buffett has said: "There is no question in my mind that mediocre CEOs are getting incredibly overpaid. And the way it's being done is through stock options."[17]

## The Managerial Power Explanation

The almost complete absence of reduced-windfall options serves the interests of managers. Options whose value is more sensitive to managerial performance are less favorable to managers for the same reasons that they are better for shareholders: Reduced-windfall options provide managers with less money or require them to cut managerial slack, or both. As long as managers can get away with the use of conventional options, they will do so.

Recall the two ways in which reduced-windfall options can benefit shareholders. First, by decoupling the options from market or sector performance, the firm can create the same incentives at lower cost, saving shareholders money. In such a scenario, managers would earn less, losing the substantial expected value of changes in the firm's stock price that are due to general market or sector movements. Alternatively, the firm can use the same amount of money to grant managers a larger number of reduced-windfall options, thereby creating more powerful incentives. In this case, the managers would not earn less, but they would be forced to reduce slack—that is, take steps that would increase shareholder value but be personally costly (such as downsizing their empires)—more than under conventional options. Therefore, for the same reasons that shareholders should favor reduced-windfall options, managers prefer conventional options.

Furthermore, some managers may resist indexing the exercise price or conditioning vesting on performance because these arrangements can shine an unwelcome spotlight on their performance relative to that of their peers. By withholding rewards for below-par performance, reduced-windfall options make relatively poor performance more transparent to outsiders. The fear of being exposed as relatively mediocre is distinct from the risk of nonpayment under an indexing regime. That is, managers would fear embarrassment even if the firm adopts a soft form of indexing that offers a greater likelihood of payout than conventional options provide.

In certain situations, one type of reduced-windfall option—indexed options—could make executives better off. In particular, if the index declines during the period between the grant date and the exercise date of the options, the exercise price will be adjusted downward, increasing the holder's profits on exercise. This feature of indexed options improves the link between pay and performance (a given increase in the firm's stock price should be rewarded more when it occurs against the background of a falling sector or market), but it also provides extra value to executives when the sector or market declines. From managers' perspective, however, this benefit does not undermine the overall superiority of conventional options. Because the market is expected to rise over time, the expected benefit to managers from increases in the company's stock price that are due to general market increases substantially outweighs the expected costs due to decreases in the stock price due to general market declines.

Furthermore, as we shall discuss in chapter 13, managers have found ways to escape some of the costs of market declines under conventional options. When such declines occur, dragging down the firm's stock price, managers often have their options repriced or replaced with new options at a lower strike price. Conventional options combined with such resetting place managers in the enviable position of "Heads I win, tails I don't lose."

The windfall gains that conventional options confer on executives are especially large during a period of booming markets. Accordingly, they have made it possible for managers to reap during the last decade large amounts of compensation that have been unrelated to managers' own performance—and to do so in a way that appears legitimate and defensible. Because the general idea behind equity-based compensation is sound, and because conventional options are the standard form of equity-based compensation, executives and boards have been able to use such options without incurring "outrage costs" for failing to use reduced-windfall options.

We are not claiming that conventional options—rather than reduced-windfall options—were initially adopted because managers pushed for the former type. Those who initially advocated the use of options—whether academics, compensation consultants, institutional investors, or even managers themselves—may not have thought much about the comparative advantages of indexed and other types of reduced-windfall options. But we believe that the persistence of conventional options, and the failure of any substantial use of reduced-windfall options to develop over time, are substantially due to the advantages that conventional options have for executives.

For some years, leading investors, business commentators, and academics have frequently emphasized the advantages of reduced-windfall options. Even though reduced-windfall options have been recognized as potentially desirable, however, all but a small fraction of firms have avoided using them. Could this pattern have been due to boards' desire to conform to "the norm," and the resulting "stickiness" in compensation arrangements, that we discussed in chapter 5? We doubt that inertia and the tendency to conform can explain the almost universal use of conventional options.

During the period in which option pay developed and became widespread, stickiness has not stopped compensation consultants from rapidly introducing and "selling" new option features—such as reloading and accelerated vesting—that make managers better off. Indexing or performance-conditioned vesting are hardly more complex or difficult to adopt than these management-favoring innovations. While management-favoring innovations emerged and spread, reduced-windfall options have not been able to make it.

Furthermore, although conventional options still enjoy sufficient legitimacy and acceptability to be adopted without shareholder outrage, the benefits of reduced-windfall options are now sufficiently recognized that a move in this direction would likely generate praise rather than criticism. If anything, boards and executives switching to such options would probably win applause from outside observers. Pressure to conform, then, cannot explain the persistent dominance of conventional option plans. Managers' interest in keeping the windfalls provided by conventional options likely plays a major role.

# 12

## Excuses for Conventional Options

Despite the obvious attractive features of relative performance evaluation, it is surprisingly absent from U.S. executive compensation practices. Why shareholders allow
CEOs to ride bull markets to huge increases in their wealth
is an open question.

From a 1999 survey of the economics of
executive compensation by John Abowd
and David Kaplan

**D**EFENDERS OF CURRENT compensation practices have attempted to
explain why companies have been rewarding managers for stock price
increases due entirely to market- or industry-wide trends. Managers and
compensation practitioners have focused on accounting considerations.
And financial economists and economically oriented legal scholars have
labored to come up with economic arguments for why such pay without
performance actually might reflect arm's-length bargaining.

### Accounting Excuses

The most common explanation given for the widespread failure of companies to adopt reduced-windfall options—whether indexed options or
performance-conditioned options—has been the unfavorable accounting
treatment these options have received.[1]

Under current FASB rules, a company that grants employees stock options need not take a charge against earnings if (1) the exercise price is
fixed and equals or exceeds the grant-date market price and (2) the expiration date is determined in advance. Under these rules, a firm is not
required to expense conventional options—either when it issues the options or when executives exercise the options, which is when the firm

147

gets a tax deduction equal to the gains reaped by the executives.[2] Accordingly, the cost of conventional stock options has not been reflected in the earnings figures reported by firms.

Indexed options, however, lack a fixed exercise price and therefore fall outside this charge-free zone. Companies issuing indexed options must mark these options against the market on a regular basis and accrue an earnings charge reflecting the increase in the stock price over the indexed exercise price. Options that do not vest unless performance conditions are met are subject to the same unfavorable accounting treatment as indexed options. Thus, it is argued, boards have preferred conventional options over reduced-windfall options because the former result in higher reported earnings, which could in turn enhance share value.[3]

Accounting considerations, however, cannot adequately explain why reduced-windfall options have been so rarely used. We accept the possibility that market pricing is not perfectly efficient and thus that investors might place a lower value on a company that expenses its options than on an otherwise identical company that uses the same amount of options but doesn't expense them.[4] If this is the case, then, as long as other firms employ nonexpensed conventional options, a firm using reduced-windfall options that must be expensed might seem less attractive to undiscriminating investors. Yet, even if this is the case, it does not follow that the lack of reduced-windfall options reflects arm's-length bargaining.

Unfavorable accounting treatment could make reduced-windfall options undesirable for a particular company only if two conditions were met: (1) the market would have to be sufficiently inefficient that moving to indexed or performance-conditioned options would cause a substantial short-term decline in the company's stock price (in the long run, the stock price presumably would reflect the fundamental value of the firm) and (2) the cost of the short-term decline in share price to shareholders (who might sell in the interim for liquidity reasons) would have to be greater than the benefit to them of using reduced-windfall options. There is little reason to expect these conditions to be met by firms in general. It therefore seems unlikely that accounting considerations can adequately explain the almost complete absence of reduced-windfall options.

It is worth noting that sophisticated institutional investors and their advisers do not share managers' negative view of indexed options. Institutional Shareholder Services, whose advice is followed by a large number of institutional investors, and the Council of Institutional Investors, which represents more than 130 pension funds, have called for the use of indexed options, even though this step would reduce reported earnings.[5] Various institutional investors have also supported the indexing of options.[6]

Institutional investors also do not share managers' negative view of expensing. Indeed, these investors see expensing options as desirable for shareholders, whether or not reduced-windfall options are adopted. In 2002, TIAA-CREF began lobbying the approximately 1,700 major public corporations in which it owns shares to begin expensing options.[7] The Council of Institutional Investors has also indicated its support for expensing.[8] And in 2003, precatory shareholder resolutions calling for expensing received more support from shareholders, on average, than did any other type of precatory resolution relating to compensation.[9]

In the wake of the corporate governance scandals beginning in late 2001, and in response to pressure from institutional investors such as TIAA-CREF, hundreds of firms, including Coca-Cola, Bank One, and the Washington Post, have decided to expense options in an attempt to placate shareholders. Tellingly, even though these firms have bowed to pressure to adopt expensing, they have not switched from conventional to reduced-windfall options—despite the fact that the accounting excuse for avoiding the latter has been eliminated. Because managers are likely to continue to have influence over their pay, we predict that, as long as there is little pressure to adopt reduced-windfall options, most of these firms will continue to use conventional options even under voluntary or mandatory expensing. Behavior consistent with this prediction would further confirm that accounting considerations have been merely an excuse and not a real impediment to the use of reduced-windfall options.

The basis underlying the accounting explanation for the widespread failure to use reduced-windfall options appears likely to disappear in the future. In March 2004, the FASB released an "Exposure Draft" of its proposed rule to require public companies to expense stock options for fiscal years beginning after December 15, 2004.[10] Despite heavy lobbying by certain firms, it appears likely that the FASB will attempt to impose such a requirement. Congress is considering legislation that would require expensing options given to the CEO and the four other highest-paid executives but allow firms not to expense options given to other employees. Assuming that firms are required to expense executives' options, this requirement will provide an additional test of whether accounting can explain the widespread lack of reduced-windfall options. Continued insistence by firms on using conventional options, despite the lack of an accounting advantage, will indicate that accounting rationales were merely a cover that afforded managers option compensation on terms most favorable to them.

## The Battle over Options Accounting

Managers have exerted much effort to prevent the FASB from requiring options to be expensed. Their efforts may well have been motivated—at least partly—by their interest in continuing to enjoy conventional options.

Under basic accounting rules, if a firm were to buy plane tickets by giving the airline options to purchase shares of the firm, the value of those options would be entered as an expense on the firm's income statement. Expensing the options would make sense because the firm would have given up something of value in exchange for the tickets. The transaction would be equivalent to a two-step process in which the firm first sells the options to a third party and then uses the proceeds to buy the tickets.

However, firms have until now been permitted not to expense certain employee options: those whose (1) strike price is fixed and not below the grant-date market price and (2) expiration date is fixed. During the last decade, reformers have attempted to require firms to expense all employee options, but managers have played a major role in blocking these attempts. In the mid-1990s, the FASB sought to have all stock-based compensation accounted for on a rational and consistent basis—that is, expensed in line with the current treatment of indexed and performance-conditioned options.[11] Heated resistance forced the FASB to stop short of requiring firms to adopt this method.[12] Instead, the FASB required companies that fail to expense options to disclose the cost of employee options in footnotes to the firm's financial statements.[13] Following the corporate governance scandals, reformers renewed their efforts; although it now appears that firms will be required to expense at least top executives' options, managers have displayed considerable resolve in fighting any move toward expensing options, investing a considerable amount of time, effort, and political capital to avoid such an outcome.

Executives claim to have fought vehemently on the grounds that expensing options reduces reported earnings, leads to a decline in share prices, and thus hurts shareholders. Because option pay now involves substantial sums of money, the effect of expensing on bottom-line earnings would be quite significant. In 1992, expensing options would have reduced earnings by approximately 2 to 3 percent.[14] A decade later, however, expensing would have produced a substantially larger reduction in earnings.[15] In the case of some firms, such as Cisco, expensing options would in fact have converted reported profits into losses.

The value of employee options must already be reported in the footnotes to firms' financial statements, and thus is already available to the market. Managers have argued, however, that the market pays little attention to these footnotes, focusing instead on reported earnings. In their view, moving the information from the footnotes to the income statement itself will alter investors' perception of the company's earnings, cause stock prices to fall, and force companies to cut back on their desirable use of options.

We are skeptical about these claims. To begin with, the FASB would require *all* firms to expense options. Thus, even if markets were sufficiently inefficient to value a firm that voluntarily expenses options less than its peer firms that report the same information in footnotes, an across-the-board requirement would not generally put firms that expense at a disadvantage vis-à-vis their peer firms. Furthermore, if expensing is necessary for the market to register the cost of conventional options, there is no reason to believe that expensing should induce companies to use too few options. Rather, expensing should cause firms to reduce the use of options only when their (newly recognized) cost exceeds their benefit to shareholders.

In any event, the main point we wish to emphasize here is that managers' campaign against expensing has certainly served their own interests in maintaining favorable compensation arrangements. Rent-seeking managers have two major reasons to oppose expensing.

First, expensing options will make the magnitude of option-based pay more transparent to a wider group of outsiders. If, as executives claim, some investors pay more attention to items expensed on the financial statement than to those detailed in the footnotes, expensing will increase overall investor attention to the costs of employee options, including executive options. Options granted to senior executives constitute a significant fraction of overall employee options.[16] Expensing options makes the costs of executives' options more salient, and this, in turn, may put pressure on compensation plan designers to reduce the use of such options.

A study by Patricia Dechow, Amy Hutton, and Richard Sloan provides evidence that camouflage considerations partly explain managers' resistance to expensing.[17] The study found that the likelihood of a firm opposing the FASB's attempt to require expensing in the mid-1990s was positively correlated with managers' total compensation and with the portion of executive compensation paid in options. In contrast, the authors found no evidence that expensing options would increase the cost of raising new capital. The authors concluded that executives were advancing the cost-of-capital argument to disguise concerns that expensing would draw attention to their pay.

Second, expensing conventional options will deprive managers of one of their main justifications for resisting any shift to some form of reduced-windfall options: that such a move would reduce reported earnings. If *all* employee options were expensed, reduced-windfall options would have the same accounting consequences as conventional options. As a result, the accounting argument against reduced-windfall options would disappear, leaving managers' personal interests in conventional options uncomfortably exposed.

If the managerial campaign against expensing were truly driven by concerns for shareholder interests, managers might have been expected to also lobby against the expensing of indexed and performance-conditioned options. No plausible financial justification requires the expensing of a performance-conditioned option when a conventional option, identical in every other respect, need not be expensed. Indeed, the performance-conditioned option represents less of a cost to shareholders than the corresponding conventional option because there is a greater chance that it will never be exercised. Yet managers fiercely opposing the expensing of conventional options have shown no interest in seeking similar treatment for reduced-windfall options. Managers' focus on maintaining the accounting advantage of conventional options is consistent with their interests. Leveling the accounting playing field for *all* options would eliminate any accounting argument against reduced-windfall options. That might be advantageous to shareholders, but it would only make managers worse off.

## Efficient after All?

Financial economists often assume that the impact of disclosure on stock prices does not depend on how the information is presented in publicly available financial statements: in other words, that it does not matter whether an expense is revealed in a footnote or on the income statement itself. They therefore have sought nonaccounting explanations for the use of conventional options that fail to filter out windfalls. As we note below, however, none of these explanations adequately explains the absence of reduced-windfall options.

*Design Costs.* Some economists have suggested that schemes that filter out industry or market effects on the stock price are too costly to design and administer.[18] The necessary administrative costs are tiny, however, compared with the stakes involved. A wide variety of sector and market indices appear daily in the *Wall Street Journal* and are available online from numerous sources. Moreover, the securities laws already require public corporations to calculate and report stock performance data relative to their industry, line of business, or peer group.[19] In short, all the requisite information is readily available, and incorporating it into option plans would involve little cost.

*Avoiding Distortions in Managers' Decisions to Enter Other Sectors.* Some economists have argued that rewarding managers for stock price rises caused by general sector movements actually provides desirable incentives. The sector to which a firm belongs, so the argument goes, is not fixed; it might be affected by managers' decisions. It is therefore desirable to offer managers incentives to adapt to poor industry conditions by shifting company resources into more profitable sectors.[20] Providing such incentives requires rewarding managers not only for the firm's performance relative to its sector, but also for sector-related price increases. Moreover, sector-indexed options not only fail to provide managers with incentives to enter high-profit industries, but also give managers a perverse incentive to remain in a declining sector if their relative performance in that sector is better than it would be in a new, more profitable sector.[21]

Even if it were desirable to provide managers with an incentive to make good sector choices by rewarding them for sector performance, however, there would still be no reason to reward managers for *market-wide* increases. Firms that wish to encourage managers to shift into more profitable sectors could filter out market-wide increases exclusively by using options linked to a broad market index rather than to an industry-specific index. Thus, sector-shifting considerations cannot fully explain the rarity of all forms of reduced-windfall options.

*Softening Industry Competition.* Strategic considerations about competition underlie another explanation offered for the near absence of reduced-windfall options. By rewarding managers for industry-related stock price movements, conventional options indirectly link executive compensation to the performance of rival firms. Some economists have suggested that implicitly linking pay to rival firms' performance serves shareholders by softening industry competition and allowing all firms in the industry to make more profits.[22]

Not all firms, however, operate in markets where this type of implicit collusion is possible. Indeed, the evidence concerning the (limited) use of explicit relative performance evaluation (RPE) in annual incentive plans is not consistent with this strategic explanation. In plans using RPE, industry peer group comparison is overwhelmingly favored over broad-based comparison.[23] Although the possible advantages of softening competition may make it desirable for some firms to tie their managers' pay to the returns of industry rivals, it cannot explain the almost complete absence of sector-indexed options. Furthermore, even if it were generally desirable to tie executive compensation to industry returns, this would not explain the widespread failure to filter out broader market increases. Therefore, the implicit collusion theory, too, fails to explain firms' almost complete failure to filter out windfalls.

*Discouraging Excessive Risk Alteration.* Saul Levmore has offered a "super-risk alteration" explanation for conventional options. According to Levmore, indexed options would encourage managers to differentiate the prospects of their firm from the index in order to increase the likelihood that their options would be "in-the-money."[24] This could cause managers to forego the best projects and strategies in favor of those that have higher volatility relative to the index.

Even if indexing did lead managers to take more risks, it is far from clear that it would worsen their decision making overall. In the absence of options, risk-averse managers tend to take fewer risks than would be optimal for their diversified shareholders. Options, which reward managers for riskier projects, counter this distortion. There is no reason to assume that indexed options would have the net effect of worsening managers' choices among projects with different risk profiles. There is even less basis for assuming that, compared with indexed options, the benefits of conventional options are so large as to justify large windfall-based rewards. Finally, even if the effect suggested by Levmore were adverse for shareholders and sufficiently large to make indexed options undesirable for some firms, it would not likely be so across the board.

*Retaining CEOs during Market Booms.* Charles Himmelberg and Glenn Hubbard have argued that conventional options provide a convenient way to retain talented managers during market booms.[25] They find evidence that CEO compensation is positively correlated with market returns, a correlation that results, they argue, from the inelasticity of the supply of individuals qualified to run public firms.[26] In their view, the better the market does, the higher the demand for executives, and the more companies must pay CEOs to retain them. Because conventional options capture market-driven stock price increases, they have a built-in mechanism for increasing pay as the market rises.

Even if an automatic mechanism that provided more pay to retain executives during market booms were desirable, conventional options would not fit the bill. Conventional options do confer additional value on executives during booms, but much of this value comes in a form— increasing the value of already vested options—that fails to strengthen managers' incentives to remain at their current firms.

Consider a company that signs a compensation agreement providing the CEO with options vesting gradually over a three-year period. Suppose also that the company seeks to address a possible scenario in which, after the first two years, the stock market rises considerably, tempting the executive to switch to a higher paying firm. And it does so by giving the CEO conventional options that rise with the market. However, by the beginning of the third year, when the executive might leave for another job, two thirds of the options will have vested. While the rising market will have increased the value of these vested options, this increased value will have no effect whatsoever on the CEO's decision to stay on the job.

The increase in value of the options that are still *unvested* at the end of the second year might provide some incentive to stay, but only for at most another year, at which time the remaining options will vest. Interestingly, however, C. Edward Fee and Charles Hadlock have found that under current compensation practices, there is no relationship between the amount an executive forfeits by leaving for another company and the likelihood of jumping ship.[27] The reason they offer: new employers are willing to fully compensate the executives for what they leave behind. Moreover, Fee and Hadlock found that the amount an executive must be compensated does not affect the willingness of new employers to hire the executive. Thus, even a CEO's unvested conventional options are unlikely to facilitate retention.

Assuming that it were desirable to have an automatic mechanism that increases pay during market booms, using reduced-windfall options for that purpose would provide better incentives. While conventional options do offer more compensation to executives during booms than reduced-windfall options, all the increase comes in the form of performance-decoupled value. Thus, conventional options do nothing to strengthen executives' incentives to produce value. A more effective automatic mechanism for creating retention incentives would be to award reduced-windfall options at intervals throughout an executive's tenure. As the market rose, the executive would get additional reduced-windfall options that would vest only after a certain period.

*Reducing Managerial Risk-Bearing Costs.* It has been argued that standard indexed options (options whose exercise price is indexed to the sector or market average) would impose too much additional risk of nonpayment on risk-averse executives. Kevin Murphy reports that the probability that a given stock will earn returns in excess of a value-weighted index is below 50 percent. In contrast, there is an 80 percent probability that by the time a ten-year conventional option expires, the stock price will exceed the exercise price, yielding a profit for the option holder.[28] Presumably, risk-averse executives provided with standard indexed options would demand indexed options with a higher expected value than the conventional options they would be replacing. The same claim could be made with respect to options subject to performance-conditioned vesting.

A lower probability of payout, however, is not an inevitable consequence of reduced-windfall options. To be sure, indexing to sector or market averages would generally reduce the probability of a payout. But as we have emphasized, standard indexing is not the only possible form of indexing. One could instead implement a more moderate form of indexing that would put a CEO in the money even if he or she outperforms less than 50 percent of the competition. In fact, one could easily design an indexed option that has the same probability of payout as a conventional option.

Suppose, for example, that conventional ten-year options have an 80 percent likelihood of payout, and one wishes to design a ten-year sector-indexed option for Firm A's CEO with the same payout probability. In addition, suppose there are ten firms in Firm A's sector. One could simply tie the exercise price of the CEO's options to the stock price performance of the second-worst-performing firm in the sector. Thus, Firm A's CEO will get a positive payout as long as Firm A is one of the eight best performers in the ten-firm sector. (Of course, the better Firm A performs, the higher the payout.) This kind of indexed option has the same payout probability as a conventional option but provides much better incentives by tying the CEO's compensation more closely to the firm-specific value he or she creates.

Furthermore, even if standard indexed options have been considered the only reduced-windfall options available, risk aversion is unlikely to explain why almost no public companies have used them. Of course, a CEO who is given standard indexed options rather than conventional options may demand options with a higher expected value to compensate for the increased risk. But in at least some cases, shareholders will likely prefer such a tradeoff. It is highly unlikely that, in almost every publicly traded firm, the CEO is so risk-averse that the additional compensation that would have to be paid to the CEO for the extra risk of indexed options would exceed the benefit from improving the CEO's incentives.

*Managers' Interest in Investing in a Market-Wide Portfolio.* Conventional options reward executives both for company-specific increases in the stock price and for general increases in sector or market levels. The problem we have focused on is that compensation based on sector- or market-wide increases has nothing to do with an executive's own performance. Economists have been puzzled by the use of conventional options also for another reason: compensation for sector or market increases exposes executives to market risk. Given that managers are risk-averse and therefore value risky compensation less, it would be cheaper for companies—at least in a taxless world—to give managers indexed options and cash equal to the value of the market component of their options.

Some economists, however, have argued that executives might in fact be interested in investing in a market-wide portfolio and, if given cash, would invest it in such a portfolio.[29] On this view, giving executives conventional options is not more puzzling than giving them indexed options plus a large amount of cash. Indeed, assuming that the managers are likely to invest the cash in a market-wide portfolio, giving compensation to them in the form of conventional options might be simpler.

We have no quarrel with this analysis. Conventional options may well be no more puzzling than a combination of indexed options and a very large amount of cash. But the large increases in pay over the past decade have often been justified on the grounds that they are necessary to provide performance incentives. This justification made investors willing to accept these pay increases, which investors would have strongly resisted had they been largely in cash. Our point, simply, is that a large portion of the value of conventional options—which have been widely considered to be "performance-based pay"—is in fact decoupled from performance.

*Saving Taxes.* David Schizer has suggested that conventional options have a potential tax advantage over indexed options.[30] Recall that, since 1994, firms have not been permitted to deduct executive compensation in excess of $1 million if it is not performance based.[31] Both conventional and indexed options qualify as performance based.[32] However, a conventional option does not screen out market or industry effects. Therefore, such an option provides managers with considerable non-performance-based value. A conventional option could be useful to a tax-paying firm that wishes to (1) give managers tax-deductible pay that is not based on their performance and (2) provide that pay in the form of a call option on the market.

Schizer's argument acknowledges that a substantial portion of the compensation delivered by conventional options isn't performance linked. He is simply pointing out that, if such performance-decoupled pay is desirable, using conventional options at least enables firms to take a tax deduction. But he does not offer any justification for providing managers with vast amounts of nonincentivizing compensation.

Furthermore, as Schizer observes, firms have largely avoided indexed options even when there was no tax advantage to delivering performance-decoupled pay through conventional options, as was the case prior to 1994, when there was no limit on the deductibility of such pay. Moreover, for the many firms that do not pay income taxes, the deductibility of executive compensation is much less relevant. Thus, Schizer's tax theory cannot explain the exclusive use of conventional options by all but a few firms after 1994.

---

It is fascinating how much intellectual energy has been invested in attempting to explain how the absence of reduced-windfall options actually benefits shareholders and is thus consistent with arm's-length bargaining. Many financial economists dissatisfied with existing explanations have simply concluded that the widespread use of conventional options "deserves further research." Their faith that additional research will yield an efficiency explanation reflects the tremendous influence that the arm's-length bargaining model has long had in financial economics. To many, the possibility that pay arrangements are not the outcome of such bargaining, and therefore may not serve shareholder interests, is difficult to accept.

# 13

## More on Windfalls in Equity-Based Compensation

[At-the-money] plans are a royalty for the passage of time.
Warren Buffett, 1998

IN THIS CHAPTER, we continue to examine the surprising insensitivity to performance of conventional equity-based compensation. We first discuss three practices relating to option compensation that have benefited managers by providing pay without performance: the near-uniform use of at-the-money options, the repricing and "backdoor repricing" of options when the firm's stock price falls, and "reload" features that enable managers to lock in and profit from temporary spikes in the stock price. We conclude by explaining how the increasing use of restricted stock in place of options will tend to increase rather than reduce executives' windfalls.

## At-the-Money Options

### The Puzzle of One-Size-Fits-All Options

Options are supposed to provide executives with financial incentives not only to exert effort but also to make the right decisions for the firm.[1] Because managers are insufficiently diversified and risk-averse, they may hesitate to take chances that would be desirable for shareholders. Options are believed to counteract this tendency by providing executives with a financial incentive to take risks. The extent to which an option encourages managers to accept additional risk depends, in part, on the exercise ("strike") price. Strike prices that are too high or too low can cause executives to take on too much or too little risk. Similarly, the cost-effectiveness of options can depend on their exercise price.

Not surprisingly, the optimal exercise price in any given case is likely to depend on several factors.[2] Analyses in the financial economics literature indicate that it is highly unlikely that the same option design will be efficient in all cases. The incentives created by options depend on a variety of grantee-specific factors, including the executive's portfolio and risk preferences.[3] At the same time, a variety of firm-specific factors, such as growth opportunities and debt load, determine which incentives will be desirable.[4] Besides differing from firm to firm, these factors may vary within a single firm over time. There is no reason, therefore, to expect the efficient exercise price to be the same for almost all executives, at all companies, and at all times.

Yet an analysis of options granted to the CEOs of 1,000 large companies in 1992 determined that more than 95 percent were granted at-the-money—that is, with an exercise price equal to the company's stock price on the date of the grant.[5] This pattern, which has since persisted, was described by Brian Hall and Kevin Murphy as "striking."[6] Although there has been some movement in the last few years to out-of-the-money options, it has been slow and grudging. In early 2004, for example, IBM attracted considerable attention when it announced that it would begin providing to top executives options with an exercise price 10 percent higher than the grant-date market price.[7] Only a handful of firms use such premium options, however.[8]

Tax and accounting rules arguably could account for the almost complete absence of "in-the-money" options (options with an exercise price below the grant-date stock price). In-the-money options are not considered "performance-based compensation" under Section 162(m) of the Internal Revenue Code and therefore are not deductible if an executive's total non-performance-based compensation exceeds $1 million a year. Additionally, options that are granted in-the-money must be charged against earnings, unlike at-the-money and out-of-the-money options.

Neither the tax nor the accounting explanation can explain, however, why fewer than 5 percent of companies have been using "out-of-the-money" options.[9] There is little reason to believe that out-of-the-money options are almost never efficient. Indeed, there is a substantial likelihood that originally out-of-the-money options will become in-the-money if the firm does well in comparison with its peers. Even if the firm does relatively poorly, there is also a good chance that, with time and in a rising market, at-the-money options will turn into in-the-money options.

As Brian Hall and others have observed, out-of-the-money options often generate much higher pay-for-performance sensitivity per dollar of expected value than do conventional options.[10] And there is some empirical evidence suggesting that giving managers out-of-the-money options rather than at-the-money options does, on average, boost firm value.[11] Thus, it is highly unlikely that out-of-the-money options are almost never efficient. According to Hall, the "almost complete absence of [out-of-the-money] options seems puzzling given their striking advantages in terms of pay to performance."[12]

The exercise prices used by firms actually display a peculiar uniformity along two dimensions: (1) each firm uses the same exercise price for all employee options, regardless of their vesting period and expiration date, and (2) almost all firms use the same formula for determining this exercise price, namely, the current market price. While the second pattern has been widely discussed, few analysts have devoted attention to the odd uniformity within each firm across vesting periods.

Because stock prices rise on average over time, an option issued at the current market price is likely to become progressively more in-the-money as time passes, and, correspondingly, to produce incentives progressively more like those of an in-the-money option. Furthermore, as time progresses, the fact that the stock price exceeds the exercise price will be less and less indicative that managers have increased shareholder value since the option was issued. Managers who received options issued at-the-money and exercisable over a ten-year period will make money as long as the stock price goes up nominally over the ten-year period. As a result, the managers can benefit even if shareholders' real returns were tiny or even negative.

For example, Apple Computer reported in a March 2001 SEC filing that in the preceding year it had granted its CEO, Steven Jobs, 20 million options. Apple estimated that if its share price increased at a rate of 5 percent a year (a rate below the historical market average and below the rate of return on long-term corporate bonds at the time), Jobs's options would be worth $548,317,503 by the time the options expired.[13]

One of many possible approaches to reducing this royalty is to have a strike price that increases over time at a predetermined rate. An option exercisable at the current market price that vests in five years will have, by the end of the vesting period, an exercise price that is in real terms much lower than the current market price. To avoid such an erosion, the exercise price could be adjusted over time for inflation. There are a variety of other possible formulas for adjusting the exercise price over time; for example, it could be increased by the T-bill rate from year to year. A number of firms in Australia and New Zealand have already employed options with an exercise price that increases over time.[14] In the United States, however, boards have thus far shown little interest in tying the exercise price to the length of time between the grant date of the option and its exercise date.

We do not attempt here to determine the optimal choice of exercise prices and their adjustment, if any, over the life of the option. The best strike price might well vary from case to case and from time to time according to multiple factors, including the time value of money and the rate of inflation. The important point is that there is little reason to expect the optimal choice of exercise price to be uniform across almost all firms, executives, times, and exercise dates.

## *The Managerial Power Explanation*

Because there is reason to believe that the value-maximizing exercise price would differ across vesting periods and across firms, the current uniformity along both dimensions poses a puzzle for believers in arm's-length bargaining. This uniformity, however, is not puzzling once managerial power is taken into account. Boards might not have been seeking the exercise prices that maximize shareholder value. On the contrary, they might have sought the prices that benefit managers the most—namely, the lowest exercise price possible in each case, consistent with other constraints.

At-the-money options may well provide the best combination of high rents and low outrage. For a given number of options, executives prefer the lowest possible exercise price. Each dollar of strike price reduction is a dollar gained once the option is in-the-money. Executives therefore prefer options that bear the lowest possible strike price without causing too much outrage.

Granting in-the-money options may increase outrage for several reasons. Though even at-the-money options may reward executives despite poor performance, it is much more obvious that this is the case when the executive receives in-the-money options. Furthermore, because in-the-money options are not considered "performance based" and are thus nondeductible under section 162(m) of the tax code,[15] their use might be perceived as particularly detrimental to shareholders. Finally, in-the-money options would force the firm to take a charge against earnings. A firm using such options would no longer have an accounting excuse for failing to adopt reduced-windfall options. The use of in-the-money options would therefore undermine one of the justifications for not using reduced-windfall options.

The above discussion explains why plan designers may be reluctant to use in-the-money options. However, this still leaves a range of possible exercise prices at or above the grant-date market price. Within this range, the lowest possible exercise price is the grant-date market price. Setting the strike price here has a superficially plausible justification: managers profit only if the stock price rises, and at-the-money options may be efficient under some circumstances. Managers' desire to have the most favorable exercise price, subject to the constraint that it not be below the grant-date price, can explain why exercise prices are almost uniformly set to the grant-date price, regardless of the vesting period, the expiration date, economic conditions, individual firm characteristics, and the identities of the executives.

At-the-money options can provide substantial windfalls even if the grant-date price represents the true value of the company at that time. But potential windfalls can be further increased through strategic timing. Managers have influence over both the timing of corporate disclosures and the timing of option grants. They can use their power to influence the release of information and the choice of the grant date to increase the likelihood that the stock price is below true value at the grant date. A lower grant-date price, of course, reduces the exercise price of the options and boosts managers' profits when the options are later exercised. Thus, managers can obtain options with exercise prices that are, on average, below the true value of the company at the grant date.

For example, on April 17, 2001, Siebel Systems issued 600,000 options to two top executives, setting their exercise price to the day's closing stock price of $33.[16] After the close of market on April 18, 2001, the company disclosed a large increase in quarterly profits and sales. That news caused the stock price to jump to $46 when the stock resumed trading on April 19, 2001. If the information had been released before the close of market on April 17—or had the option grant been postponed until April 19— the executives would have received options with an exercise price $13 higher. By granting the options before the news release, Siebel Systems effectively gave the executives a $13 discount on each of their 600,000 options—a benefit of about $8 million.

To be sure, the sequence of events does not prove any wrongdoing by

Siebel's executives. The dates of the option grants and the news release could have been fixed long before anyone knew that the timing would provide a multimillion-dollar windfall to the Siebel executives. The executives' large gains could have resulted from pure luck. But a number of studies find a systematic connection between option grants and corporate disclosures.[17] Specifically, companies are more likely to release bad news and less likely to release good news just before options are granted.

A study by David Yermack focuses on earnings announcements, which tend to occur at scheduled times throughout the year. He finds that managers are more likely to be awarded options in advance of the release of favorable earnings results that boost the stock price than in advance of unfavorable announcements. Yermack concludes that managers are able to influence the compensation committee to give them options when they know that the next earnings announcement will be favorable and therefore likely to boost the stock price. Executives effectively award themselves in-the-money options camouflaged as at-the-money options. Yermack's study also finds, consistent with the prediction of the managerial power approach, that more powerful CEOs are able to obtain larger "discounts" on their options.

David Aboody and Ron Kasznik examine companies whose option grant dates were scheduled in advance—that is, companies where managers do not appear to have control over the timing of their option grants. They find that managers time voluntary disclosures to reduce the stock price before getting their at-the-money options.[18] Among other things, managers delay the release of good news until after the grant date. According to the findings of a study by Steven Balsam, Huajing Chen, and Srinivasan Sankaraguruswamy, executives also manage earnings in order to depress the grant-date price.[19] They find that managers boost income-decreasing accruals prior to stock option grants.

Like managers with control over the timing of their option grants, managers with control over the timing of disclosures and earnings accruals receive options with an exercise price below the company's true value at the grant date. In either case, managerial influence increases the extent to which at-the-money options provide pay without performance.

## Repricing and Backdoor Repricing

We have discussed how an at-the-money exercise price allows managers to benefit from stock price gains unrelated to their own performance. We now examine what happens when the stock price falls below the exercise price. Contrary to what one might expect, current practices do not leave executives empty-handed in such situations. Firms have either repriced executives' options or engaged in "backdoor repricing" by issuing new options at a lower exercise price. The prospect of receiving some value from the firm in such circumstances has further weakened the link between option pay and managerial performance.

## Rewarding Managers When Stock Prices Fall

Until the late 1990s, the main way in which firms "made up" for options that had fallen out-of-the-money was to reduce the exercise price. Examining the S&P ExecuComp database for 1992–1995, Menachem Brenner, Rangarajan Sundaram, and David Yermack found that in each of those years an average of 1.3 percent of executives had their options repriced.[20] Of 806 individual option repricings, they found that the strike price was reduced in all but two cases, with an average reduction in exercise price of 39 percent.[21] The S&P 500 Index rose by about 50 percent during the period studied by the authors, with no significant downturns. The frequency of repricing would presumably have been even higher if the markets had not risen as quickly and as consistently as they did during that period.

Since the FASB required firms to expense options that were repriced after December 15, 1998, firms have become more reluctant to reprice.[22] However, they have found other ways—methods that Brian Hall and Thomas Knox call "backdoor repricing"—to achieve the same result without having to expense the options.[23]

When executives are left holding options that are out-of-the-money, firms often engage in backdoor repricing by replenishing the executive with additional options that have a lower exercise price. In some cases, the new option grants are preceded by cancellation of the old, out-of-the-money options.[24] In other cases, the old options remain. The latter, of course, is better for the executives. Though the old options are "underwater" (that is, out-of-the-money) at the moment, they may still have value, especially if the option expiration date is far in the future. Although the various forms of backdoor repricing differ somewhat from each other and from standard repricing, for simplicity we will use the term "repricing" to refer to all the ways in which additional value is given to executives whose options have fallen underwater.

The problem with any form of repricing is that it weakens the link between pay and performance. Indeed, repricing does not simply provide pay independent of performance; it rewards poor stock performance. Thus, the expectation that firms will engage in repricing to offset the consequences of adverse stock price movements reduces managers' incentives to perform. Conceivably, executives anticipating a repricing if the stock price falls may even have an incentive to create a short-run decline in stock price. Repricing therefore undermines the incentive justification for the use of stock option plans in the first place.[25]

Defenders of repricing argue that these adjustments help retain and motivate executives when prices fall to levels that make existing options far out-of-the-money. In their view, although ex-post repricing undermines ex-ante incentives, companies might determine that the ex-post retention and incentive benefits outweigh the ex-ante costs. But many firms have engaged in repricing even when executives' existing options still had significant value; underwater options may still retain significant value if they have a long maturity and the stock is highly volatile.[26] Thus, the retention and incentive justifications did not apply in many cases where firms hurried to reprice following a sharp stock decline. Indeed, a study by Mary Ellen Carter and Luann Lynch found little evidence that repricing underwater stock options affected executive turnover.[27] And even if repricing does on the margin have a positive effect on executives' incentives going forward, there is still the question of whether these beneficial incentive effects are worth the costs to ex-ante incentives resulting from paying for poor stock performance.

Defenders of repricing can argue that it is especially justified in situations where the firm's stock decline is due to a general market or sector downturn, an event that is outside the executives' control. Because such a downturn is not the product of managers' actions, protecting managers from its consequences does not dilute their ex-ante incentives to perform.[28] But repricing conventional options in the wake of a market downturn seems inferior to indexing the options against market movements in the first place. Using indexed options that automatically correct for market-wide and sector-wide shocks in both directions will generally ensure that options remain valuable, and that managers continue to have incentives to perform, when markets decline. Moreover, the protection will come more cheaply and with fewer complications than if conventional options are coupled with ex-post repricing.

Consider executives holding standard indexed options whose exercise price is tied to the sector or market average. The executives are insulated from sector or broad market swings. As a result, there is never a need to engage in repricing to protect them from a general market or sector slide. The options will automatically "correct" for such a slide, and executives who perform adequately relative to their peers will always be rewarded.

Under current arrangements, executives receive conventional options and fall back on repricing when the market moves against them. As a result, managers reap the gains of a sector- or market-wide rally, while being protected from sector- or market-wide downturns. Once again, for executives it's "Heads I win, tails I don't lose." When a market slide is accompanied by repricing and followed by a market rise, executives enjoy the best of both worlds, reaping a windfall from a rally that begins at the bottom of the market and ends at the top. The combination of conventional options and repricing is much more costly to the firm and provides no additional incentive for managers to boost shareholder value.

## The Managerial Power Explanation

Because the anticipation of repricing can dilute ex-ante incentives, firms' eagerness to reprice does not square well with the arm's-length bargaining view. Repricing can be justified as protection against general market or sector downturns if the use of conventional options is taken as given. But this justification simply underscores the potential value of using indexed options, making the persistent failure of firms to use them all the more puzzling. Not surprisingly, shareholder groups have expressed concern about repricing and have sometimes opposed the practice directly.[29]

Seen from the managerial power perspective, however, the practice of repricing is easy to explain. Although indexed options could yield at less cost much of the potential benefit of repricing conventional options, executives clearly have a substantial preference for the latter. Executives benefit from conventional at-the-money options and from repricing. Thus far, they have been able to enjoy both.

It is worth noting that while standard repricing has met increasing resistance from shareholders,[30] back-door repricing has thus far largely escaped their scrutiny. Firms are therefore able to engage in repricing without much outside attention. When executives benefit from large option gains due to market-wide stock price increases, their windfalls can be easily justified to outside observers. After all, the firm and its executives had a contract that provided incentives; all parties to the contract, including shareholders, enjoyed gains; and the firm adhered to its contract. When stock prices decline, the replenishing of options can be justified by referring to the need to retain and motivate executives going forward. The absence of formal repricing also helps, of course.

The managerial power explanation is consistent with some existing empirical evidence. For example, Donald Chance, Raman Kumar, and Rebecca Todd have found that repricing is more common among smaller firms with insider-dominated boards and greater agency problems.[31] Brenner, Sundaram, and Yermack found that repricing does not in fact occur as a result of industry-wide shocks, despite firms' claims that the practice is used to avoid penalizing executives for trends beyond their control.[32] On the contrary, the authors found that repricing is associated with poor stock price performance specific to the individual firm, thus rewarding managers for poor performance. Two other studies, one by Chance, Kumar, and Todd and the other by Mary Ellen Carter and Luann Lynch, also found that repricing is not driven by market or industry factors, but rather follows poor firm-specific performance.[33]

Yet another study, by Sandra Callaghan, Jane Saly, and Chandra Subramaniam, found that repricing frequently occurs after the release of bad news or just prior to the release of good news.[34] This suggests that managers tend to time either the release of information or the repricing (or both) so that the repricing occurs when the stock price is particularly low—and that managers can therefore reap larger gains afterward. This is similar to the findings described in our earlier discussion of at-the-money options—that managers time the release of information or the option grant-date in order to receive new at-the-money options with an exercise price below the stock's true value.

Interestingly, Chance, Kumar, and Todd found that half of the repriced options in their study would have subsequently become in-the-money even if they had not been repriced. This finding suggests that many re-pricings are not needed to motivate and retain executives. Furthermore, the authors found no evidence that lowering the exercise price led to an increase in future stock prices. In other studies, Timothy Pollock, Harold Fischer, and James Wade found that the presence of institutional investors reduces the likelihood of repricing,[35] and Brenner, Sundaram, and Yermack found that the presence of a nonindependent board member on the compensation committee increases it.

## Reload Options

A significant number of firms automatically grant new options to executives who exercise their existing options. This practice of "reloading" is yet another twist on conventional option plans that further facilitates managers' ability to reap benefits even when they do not perform well.

Basic reload options operate as follows: The holder of an option with a reload provision exercises that option before expiration and pays the exercise price with already-owned stock. In return, the manager receives not only the shares that result from the exercise of the options but also a new option for each share tendered in exercising the options. The new reload options carry the same expiration date as the original options, but the exercise price is set to the stock price on the date of the reloading.

For example, a CEO who held ten reloadable options with a $20 strike price would surrender five shares of stock to exercise the options if the market price at exercise was $40 per share. That would yield ten shares from exercising the options, plus five new options with a $40 strike price.[36] Reload options often allow multiple reloading—the new options that the executive receives are themselves reloadable, providing the same reload rights as the original options.

Reload options are worth more than conventional options. By exercising the first-generation options after a price spike, the recipient locks in a portion of the gain against a subsequent share price decline, while maintaining some of the upside potential thanks to the reload feature.[37] Indeed, it is optimal for the holder of a multiple-reload option to exercise whenever the stock price exceeds the previous high since the original grant date.

Reload options therefore enable executives to profit from share price volatility by allowing them to capture temporary gains even if long-term share performance is flat. The incremental value of the reload feature depends on the volatility of the firm's stock price and on other factors. Examining one executive at one firm by way of example, Jane Saly, Ravi Jagannathan, and Steven Huddart estimated that basic reload options in that case were worth about 15 percent more than conventional options.[38] Furthermore, a large percentage of firms with reload programs issue additional options to cover the shares that must be set aside to pay the executive's taxes upon exercise of the options.[39] Saly, Jagannathan, and Huddart estimated that this feature further increased the value of the reload options by an average of 9 percent.[40]

Reloads are difficult to explain under the arm's-length contracting approach. They clearly increase the likelihood that the executive will benefit from temporary stock price spikes. Reloads thus reward managers for stock price volatility and further decouple pay from performance. Not surprisingly, institutional investors object to their use.[41]

Defenders of reload options argue that the reload feature encourages executives to exercise options earlier and therefore to hold more shares.[42] However, if the executives are not prevented from selling the shares they receive on exercise, the reloads do not necessarily promote this result. Generally, executives are free to sell shares they obtain as a result of the exercise of options, and they do in fact sell most of these shares.[43]

In any event, if the goal is to increase managerial ownership, there are cheaper, more direct, and more effective ways to achieve it. As we discuss in the next chapter, firms could simply reduce executives' currently broad freedom to unwind equity incentives as soon as they vest. In some cases, the reload feature may actually reduce an executive's shareholdings by giving him or her an incentive to "pay" for reload options with existing shares, rather than with cash.

Although arm's-length contracting cannot easily explain reloads, managerial influence can. The reload feature makes the options more valuable to the executives but does so in complex ways that are difficult to evaluate. Furthermore, although reloads are not necessary to promote increased stock ownership by executives and may in fact reduce such ownership, the increased ownership justification given for reloads is not patently incorrect. As a result, managers can reap substantial benefits from stock volatility rather than good performance and do so without risking significant outrage.

## The Move to Restricted Stock

Signs of managerial influence can be found not only in the attachment that firms have displayed to conventional option plans but also in the changes companies are making in response to recent criticism of such plans. Under pressure from shareholders, the use of performance-based options is now picking up a bit. But firms are displaying much greater willingness to replace conventional options with restricted stock than to replace them with reduced-windfall options. This pattern should not be surprising: restricted stock grants tend to increase windfalls rather than reduce them.

According to various observers, the use of restricted stock grants is increasing significantly.[44] The increased use of restricted stock is generally viewed as a response to shareholder concern about conventional options. "With Options Tainted, Companies Award Restricted Stock," runs the headline of a *Wall Street Journal* article on the subject.[45] Unfortunately, however, firms replacing conventional options with restricted stock are ending up with an equity-based incentive plan that contains an even larger windfall element.

It is important to recognize that, although restricted stock is not usually labeled an "option," it is in fact an option. Consider a company that issues an option to an executive on a day when the market price is $100. If the option is issued at-the-money, it will have a strike price of $100. Should the executive exercise the option at a later date when the stock price is $V, the executive will make a profit of $V–$100. In contrast, a restricted share that is sold when the stock price is $V will provide the executive a benefit of $V. A restricted stock, then, is simply an option with an exercise price of $0.

Are there reasons to believe that the optimal exercise price of options is zero? In fact, even an exercise price equal to the grant-date price— $100 in our example—might well be too low in many cases, especially when the exercise takes place years after the grant date. As we have seen, using the grant-date price as the strike price may well provide an executive with large gains from market or sector movements even if the executive has substantially underperformed compared to industry peers.

Reducing the exercise price from $100 to $0 makes the windfall problem worse. The reduction boosts the windfall captured by an executive who performs poorly relative to the rest of the industry but whose firm's stock price goes up in a rising market. Indeed, it enables poorly performing executives to capture a windfall even when the stock falls below its grant-date price.[46]

It might be argued that restricted stock awards can be superior to conventional options if executives given these shares are precluded from selling them for a long period of time. Such a feature could provide executives with incentives to focus on long-term value and avoid the short-term gaming that is encouraged by executives' broad freedom to unload their options. But this benefit can be obtained without conferring on managers the big windfalls generated by restricted stock. Any option plan can be structured to include restrictions on managers' ability to unload the options quickly.

It is important to distinguish between two dimensions of equity-based plans. One dimension is their holding period—how long the executive must wait before cashing out the equity by, for example, exercising options and selling the acquired shares. The longer the holding period, the greater the executive's incentive to focus on long-term share value. A completely separate dimension is how the executive's payoff from the equity instrument is determined. Tying payoffs to long-term value does not require using options with an exercise price of zero—that is, restricted stock. It can be done by using options with a positive exercise price, as long as the option plan makes the options "restricted" and precludes managers from unloading them for a long period even after the options have vested.

Some supporters of restricted shares also praise them for continuing to provide incentives to executives in the event of a stock price decline.[47] When a firm's stock price falls due to general market or sector developments, conventional options may become worthless, penalizing executives for a decline that was not due to their own poor performance and possibly leaving them with insufficient incentive to create value. In contrast, no matter how steep the decline in nominal stock price, restricted stock will continue to provide executives with some value and incentive going forward.

But this nonfragility advantage of restricted shares comes at a steep price. Consider again the example of a firm whose nominal stock price is now $100. Suppose that the likelihood of the firm's price falling and staying below $100 during a specified period is only 20 percent. Lowering the exercise price from $100 to $0—that is, moving from conventional options to restricted stock—would ensure that the equity compensation retains value and continues to provide incentives to an executive even if the stock price falls below $100. But this would come at the price of paying the executive an additional $100 per option in the (four times more likely) event that the stock price does not fall below $100 during the specified period.

There are other ways to address the fragility problem of conventional options that do not involve such a high cost. However, firms have made no effort to use any of these methods. To illustrate the wastefulness of the restricted stock "solution," compare restricted stock to an option with an exercise price indexed to the performance of the bottom 5 percent of the firm's industry. This option will not become worthless and will continue to provide incentives as long as the firm's performance does not fall below this rather low benchmark. However, such an option will generate smaller windfalls than restricted stock.

In sum, boards' substantial willingness to move to restricted shares, which contrasts sharply with their reluctance to adopt certain other innovations in equity compensation, should not be viewed as a sign of dwindling managerial influence. Any arrangement that imposes more meaningful limits on managers' ability to unwind incentives would be a positive development for shareholders. But even if managers must wait longer before cashing out restricted stock than they had to wait before liquidating their options, a move to restricted stock does not reduce, and might even increase, managers' ability to enjoy equity-based compensation that provides substantial pay without performance.

# 14

## Freedom to Unwind Equity Incentives

> For every 1000 new options awarded, an executive sells 684 shares of stock.
>
> From a 1997 empirical study of equity-based compensation by Eli Ofek and David Yermack

IN THIS CHAPTER, we discuss another key reason why existing equity-based compensation arrangements have failed to produce cost-effective incentives. Until very recently, firms have taken surprisingly few steps to prevent or to regulate the unwinding of the incentives created by option and restricted-stock grants. Managers thus have been enjoying broad freedom to unload their options and shares. Such unloading either weakens managers' incentives or forces the firm to provide additional options or shares to restore incentives. Shareholders therefore either get weaker incentives for a given level of compensation, or must pay more for a given level of incentives. Furthermore, managers' freedom to unload options and shares has also provided them with perverse incentives to produce transient, short-term stock price increases.

### Benefits of Restricting Early Unwinding

Options and restricted shares are awarded to provide executives with stronger incentives to generate shareholder value. Because executives are risk-averse, they would prefer to receive the expected value of these incentive instruments in cash. They might well prefer a smaller amount of risk-free cash to risky incentive compensation that has a higher expected value. For this reason, once the options and restricted shares vest, executives often wish to convert them into cash. Such unwinding, however, eliminates the incentive benefits of these instruments. An efficient con-

174

tract can be expected to strike a balance between maintaining these incentives and satisfying managers' legitimate liquidity and diversification needs.

The rationale for limiting executives' freedom to unwind vested options is wholly separate from the rationale for vesting periods themselves. The purpose of a vesting period is to prevent an executive who has just been granted options from immediately resigning and walking away with the options (or underlying shares). Once the incentives vest, the executive has "earned" them; they can no longer be taken away.

However, the fact that, upon vesting, the options cannot be taken away from the executive does not necessarily imply that the executive should be permitted to immediately exercise the just-vested options and sell the acquired shares. In at least some cases, it might be efficient to pay the executive with options that cannot be exercised for a specified period even after they vest; options, for example, that vest in three years but can be cashed out only after, say, three additional years. If the executive continues to work for the company after the vesting date, the options (or, if exercised, the underlying shares) would provide beneficial incentives during that period.

Compare this restricted-unwinding arrangement to a situation in which such options can be exercised, and the underlying shares sold, immediately upon vesting. Suppose the executive does in fact exercise the options and sell the underlying shares at once. In this scenario, shareholders must either (1) provide the executive with new options—and bear substantial additional cost—to maintain the same amount of incentives or (2) bear the costs associated with the executive having weaker performance incentives than under the restricted-unwinding arrangement.

In addition to increasing the amount of equity incentives held by executives at any given point in time, an arrangement barring the sale of shares for some time after options and restricted shares have vested offers another advantage over unrestricted unwinding. Executives holding options and shares that cannot be cashed out for some time are more likely to focus on long-term value. To the extent that an executive's performance becomes fully reflected in the company's stock price only after the passage of time, such restrictions provide the executive with better incentives. In contrast, an executive who is free to cash out options and shares as soon as they have vested will be able to gain from short-term spikes in the company's stock price even when the company does not perform well in the long term. As we further discuss below, rewarding managers for short-term stock improvements that do not reflect increased long-term value can lead them to take steps that reduce shareholder value.[1]

To be sure, restrictions on executives' ability to cash out vested options and shares have their drawbacks. They impose liquidity and diversification costs on executives. When devising such restrictions, boards would need to balance these costs against the incentive benefits of restricting the unwinding of these instruments. Given an executive's liquidity and diversification needs, boards could choose the fraction of options or shares that must be held after vesting, the length of the holding period, and whether the executive may unload the options and shares all at once or only gradually when that holding period ends. The efficient parameters are likely to vary from firm to firm and from executive to executive, depending on, among other things, the expected length of the executive's tenure at the firm and his or her personal diversification and consumption needs. What is clear, however, is that it is unlikely that for all firms and all executives, the efficient contract is one that allows an executive to unwind options and shares as soon as they vest.

## Managers' Widespread Freedom to Unwind Early

Until recently, firms rarely prevented executives from unwinding options and restricted shares once they vested. Thus, it is not surprising that executives have been exercising many of their options and selling the underlying shares well before expiration.[2]

A study that examined ten-year options granted to the executives of 40 large companies determined that the options were exercised after an average of 5.8 years.[3] Once they exercise options, executives sell, on average, more than 90 percent of the acquired shares.[4] Even before unloading vested options and shares, executives often hedge them fully or partially in transactions that do not generate taxable income and are not always reported to the SEC.[5] For example, executives often utilize collars and equity swaps to lock in gains on their shareholdings following a stock price increase.[6] Such transactions, of course, weaken the link between executives' wealth and shareholder value, diminishing their incentives to increase this value.

In addition to granting executives broad freedom to unwind vested options and shares, firms have failed to restrict the use of financial instruments that can weaken or eliminate entirely the incentive effects of options and shares that are still unvested. Executives generally have been allowed to hedge away their equity exposure before these instruments vest.[7] In fact, boards often do not even request restrictions on hedging when negotiating with CEOs.[8] At the moment, several serendipitous features of the federal income tax code may well reduce the attractiveness of hedging unvested options and (to a lesser extent) restricted stock through the derivatives market.[9] But even modest changes in tax rules could eliminate this desirable disincentive. In any event, there has been little reason for arm's-length contracts not to include prohibitions on such unwinding.

When executives already hold options and shares, it may be worth granting them additional options and shares in order to strengthen the link between managers' and shareholders' interests. Surprisingly, however, firms granting such additional options and shares rarely prohibit managers from offsetting the effects of such equity grants by selling shares they previously held. As a result, when firms grant options, executives often sell stock they already hold. A study by Eli Ofek and David Yermack found that, on average, managers sold approximately 680 already-owned shares for every 1,000 new options granted, and sold 940 already-owned shares for every 1,000 new restricted shares granted.[10] These sales undid much of the beneficial incentive effect of the grants.

A number of firms have created "target ownership plans" that either encourage or require managers to hold a certain amount of shares—usually expressed as a multiple of the executive's salary.[11] But the targets have tended to be low. In an examination of 195 firms adopting such plans between 1991 and 1995, John Core and David Larcker found that only 138 disclosed the ownership target. Among these 138, the minimum level of ownership for the median CEO was four times his or her base salary. Although this target may seem to mandate substantial stock ownership, it does not. An executive's base salary is commonly dwarfed by other elements of the compensation package, such as the bonus and equity compensation. As a result, the target ownership amount may be less than one year's compensation. Furthermore, only 23 percent of the 195 firms imposed a penalty for not meeting the target. In many cases, the targets were purely voluntary.

To illustrate the general weakness of these ownership requirements, let us consider a firm that appears to have a substantial ownership target for its CEO. American Express requires its top executives to meet share ownership targets that are a multiple of their base salary. The targets range from three times base salary for lower ranking executives to twenty times base salary for the CEO. The base salary of Harvey Golub, the American Express CEO who retired in 2000, was approximately $1 million in each of the years 1998, 1999, and 2000.[12] Thus, American Express's ownership guidelines required him to hold approximately $20 million worth of shares, a seemingly substantial amount. However, in 2000 Golub's base salary was only 4 percent of his total compensation of approximately $25 million. More important, he received more than $130 million in compensation during the period 1993 to 2000.[13] Thus, in 2000 Golub was required to hold equity worth less than 16 percent of the total compensation he had received as CEO of his company.

Furthermore, American Express, like many other firms, allows executives to count toward their "target" some of the value of unvested options and restricted stock: the executives of American Express can count 50 percent of unrealized stock option gain and 50 percent of the market value of restricted shares.[14] Because executives cannot sell unvested options and restricted shares anyway, the target ownership requirements often impose little additional constraint on managers' ability to unwind their equity incentives.

Given managers' consumption and diversification needs, an efficient contract might permit some unwinding before they leave the firm. Still, arm's-length contracting cannot easily explain the almost universal absence of restrictions on the unwinding of vested options and shares, on the hedging of unvested options and restricted shares, and on the unloading of existing options and shares when new options and shares are granted.

In contrast, the absence of such restrictions can be explained readily under the managerial power approach. Broad freedom to unwind incentives by unloading options and shares early provides managers with inconspicuous diversification benefits; the costs imposed on shareholders by diluted incentives are hardly salient. Furthermore, managers' unwinding provides a convenient justification for granting new options and restricted stock to restore incentives. Although the need to continually replenish managerial options and restricted shares considerably raises the costs to shareholders, it also clearly increases the benefits to managers.

In the wake of the corporate scandals that begun erupting in late 2001 and the resulting shareholder outrage, some boards are now imposing new restrictions on executives' unwinding.[15] More firms are adopting ownership mandates (although, as we saw with American Express, such mandates may not always be meaningful). Some boards are also imposing stock retention mandates—requirements that executives retain a specified fraction of the stock they receive directly from the firm or acquire through the exercise of options. One firm, Cinergy, even decided to prohibit its CEO from selling shares received through option exercises (except to cover certain costs) until 90 days after leaving the company.[16] But until outside pressure became sufficiently intense to cause these boards to place limits on unloading, the managers of these firms had been able to benefit from a broad freedom to unload equity incentives. And even now, most firms still do not place meaningful restrictions on such unwinding.

## Managers' Freedom to Time Their Sales

Even if an efficient contract permitted managers to cash out a certain amount of their options and shares at a specified stage of their contract, it does not follow that it would grant them control over the exact time of the unloading. Compensation contracts, however, often provide managers with broad freedom to cash out whenever they choose. When managers can control the timing of trades, they can use inside information to make additional gains. For example, they can sell early if they know the price is too high and is likely to fall.

Under U.S. securities laws, it is illegal for executives to trade on "material" inside information. However, these laws do not prevent managers from using private information to make significant profits when trading in their firm's shares.[17] Managers are able to put together many kinds of inside information. Even when no single piece of data is sufficiently concrete and important to be legally "material," knowledge of all those individual pieces of information and how they fit together often enables managers to form a better overall understanding of the firm's situation.

In addition, the SEC, which is responsible for enforcing insider trading laws, has a relatively small enforcement budget. The agency can afford to pursue only those cases that are easily won—cases usually involving abnormally heavy trading by executives several days before an important news announcement. As a result, many executives can use even their "material" inside information without much fear of detection. This may help explain the body of evidence indicating that managers are able to make considerable abnormal profits—that is, higher than market returns—when trading in company stock.[18]

The magnitude of managers' insider trading profits is largely a function of their informational advantage, not a function of their own performance. Permitting managers to make such gains is unlikely to be an efficient way to reward them for good performance. Of course, an arm's-length contract might allow an executive to sell a certain number of shares in a given year for liquidity or diversification reasons—but that does not mean the executive should choose the exact timing of the sale. After all, most liquidity and diversification needs can be anticipated and planned for. One could adopt a variety of restrictions on the timing of sales without hindering an executive's ability to satisfy legitimate liquidity and diversification needs.

One approach would require that stock sales be carried out gradually, over a specified period according to a prearranged plan. Managers required to sell company stock under such a plan could not easily exploit their access to inside information.[19] Executives and directors of public companies have been well aware of this possible approach—and its potential benefits for shareholders—for at least several years: in 2000, the SEC adopted Rule 10b5-1, which creates a safe harbor for insider trading liability for managers trading according to such a plan, as long as they do not adopt the plan while aware of material inside information.[20] Since then, many law firms have advised their public company clients to use such so-called 10b5-1 plans.[21] However, few (if any) firms have required executives to sell their shares according to a prearranged plan.

Alternatively, as one of us proposed in earlier work, executives could be required to disclose their intended trades publicly and in advance.[22] Under such a pretrading disclosure requirement, the announcement of an unusually large sale would signal the possibility that the executive knows bad news about the firm. This would drive the price down, reducing executives' ability to make a profit by trading on inside information.

We know of only one firm, Ameritrade, that has ever imposed a pretrading disclosure requirement on executive trading—and it did so only briefly and as a result of shareholder outrage.[23] In early February 1999, ten Ameritrade insiders and one relative of an insider sold tens of thousands of shares just as the price hit a peak and right before the stock price plummeted. At the time, Section 16(a) of the Securities Exchange Act of 1934 required that executives disclose their trades by the tenth day of the month following the trade. When the Ameritrade insiders' sales were revealed in early March, shareholders were outraged. To mollify them, Ameritrade announced several days later that, in the future, it would require insiders to announce in advance any plans to sell shares. Executives would even have to announce the number of shares they planned to sell. Ameritrade's chairman of the board explained, "I feel that instituting a policy which ensures [that shareholders] know in advance when insiders intend to sell stock is simply the right thing to do." After some time had passed, however, Ameritrade quietly canceled the policy. There does not appear to be a single case of an Ameritrade insider providing advance notice of selling.

To be sure, many firms have for years employed "trading windows" and "blackout periods" to restrict the times when a manager can sell or buy shares. Many companies, for example, permit managers to trade only during the two- or three-week period after quarterly earnings have been released. But most of these restrictions were not put in place until Congress enacted insider trading laws during the 1980s that made firms liable for not taking reasonable steps to prevent illegal insider trading by their employees.[24] Firms' goal in adopting these restrictions was to reduce the possibility of being held liable for an employee's insider trading violation.[25] As a result, these trading windows and blackout periods have not been designed to effectively prevent managers from trading profitably on their inside information.[26] Executives subject to these restrictions are still frequently able to sell their shares before dramatic stock price declines, thereby avoiding major losses.[27]

Recent years have provided dramatic examples of managers profiting from their access to inside information. Examining the 25 largest U.S. public firms that went bankrupt between January 2001 and August 2002, the *Financial Times* found that executives of these firms sold almost $3 billion of stock between 1999 and 2001 as the market value of the firms dropped from $210 billion to zero.[28] For example, Gary Winnick, the CEO of Global Crossing, sold more than $700 million worth of shares in the year before the firm filed for bankruptcy, at a time when the company was allegedly inflating sales revenues.[29]

There are also examples of considerable selling before dramatic stock price declines in firms that did not end up filing for bankruptcy. A study published by *Fortune* in September 2002 examined trading by executives in the shares of publicly held firms that had reached a market capitalization of at least $400 million and whose shares had subsequently fallen at least 75 percent.[30] The firms were ranked by the amount of executive sales. At the top 25 firms, 466 executives collectively sold $23 billion before their stocks plummeted. At the top of the list was Qwest Communications. Qwest insiders sold more than $2 billion while they were overstating revenues. Shortly thereafter, Qwest stock fell more than 95 percent. Other examples are almost as dramatic. JDS Uniphase insiders and controlling shareholders sold almost $2 billion worth of stock as the price plummeted. AOL Time Warner insiders sold $1.5 billion in shares before the stock price dropped more than 80 percent.[31]

Research suggests that this pattern is systemic and long-standing. One recent study found that executives of small publicly traded companies exercise their options and sell the underlying stock shortly before the price of the stock underperforms the market.[32] Another study reported that insiders sell heavily before earnings declines.[33] A third study concluded that insiders manipulate earnings to delay the onset of bond default and sell their own shares at higher prices.[34]

Although the broad freedom to make such profits is difficult to explain from an arm's-length bargaining perspective, it is not at all puzzling from a managerial power perspective. These insider trading profits, which ultimately come at the expense of public shareholders, provide extra value to executives in a form likely to go unnoticed by shareholders because the costs do not show up in any of the firm's publicly disclosed accounting information or in compensation figures. Such profits are generally well camouflaged except in notorious cases in which large sales of stock preceded dramatic declines in the stock price.

Given managers' interest in camouflaging these transactions, it is not surprising that, until the Sarbanes-Oxley Act closed the loophole in 2002, many firms took advantage of a rule that enabled them to delay reporting insider sales for up to a year. Before the reforms took effect, Section 16(a) of the Securities Exchange Act of 1934 generally required executives to disclose their trades to the SEC by the tenth day of the month following the trade. Under that regime, many firms permitted or even facilitated transactions that were economically equivalent to sales but that allowed executives to avoid making the usual posttrade disclosure to the SEC. An example of such a transaction is the use of company stock to repay executive loans. Although using stock in this way is economically equivalent to selling stock to shareholders, these transactions were not covered by Section 16(a) and so did not need to be reported to the SEC by the tenth day of the following month. Instead, firms were required to disclose these transactions only by the forty-fifth day after the end of the company's fiscal year.[35]

The evidence indicates that stock sales back to the firm are followed by greater than average negative stock returns in the next one or two years.[36] This evidence is consistent with the hypothesis that managers who sell on particularly bad news would seek to camouflage their sales through such hidden transactions. Tyco was one firm that enabled executives to use the repayment of loans to hide executive stock sales. Dennis Kozlowski, Tyco's chairman, and Mark Swartz, its CFO, sold $105 million in shares to the company in late 2000 and 2001, before Tyco's accounting irregularities were revealed and the stock price plummeted. These sales to the company took place even as Kozlowski was publicly announcing that he rarely sold his shares.[37]

Looking ahead, the 2002 Sarbanes-Oxley Act's stricter insider trading disclosure rules will reduce firms' ability to let managers profit from trading on private information. Sarbanes-Oxley requires executives to report a trade to the SEC by the end of the second business day following the transaction.[38] These reports to the SEC must be filed electronically and also posted on the company's Web site within one day of the filing.[39] If the trades are suspiciously large or otherwise unusual, the market will likely intensify its scrutiny of the firm and bid the stock price lower. This stock price adjustment, in turn, will reduce managers' profits from any subsequent sales. However, managers aware that bad news will emerge can still try to unload their shares on a single day or on two consecutive days; in such a case, the price adjustment that occurs on the third day, after the market learns of the managers' trades, will come too late to have any effect on their insider trading profits. The Sarbanes-Oxley Act's stricter disclosure rules will therefore reduce insider trading profits only when managers cannot sell all the shares they wish to unload before they must disclose the trades.[40]

Our main interest, however, is not in assessing managers' ability to make insider trading profits in the future; rather, it is in examining whether compensation arrangements reflect arm's-length contracting. For this purpose, what is critical is that boards on their own have done little to constrain managers' ability to profit from timing their sales. They did not require managers to sell shares according to a prearranged schedule or to announce their intended trades in advance (or even immediately afterward). In fact, many companies took active steps to delay as much as possible the disclosure of insider trades.

## Perverse Incentives

We have discussed how managers' broad freedom to unload options and shares has provided them with personal gains while failing to strengthen their incentives to benefit shareholders. In fact, this freedom has created perverse incentives.[41]

Executives who are free to unload shares or options may have incentives to jack up short-term stock prices by running the firm in a way that improves short-term results at the expense of long-term value. They may also seek to provide the market with an overly positive picture of short-term results and long-term prospects. In addition, they may have incentives to choose projects that are less transparent, or to reduce the transparency of existing projects, because lack of transparency enables them to profit more from their freedom to unload their holdings in the short run. The costs to shareholders of such distortions might exceed, possibly by a large margin, whatever liquidity or risk-bearing benefits executives obtain from being able to unload their options and shares at will.

A growing body of empirical work supports the view that managers' freedom to unload options and shares has provided them with undesirable incentives. Several studies find evidence that managers whose compensation is more directly tied to share prices are more likely to manipulate earnings.[42] The empirical evidence also suggests that managers engage in earnings manipulation and fraud in order to unload shares at a higher price.

Messod Beneish found that managers of firms whose earnings were overstated sold at a high rate before the overstatement was corrected.[43] Scott Summers and John Sweeney determined that firms that fraudulently misstated their earnings had a higher level of insider selling activity—measured by number of transactions, number of shares sold, or the dollar amount of shares sold.[44] Shane Johnson, Harley Ryan, and Yisong Tian found that executives at firms that committed fraud exercised significantly larger fractions of their vested options than other executives.[45] This pattern indicates to us that it is not the mere holding of options and shares—but rather the freedom to unload them in the short run—that produces incentives to engage in misreporting.

Finally, there is evidence that executives' freedom to unload holdings has provided incentives to improve financial results in ways that reduce shareholder value. Merle Erickson, Michelle Hanlon, and Edward Maydew studied firms that restated their financial statements following SEC allegations of accounting fraud during the years 1996 to 2002. They found that these firms collectively paid an extra $320 million in taxes—but only after they had overstated their earnings by $3.36 billion, which in turn allowed managers to sell their shares at a higher price.[46]

In the future, the Sarbanes-Oxley Act will reduce executives' incentive to inflate short-term stock prices. In addition to making it more difficult to misreport, this act also seeks to prevent executives from being able to profit by doing so. Under the Sarbanes-Oxley Act, the CEO and CFO of a firm required to restate earnings under certain conditions must give back to the company any bonus or other incentive or equity-based compensation received during the 12 months following the filing of the misleading financial statement, or any profits realized from the sale of stock within that 12-month period.[47] What is interesting, however, is that boards have never imposed such a requirement themselves. One would think that under an arm's-length contract, boards would not permit executives to benefit from short-term increases in stock price that turn out to have been produced by misreporting.

# Part IV

## Going Forward

# 15

## Improving Executive Compensation

> One of the great, as-yet-unsolved problems in the country
> today is executive compensation and how it is determined.
> SEC Chairman William Donaldson, 2003

EXECUTIVE COMPENSATION ARRANGEMENTS, we have concluded, have deviated substantially from arm's-length outcomes. We now turn to the implications of our analysis for the study, practice, and regulation of executive compensation—and of corporate governance more generally. What can be done to improve executive compensation and induce boards to serve shareholders' interests?

We should make clear at the outset that the main aim of this book is not to provide a detailed blueprint for reform. Rather, our primary objective is to improve understanding of the problems that have plagued executive compensation. In our two concluding chapters, however, we do wish to sketch some of the main implications of our analysis.

In our view, the problems of executive compensation arise from a basic corporate governance problem. Under current arrangements, directors' incentives to enhance shareholder value are not generally sufficient to outweigh the various factors that induce boards to favor executives. Thus, the problems of executive compensation can be fully addressed only by adopting reforms that would confront boards with a different set of incentives and constraints. We discuss such reforms in the next chapter. We start here, however, by considering several partial remedies that can be applied specifically to executive compensation.

### Paying for Performance

Well-designed executive compensation can provide executives with cost-effective incentives to generate value for shareholders. Unfortunately, the promise of such arrangements has not yet been fully realized. In examining executive compensation, investors should be wary of pay arrangements that fail to reward performance and should encourage those that do so in a cost-effective way.

What practices should investors support? Which ones should they oppose? As we have seen, compensation arrangements fail to provide executives with cost-effective incentives to increase shareholder value. The fraction of executives' compensation that rewards their own performance is significantly smaller than has been commonly recognized. A large part of both equity-based compensation and non-equity-based compensation provides value to managers regardless of their own performance, diluting and distorting incentives. In this book, we have identified various ways in which current schemes fail to perform well and could be improved. To illustrate, let us note some important changes that investors should support to improve executives' incentives.

*Reducing Windfalls in Equity-Based Plans.* Investors should encourage equity-based plans that filter out at least some of the gains in the stock price that are due to general market or industry movements. With such filtering, the same amount of incentives can be provided at a lower cost, or more incentives can be provided at the same cost. Investors must recognize that a move to restricted-stock grants, which provide an even larger windfall than conventional options, is not necessarily in the interests of shareholders.

To reduce windfalls, investors should press boards to consider schemes (such as those we discussed in chapter 11) under which the exercise price is adjusted to filter out general market or industry movements. At the minimum, option exercise prices should be adjusted so that managers are rewarded for stock price gains only to the extent that they exceed those gains (if any) enjoyed by the most poorly performing firms.

*Improving the Link between Bonus Plans and Performance.* In assessing whether executive pay is adequately tied to performance, investors should scrutinize whether firms' bonus plans actually reward good performance or do so in name only. They should be wary of boards that give bonuses to managers for accomplishments, such as acquiring other companies, for which no special incentive is needed.

As part of the effort to strengthen the link between bonus plans and performance, investors should resist bonus plans that include discretionary elements. While such discretion in bonus plans could be desirable if exercised by boards solely guided by shareholder interests, it might be counterproductive if given to boards as they currently operate.

*Limiting and Regulating the Unwinding of Equity Incentives.* Investors also should seek to limit executives' broad freedom to unwind the equity-based incentives created by their compensation plans. It may well be desirable to separate the vesting and unwinding of options. With such separation, options that have already vested and become the executives' property (on the shares received upon exercising these options) will remain in their hands for some time, continuing to provide incentives to increase shareholder value. To prevent executives from circumventing such limits on unwinding, executives should be prohibited from engaging in any hedging or derivative transactions that reduce their exposure to fluctuations in the company's stock price.

In addition, whenever executives are allowed to sell shares, they should be required, as one of us proposed some time ago, to disclosure *in advance* of their intention to sell shares. When making such pre-trading disclosure, executives should provide detailed information about the intended trade, including the number of shares to be sold.[1] Limiting and regulating the unwinding of equity incentives will reduce the ability of managers to profit from short-term gains that do not reflect the company's long-term prospects, thus reducing the various perverse incentives we discussed in chapter 14.

*Avoiding Soft Landing in Case of Failure.* Investors also should be wary of practices and arrangements that reward failing managers. They dilute incentives to enhance shareholder value—and thus undermine some of the incentives to increase value that other elements of the compensation package attempt to provide. Investors should scrutinize generous severance provisions to ensure that they do not provide large payments to executives when they depart with a record of poor performance. Investors also should oppose golden goodbyes to departing executives, including gratuitous payments beyond those required by their contracts.

*Scrutinizing the Magnitude of Nonperformance Pay.* Investors should attempt to assess the overall magnitude of nonperformance pay given to executives. In doing so, investors should take into account the various hidden forms of nonperformance pay we discussed (such as retirement benefits). Once the total amount spent on pay unrelated to performance is identified, investors should assess whether it is possible to enhance shareholder value by making total compensation more sensitive to performance.

In scrutinizing the compensation arrangements approved by the board, investors should be well aware of both directors' limitations and their own. Given the many factors that currently induce directors to favor executives, investors should not presume that directors' compensation choices are those optimal for shareholders. At the same time, although shareholders can and should try to influence the general contours of compensation plans, they should recognize that they lack company-specific information and are hardly in a position to fine-tune the details of these arrangements. These competing considerations should shape the extent to which investors second-guess (and, if need be, criticize) the choices made by directors.

## Improving Transparency

We argue in the next chapter for reforms that would increase shareholder power. But shareholders do already have some power. This power is in part why the outrage constraint matters. The greater outsiders' under-standing of compensation arrangements, the tighter the outrage con-straint. Improving the transparency of compensation arrangements is therefore desirable.

Financial economists have paid insufficient attention to transparency because they often focus on the role of disclosure in getting information incorporated into market pricing. It is widely believed that information can be reflected in stock prices as long as it is known and fully understood by even a limited number of market professionals.

In the case of executive compensation, there is already significant dis-closure. As we have discussed, SEC regulations require detailed disclosure of the compensation of a company's CEO and of the four most highly compensated executives other than the CEO.[2] In our view, however, is it important to recognize the difference between disclosure and transpar-ency, and it is transparency that should receive more attention.

The main aim of requiring disclosure of executive compensation is not to enable accurate pricing of the firm's securities. Rather, this disclosure is primarily intended to provide some check on arrangements that are too favorable to executives. This goal is not well served by disseminating information in a way that makes the information understandable to a small number of market professionals but opaque to others.

The ability of plan designers to favor managers depends on how com-pensation arrangements are perceived by a wide group of investors and other outsiders. Because of market forces and social dynamics, managers and directors are concerned about possible disapproval from institutional investors and other reference groups, such as the business press. We have seen that compensation designers often seek to make the amount of pay, or the extent to which pay is decoupled from performance, less transparent. For disclosure to constrain compensation effectively, the disclosed information must reach more than just a select group of market professionals and arbitrageurs. Raw facts buried in a mountain of technical disclosure probably will not suffice. The salience of disclosure and degree of transparency are important.

Public officials and governance reformers, therefore, should work to ensure that compensation arrangements are and remain transparent. Several transparency-boosting measures are worth considering.

*Accounting Treatment of Options.* Employee options should be expensed. As we discussed in chapter 12, the FASB, which in the past was pressured by managers not to require the expensing of options, is now expected to try to adopt such a measure. Congress is considering legislation that would force firms to expense the option compensation given to their five highest-paid executives (but allow them not to expense other employee options). From an accountant's perspective, expensing is desirable because it leads to a more accurate reflection of the firm's financial situation. For our purposes, however, expensing executives' options is beneficial because it makes the costs imposed by these options more evident to investors on an ongoing basis.

Rationalizing the accounting treatment of option plans would also level the playing field among different types of options. It would eliminate a major excuse used to avoid reduced-windfall options. The fact that reduced-windfall options must be expensed while conventional options need not has long been a convenient excuse for using the latter and failing to filter out gains due to general market or sector rises.

*Placing a Monetary Value on All Forms of Compensation.* Companies should be required to place a dollar value on all forms of compensation and to include these amounts in the compensation tables contained in company disclosures. Companies have been able to provide executives with substantial "stealth compensation" by using pensions, deferred compensation, and postretirement perks and consulting contracts. Although some details of these arrangements have appeared elsewhere in companies' SEC filings, firms have not been required to place a dollar value on these benefits and to include this value in the tables. These benefits have not even been included in the standard database used by financial economists to study executive compensation.

In our view, companies should be required to place a monetary value on each benefit provided or promised to an executive and to include this value in the compensation table in the year in which the executive becomes entitled to it. Thus, for example, the compensation table should include the amount by which the expected value of the executive's promised pension payments increased during the year. In addition, it might be desirable to require companies to place a monetary value on any tax benefit that accrues to the executive at the company's expense (for example, under deferred compensation)—and to report this value.

These measures would provide shareholders with a more accurate picture of total executive compensation. They also would eliminate distortions that might arise when companies choose particular forms of compensation for their camouflage value rather than for their efficiency.

*Placing a Monetary Value on Total Compensation from All Sources.* By paying executives in many different forms, with some of them not even given a monetary value, companies make the total amount of compensation less salient that it should be. Companies should be required to indicate in the executive compensation section of their filings the total amount of compensation that each of its top executives earned in that year as well as since coming into office.

*Pay and Performance.* It might be worthwhile to require companies to disclose to shareholders in a transparent way how much of the gain that managers make on their options is due to general market and industry movements. This could be achieved by requiring firms to calculate and report the gains made by managers from the exercise of options (or the vesting of restricted shares, in the case of restricted-share grants) and to report what fraction, if any, resulted from the company's superior returns over its industry peers. Such disclosure would make much more transparent the extent to which the company's equity-based plans reward the managers' own performance.

*Unloading of Options and Shares.* Companies should be required to make transparent to shareholders on a regular basis the extent to which their top five executives have unloaded any equity instruments received as part of their compensation. Athough a diligent and dedicated researcher can obtain this information by sifting through stacks of executive trading reports filed with the SEC, requiring the firm to compile and report such information would highlight for all investors the extent to which managers have used their freedom to unwind incentives.

Of course, designers of compensation plans may find new ways to make compensation, or its insensitivity to performance, more opaque. As new practices (and new means of camouflage) develop, disclosure arrangements should be updated to ensure transparency.

## Compensation Committee Procedures

The recently adopted stock exchange requirements seek to make more formal the process used by compensation committees to determine executive pay. According to the NYSE requirements, each compensation committee must have a written charter.[3] The committee is also required to review and approve corporate goals and objectives relevant to CEO compensation, and to produce a report on executive compensation for the company's annual proxy statement or annual report. Institutional investors have for some time been urging all companies to use such procedures.[4]

Requiring compensation committees to follow certain steps is a measure we find acceptable but not particularly beneficial. Such requirements may force committee members to devote more attention to executive compensation than they have in the past. For directors solely focused on shareholder interests, being required to take certain steps and to articulate what they are doing could be a useful way to make their work more careful and methodical.

While procedural requirements may mitigate problems arising from carelessness and insufficient attention, however, they do not address those arising from directors' incentives and tendencies to use their discretion in ways that favor executives. The need to follow certain steps and to write a report would not place a meaningful limit on directors' discretion. With the help of lawyers and compensation consultants, directors who wish to favor executives will usually be able to offer justifications for their choices, sometimes by merely using boilerplate language. Thus, the key issue of directors' incentives remains.

## Requiring Shareholder Approval

In addition to improving director incentives—the subject of the next chapter—it might be worthwhile to place some limits on directors' discretion. The risk of any such limits, of course, is that directors might be prevented from structuring compensation in a way that is desirable for shareholders. The most natural way to limit director discretion without preventing the board from adopting good arrangements is to require shareholder approval of certain board decisions. Two approaches in particular are worth discussing—requiring shareholder approval of equity-based plans and requiring shareholder approval of compensation agreements that include specified "suspect" features.

## Approval of Equity-Based Plans

In 2003, the major national stock exchanges adopted requirements that obligate listed companies to obtain shareholder approval of equity-based compensation plans.[5] Although these requirements have been hailed by some as very important measures,[6] they cannot ensure that executive compensation, or even just equity-based compensation, is designed to serve shareholders' interests.

To put these requirements in perspective, we must recall that many companies have already been putting equity-based compensation plans to a shareholder vote. As we discussed in chapter 3, a major impetus for doing so was a desire to avoid the tax penalty imposed on plans lacking shareholder approval. Thus, the new requirements will merely expand an already common practice that has not proven to be an effective constraint on boards.

Shareholder voting on plans gives shareholders who are unhappy with executive compensation (or other matters) an opportunity to register their dissatisfaction. It may also enable them to block the issuance of more shares and options when they find executive pay practices especially outrageous. But voting on equity compensation plans does not provide shareholders in normal circumstances with substantial influence over the design of compensation arrangements.

To begin with, shareholders are asked to vote on plans that are broadly worded and therefore leave the board substantial discretion. Shareholders are asked to approve the board's use of a particular number of options or restricted shares for employee compensation, but there are important features of equity-based plans for which no approval is or will be sought. For example, shareholders are not asked to approve the number of options that any given executive will receive from the total at the board's disposal, and what limits on vesting and unwinding, if any, will be imposed in connection with the given options or shares. As one prominent law firm advised its clients in a memo, "In light of the new NYSE and NASDAQ shareholder approval rules, stock plans should be drafted broadly so that the company may change the terms of grants without having to amend the plan in a manner that may require shareholder approval under the new rules."[7]

Moreover, even though shareholders can collectively veto the use of options and restricted shares, they will have little control over how executives are compensated if they turn down the plan proposed by the board. If, for example, shareholders oppose a plan based on conventional options because such options provide excessive windfalls from market and sector rises, they have little assurance that the board will not instead adopt arrangements that may be even worse for shareholders—such as very large bonus plans. For this reason, we expect shareholders to approve proposed plans in many cases in which they would have liked the board to design compensation agreements differently. All in all, we expect the expansion in shareholders' veto power over equity-based compensation plans to leave boards with substantial control over equity-based compensation.

### Voting on Specific Features of Compensation Agreements

Allowing shareholders to vote on compensation agreements that include certain potentially problematic features might be useful. Consider an arrangement requiring shareholder approval for executive compensation plans that include one or more items from a list of "suspect" features. Shareholder approval could be required, for example, for conventional options that do not filter any windfalls from general market or sector movements, for options that can be unwound shortly after vesting, for any equity-based compensation plan that does not require executives to provide pretrading disclosure of intended sales of shares, or for severance benefits that are very large relative to annual compensation. Some shareholder resolutions, and the Council of Institutional Investors (CII), have recommended such requirements. For example, the CII has recommended that "underwater" options should not be repriced or replaced unless management obtains shareholder approval.[8]

We believe that such shareholder approval requirements can be beneficial if applied to provisions that have a high likelihood of being undesirable. In such cases, this type of arrangement can be regarded as striking a middle course between outright prohibition and unqualified acceptance of such features. If a particular feature appears undesirable, both complete prohibition and unfettered freedom could be costly. Allowing the feature to be included only if approved by shareholders may strike a sensible balance.

Of course, whether such arrangements benefit shareholders will depend very much on which provisions are designated as requiring shareholder approval. Imposing shareholder approval requirements on provisions that are likely to be desirable imposes unnecessary costs. And neglecting to impose such requirements on provisions that are likely to be undesirable fails to capture the potential benefits of such an arrangement. Regulators or exchange officials are not in a good position to determine which features are suspect, because they would not be able to make choices on a company-specific basis or to easily adjust the set of arrangements for which shareholder approval is required as new information emerges.

Thus shareholders themselves should decide what limits on directors' discretion to impose and how to modify them as new information arrives. The problem, however, is that corporate law currently does not enable shareholders to propose and vote on rules relating to executive compensation that are binding on the board. With respect to executive compensation, a subject presently left by corporate law to the discretion of the board, shareholders can only initiate and vote on precatory resolutions that are merely advisory. In our view, it would be desirable to permit shareholders to initiate and approve binding rules for executive compensation arrangements. Among other things, giving shareholders such power would enable them, if they so choose, to adopt rules prohibiting the board from adopting certain compensations arrangements without shareholder approval.

### The Limits of Voting on Executive Pay Arrangements

We view the shareholder voting mechanism as very important. In the next chapter, we argue for strengthening shareholders' ability to vote in new directors and to vote on the basic ground rules of corporate governance. The design of executive pay arrangements, however, is not an area in which shareholder intervention via voting can completely substitute for the decision making of a board that effectively guards shareholder interests.

Shareholder voting could establish some outer limits to what boards can do without specific shareholder approval. In defining these outer limits, shareholders would rely on their general knowledge about the basic structures of compensation arrangements. But good directors are still needed to make the many and complex choices within these outer limits and to negotiate with executives. These are tasks that require case-specific detail and back-and-forth discussion. Shareholder voting cannot substitute for all this.

## Executive Compensation and Corporate Governance

Our analysis in this chapter brings us back to the basic corporate governance problem. How do we improve the incentives of directors and make them more likely to focus on shareholder interests? Although the potential changes we have discussed would improve executive pay arrangements, they would not address the problems fully. A more complete solution would require improving corporate governance generally.

The measures we have looked at would all leave directors with significant discretion, as well they must. They would not by themselves provide directors with a new set of incentives. Further improvements in the design of executive compensation would require increasing directors' incentives to serve shareholders. Such improved incentives would have a beneficial effect not only on executive pay arrangements but also on other decisions made or reviewed by the board. An analysis of the problems with executive compensation, therefore, suggests the need for fundamental corporate governance reform, which is the subject of the next chapter.

## Recognition and Reality

We end this chapter by emphasizing how important it is to recognize the critical role of managerial influence in determining executive compensation. Widespread recognition of current problems with executive compensation, which we seek to advance with this book, can by itself have an effect on the severity of these problems.

Widespread acknowledgment of managers' influence over their compensation—especially by institutional investors—may do much to limit these problems. We have argued that managers' ability to overpay themselves and to decouple their pay from performance, and the magnitude of the resulting costs to shareholders, depends on the extent to which flaws in compensation arrangements are widely recognized by outsiders. Thus, how much executives can get away with depends on the degree to which outsiders are aware of the distortions in compensation arrangements that managers seek to camouflage. Simply increasing awareness of these distortions can reduce the problems we have identified.

To improve executive compensation practices, investors and reformers need more than power alone. They also need information and an awareness of what to look for and what to focus on. They must recognize the key role that managerial influence has played and continues to play in executive compensation, the myriad factors that contribute to managerial influence, and the range of ways in which this influence manifests itself.

We believe it is also important for our fellow academic researchers to appreciate fully the magnitude of the agency problems involved in executive compensation. Financial economists have been great supporters of equity-based compensation schemes, appreciating their promise of providing desirable incentives to management. This enthusiasm has added legitimacy to the large increases in executive compensation during the past decade.

Financial economists should recognize that incentive schemes also have, as it were, a "dark side." Their design may sometimes be a product of agency problems within the firm, rather than an instrument for combating them. Because of these agency problems, executive compensation has yet to fulfill its promise and has even created some perverse and distorted incentives. We are pleased to see financial economists now spending more time examining some of the adverse effects that compensation arrangements have had on management behavior. We hope they will focus more closely on the role of managerial influence and devote as much attention to studying it as they have to the model of arm's-length contracting.

# 16

## Improving Corporate Governance

The shareholder franchise is the ideological underpinning upon which the legitimacy of directorial power rests.
Delaware chancellor William Allen,
in Blasius v. Atlas, 1988

THE PROBLEMS OF executive compensation arrangements, we have seen, are rooted in boards' failure to bargain at arm's length with executives. Greater transparency, improved board procedures, additional shareholder approval requirements, and a better understanding by shareholders of the desirability of various compensation arrangements all can help improve the situation. But these remedies cannot substitute completely for effective decision making by directors striving to serve shareholder interests.

After all, executive compensation requires case-specific knowledge and thus is best designed by informed decision makers who have some discretion and use it to enhance shareholder value. The problems discussed in this book therefore would be best addressed by improving the incentives of directors. We need to turn the official story of executive compensation and board governance, which features directors as the dedicated guardians of shareholder interests, from fiction into reality.

Directors who safeguard shareholder interests are needed not only to address executive compensation problems but also to tackle the myriad corporate governance problems that would continue to arise even if compensation arrangements were optimized. For example, having such directors is essential for our ability to rely on boards to prevent managers from engaging in empire building or from impeding acquisition offers that would benefit shareholders. The foundation of our board-monitoring system of corporate governance is the existence of directors who select, supervise, and compensate executives with shareholder interests in mind.

Shareholders' ability to rely on such directors is, so to speak, the Archimedean point on which this system stands.

The critical question, then, is how to make directors more focused on shareholder interests. The most promising approach for achieving this result is to alter the current allocation of power between boards and shareholders. We offer below an outline of the case for such reform, and we provide further details in other work.[1]

## The Limits of Director Independence

The main way in which the corporate governance system has recently responded to perceived governance problems is by trying to bolster board independence. Recent reforms have sought to make nominally independent directors more independent and to expand the presence and role of such independent directors on the board. Strengthened director independence is now widely believed to be key to the effectiveness of the board-monitoring model. Attributing past governance problems to insufficient director independence, many believe that strengthened independence will prevent such governance problems in the future.

As we discussed in chapter 2, in 2003 the stock exchanges adopted listing standards that require boards of listed companies to have a majority of independent directors, tighten the definition of independent directors, and mandate that compensation and nomination committees be composed solely of independent directors. Supporters of management have used these reforms as a basis for arguing that no more changes are necessary.[2] In their view, even if the official model of board oversight of management has not worked well in the past, these reforms adequately address concerns about the quality of board decision making. The rules strengthen board independence, and such strengthening is all that is necessary.

We agree that recent reforms are likely to be beneficial. But we see no basis for complacency. The adopted rules, and the increased attention to director independence accompanying them, cannot by themselves ensure that boards properly carry out their critical role. Rules governing director independence cannot deliver nearly as much as their enthusiastic supporters claim.

There are some preliminary reasons for skepticism about how much the new director independence requirements can deliver. Clearly they will exclude some individuals from serving on the board of a particular company. However, a vast number of individuals will still qualify as independent directors. The independence requirements do not resolve which few individuals will be selected from this vast pool of "independent" candidates. Furthermore, even though the independence requirements may eliminate some forms of managerial influence over individual directors, they hardly ensure that directors will be dedicated to shareholder interests.

When filling other high-level positions, companies generally recognize that selecting the right person for the job and providing that person with appropriate incentives is very important. This should be no less true with respect to directors, especially given their critical roles. Thus, the fact that director independence alone ensures neither the selection of the best people nor the provision of good incentives for those selected should be disconcerting.

A fundamental limitation of independence requirements is that they fail to provide affirmative incentives for directors to enhance shareholder value. As long as these requirements merely reduce directors' incentives and inclinations to favor executives, but do not fully eliminate them, any residual tendency among directors to favor executives may have a substantial impact in the absence of any countervailing incentive to enhance shareholder value.

As we discussed in chapter 2, recent reforms do not eliminate the myriad factors that lead directors to favor executives. To begin with, the reforms do not change the reality that the key to reelection is remaining on the company's slate. The CEO and his or her director allies may not fully control board nominations in the future, but remaining on good terms with them is likely to continue to increase a director's chances of being renominated.

Furthermore, even though the recent reforms place considerable limits on the CEO's power to reward directors, they certainly do not eliminate it. Indeed, it will be difficult to prevent a CEO from rewarding board members as long as CEOs retain some influence over director compensation and as long as board seats are not closed to the large set of individuals whose business interests might be influenced—either while serving as directors or afterward—by the CEO's decisions and actions.

Finally, even if reforms could make it impossible for the CEO to reward directors, the latter would still be subject to social and psychological factors inducing them to remain on good terms with the CEO. As long as directors are supposed to act collegially and feel like part of a team of which the CEO is for many purposes the leader, they will feel more comfortable accommodating his or her wishes than opposing them. There is little in the recent reforms to counteract directors' very human tendency to avoid conflict with their colleague and leader.

This last point is worth emphasizing: it suggests that merely reducing managers' ability to reward directors—without providing significant affirmative incentives to serve shareholders—may not be sufficient to induce directors to focus on shareholder value. Because most directors hold only a tiny fraction of the company's shares, the direct personal cost to them of giving executives generous compensation and too much leeway in running the company may be rather small. Thus, economic incentives or social ties of even modest magnitude may be enough to tilt directors toward executives.

The analysis above should make clear the limits of the new independence requirements. Directors lacking strong incentives to serve shareholders are unlikely to be independent from executives. It is worth noting, however, that even if directors were completely insulated from managerial influence, the absence of such incentives would still be detrimental to shareholders.

Consider the hypothetical scenario in which the board is largely composed of independent directors who somehow have neither the incentive nor the inclination to remain on good terms with the CEO. Suppose that a group of such directors comes to control the board and its committees and, by virtue of its control of the company's slate, can self-perpetuate. And suppose that members of this group cannot be moved by CEO rewards. In this hypothetical scenario, the directors will not serve managers' interests. But in the absence of sufficient pro-shareholder incentives, the directors will not serve shareholders either, despite the directors' complete independence from executives. They may pursue their own preferences and interests—say, by seeking to appoint executives they favor for personal reasons, by increasing directors' compensation, by expanding their empire, or by encouraging the firm to invest in pet projects. In short, even in the hypothetical case of totally independent directors, shareholders may still have substantial grounds for concern as long as directors do not have substantial affirmative incentives to enhance shareholder value.

## Director Compensation Schemes

Companies have compensated directors with equity for some time, and various observers have called for greater reliance on equity grants in compensating directors.[3] Can equity compensation, perhaps with some increase in the amounts of stock involved, provide independent directors with adequate affirmative incentives to focus on shareholder interests?

As long as director compensation remains within existing ranges, the financial cost to directors of many value-reducing steps (though not all) would remain small even if more or most of their compensation were equity based. Consider a compensation scheme under which directors receive each year restricted stock awards worth $100,000 for their services. And consider a director who has accumulated stock worth $300,000. Such holdings would surely provide directors with substantial incentives to oppose a CEO-favored course of action that could halve the value of shareholders' (and directors') holdings. However, there would be little incentive to fight the CEO over a compensation arrangement or a pet project that would reduce shareholder value by, say, 1 or 2 percent. In such a situation, confronting the CEO is unlikely to increase the value of the director's holdings by more than the amount board members are paid for attending a single board or committee meeting.

Providing directors with meaningful equity incentives would require greatly increasing their compensation for serving on the board. But increasing the size of equity grants to directors may have unintended negative consequences. The more directors are paid, the greater is their desire to be reelected. Boosting compensation may therefore lead directors to focus not on the difficult task of increasing share value but rather on that of remaining on the board and enjoying the increased stream of compensation, as well as obtaining (now more lucrative) directorships on other boards. As long as board appointments depend not on the preferences of shareholders but on those of nominating committees, increased motivation to get reelected is not the same as increased motivation to enhance share value. Furthermore, very highly paid independent directors may become more concerned with finding ways to justify increasing the number of their options or shares than with improving the per-share value of the company.

This last point reveals a basic difficulty with trying to solve the problem of director incentives with an equity-based compensation scheme. At first glance, one might hope that such a scheme will, by aligning the interests of directors with those of shareholders, induce the board to carry out its oversight duties well and, in particular, to bargain with executives at arm's length and solely with shareholder interests in mind. But closer inspection suggests that this approach simply re-creates, one level up, the very problem concerning executive compensation with which we began.

Under the arm's-length bargaining view, executive compensation is assumed to address the agency problem between managers and shareholders. Managers' interests can be aligned with shareholders', so the argument goes, by an incentive compensation scheme that induces managers to use their discretion in shareholders' interest. But the problem, as we have seen, is that someone other than the managers must come up with the right pay package, and there are reasons to believe that directors have not been designing executive compensation with shareholders' best interests in mind.

Could we address this agency problem between directors and shareholders by providing the directors themselves with well-designed equity-based compensation schemes? Well, someone would need to design the directors' incentive compensation. Directors currently set their own compensation. As long as directors' compensation is in their own hands, legitimizing the provision of large equity-based compensation might not eliminate, and could even worsen, the agency problem in the relationship between boards and shareholders. In this state of affairs, directors' incentives to boost their compensation might adversely affect their performance.

Should we, then, have another independent group of "super-directors" set the compensation of the independent directors? And to make sure that the super-directors exercise their discretion in the interest of shareholders, should they be given an incentive scheme set by super-super-directors, and so forth? The futility of such an infinite chain is quite apparent, and it illustrates the key problem with relying on director independence by itself: Independence, even coupled with incentive schemes, cannot secure shareholder interests unless there is some mechanism at the end of the chain that makes the designers of incentive schemes designers accountable to shareholders. This basic point highlights the importance of making directors dependent on shareholders.

## Making Directors Dependent on Shareholders

The problem with an approach that focuses on director independence is that, by itself, it does not reduce directors' insulation from shareholders.

As long as directors' election and compensation ultimately depend on other directors, even if not on the firm's executives, the corporate governance system lacks an anchor that would securely tie board decisions to shareholder interests.

In our view, the most effective way to improve board performance is to increase the power of shareholders vis-à-vis directors. We should make directors not only more independent of executives but also less independent of shareholders. This second step would give directors better incentives to serve shareholder interests.

Although shareholder dependence could be created by giving shareholders a major role in setting director compensation, we will focus on increasing shareholders' role in the appointment and reappointment of directors to the board. The current system—under which the key to a board seat is pleasing the board members who make nomination decisions—should be replaced. The appointment of directors should substantially depend—in fact and not only in theory—on shareholders.

Making directors dependent on shareholders could counter some of the factors that incline directors to pursue their own interests or those of executives rather than serve shareholders. It could make the desire to be re-elected a positive force rather than a negative one. It could provide directors with an incentive to develop a reputation for serving shareholders. It could perhaps instill in directors a sense of loyalty toward shareholders, especially if institutional investors take an active role in putting directors on boards.

For this reason, we support removal of the barriers that have until now insulated directors from shareholders. Because of shareholders' collective action problems, increasing shareholder power vis-à-vis directors would hardly be a perfect solution. But movement in this direction has substantial potential for improving the incentives and performance of boards.

## The Myth of Corporate Elections

Shareholders' power to replace directors plays a critical role in the accepted view of the corporation. Although this power is not supposed to be used regularly, it is expected to provide a critical safety valve. "If the shareholders are displeased with the action of their elected representatives," emphasized the Delaware Supreme Court in its well-known opinion in the case of *Unocal Corp. v. Mesa Petroleum Co.*, "the powers of corporate democracy are at their disposal to turn the board out."[4]

In reality, however, this safety valve is largely a myth. Indeed, attempts by shareholders to replace incumbents with a team that would do a better job—the kind of action referred to in the *Unocal* opinion above—are even more rare than is commonly recognized.

The dearth of electoral challenges is documented in a recent study by one of us.[5] During the seven-year period 1996–2002, proxy contests over who would run the (stand-alone) firm in the future occurred in only about 80 companies among the thousands of publicly traded firms.[6] Furthermore, most of the firms in which these contests took place were small companies. Only about ten firms had a market capitalization exceeding $200 million in the year of the proxy fight over control. Thus, for firms with a market capitalization exceeding $200 million, the incidence of such contests was practically negligible—less than two a year on average.

This means that the safety valve of potential ouster via the ballot box— on which our corporate governance system is supposed to rely—has been all but shut off. The risk of being removed in a proxy contest is far too remote to provide a strong incentive for directors to focus fully on shareholder interests.

To be sure, it is difficult to determine precisely the optimal incidence of electoral challenges—the one that would provide directors with sufficient incentives without imposing excessive costs. But there are strong reasons to doubt that this optimal incidence is, essentially, zero. The case for reforms that would make the electoral threat more meaningful is thus strong.

## Invigorating Corporate Elections

### The SEC's Mild Step under Fire

The SEC is now considering a rule that seeks to lower, in a narrow range of cases, the hurdles impeding electoral challenges to incumbents. The rule would enable shareholders in some special circumstances to place candidates for a small number of board seats on the corporate ballot. Although its practical effect is likely to be rather limited, the rule has been strongly resisted by management groups. For example, the Business Roundtable, the influential association of CEOs of leading companies, has vigorously attacked the proposal.[7]

Several aspects of the proposed rule make it a very timid first step toward making electoral challenges more viable. First, the proposed direct access procedure would be available in a corporate election only if a triggering event indicating massive shareholder dissatisfaction had occurred in the preceding annual meeting. The triggering events listed in the proposal are a majority vote in favor of a shareholder proposal seeking shareholder access, or a 35 percent vote to withhold support from one of the directors. Even if a triggering event makes shareholder access to the ballot available, shareholders still need to satisfy substantial ownership and holding requirements to be able to place candidates on the ballot.

Furthermore, those shareholders (or groups of shareholders) eligible to place a candidate on the ballot would still bear their own "campaign costs" even if they win, whereas incumbents' costs would be fully borne by the company. This financing disadvantage both strongly discourages challenges and makes those that do occur less likely to succeed.[8] Without such reimbursement, challenges to incumbents will still confront excessive impediments.

Finally, the proposed rule makes only a small minority of board seats available to candidates placed on the ballot by shareholders and then elected by a majority vote. Only one shareholder-nominated candidate can be placed on the ballot when a board has up to 9 seats, and only 2 when a board has between 10 and 19 seats.

Shareholders dissatisfied with incumbents' performance must therefore (1) garner sufficient support from normally passive fellow shareholders to reach one of the triggering thresholds, (2) wait for the next election, (3) satisfy the substantial ownership and holding requirements for nominating a candidate, (4) bear the costs involved in persuading other shareholders to vote for their candidates in a campaign against incumbents who are fully financed by the company itself, and (5) win majority support for their candidates. And if they are successful in each of the demanding steps of this long and costly process, they will be able to place on the board only a relatively small number of directors; these directors may have influence by virtue of their presence at board meetings, but will be far from having a decisive say.

Conversely, from the perspective of incumbent directors, the proposed change would not expose them to a substantial risk of replacement in the event of dismal performance. Even in the face of widespread dissatisfaction, they could not be replaced unless they fare badly in two votes spaced at least a year apart and, as incumbents, they would have the advantage of being able to outspend their challengers by using corporate funds in each of those votes. In any event, only a limited percentage of the board would be vulnerable to replacement in this way. Thus, the proposed rule would produce little pressure on directors to be attentive to shareholder interests.

Given that the proposed rule would lack real force, why has it become the subject of a fierce battle between management groups and some institutional investors and shareholder activists? The reason may well lie in its symbolic significance, rather than in its practical consequences: it would be a step toward relaxing management's powerful hold on the proxy machinery. We very much support this rule, mainly because we hope it will facilitate additional steps in this direction in the future.[9] By itself, however, the SEC's shareholder access proposal is unlikely to make directors sufficiently accountable to shareholders.

## What Should Be Done

What, then, should be done? First, shareholder access to the ballot should be made much easier than it is under the SEC's proposed rule. When a significant group of shareholders wishes to place a candidate on the ballot, there is absolutely no reason to force them to win a victory of sorts in one election and then to wait a year until the next election. Indeed, in some cases where past board performance makes shareholder intervention especially necessary, a long delay may be particularly costly to shareholders. Therefore, in each board election, access to the ballot should be granted to any group of shareholders that satisfies certain ownership and threshold requirements (say, ownership of 5 percent of the shares for at least one year prior to the election).

In addition, access should not be limited to attempts to elect a "short slate" that will constitute a small minority on the board. Shareholders satisfying threshold requirements should be able to place on the corporate ballot a slate that would replace all or most of the incumbent directors. The threat of such a "long slate" challenge is likely to make current directors more responsive to shareholder interests. Of course, the success of such a challenge is likely to have a greater impact on the corporation and its shareholders than one involving a short slate. Thus, a long slate would require more expansive disclosure, but given the dearth of electoral challenges outside the hostile takeover context, lowering the current impediments to "long-slate" challenges would be desirable.

Beyond providing shareholders with easier access to the corporate ballot, additional measures to strengthen the electoral threat should be adopted. Under existing rules of corporate law, incumbents' "campaign" costs are fully covered by the company—providing them with a great advantage over outside candidates, who must pay their own way. To lower the financial barrier for challengers, companies should be required to distribute proxy statements by independent nominees who have sufficient initial support and who wish to have such materials distributed. Furthermore, companies should be required to reimburse reasonable costs incurred by such nominees when they garner sufficient support in the ultimate vote.

These measures could be opposed, of course, on grounds that they would be costly to shareholders. But an improved corporate elections process would be in the interests of both companies and shareholders. The proposed measures would not expend corporate resources on nominees whose initial support and chances of winning are negligible; the limited amounts expended on serious challenges would be a small and worthwhile price to pay for an improved system of corporate governance.

Incumbent directors are currently protected from removal not only by the substantial cost to challengers of putting forward a competing slate, but also by staggered boards. In a staggered board, only one third of the members come up for election each year. As a result, no matter how dissatisfied shareholders are, they must prevail in two annual elections in order to replace a majority of the incumbents and take control way from current management. A majority of public companies now have such an arrangement.

Staggered boards offer directors insulation not only from proxy contests but also from a hostile acquisition of a large block of shares in their company. Corporate law now allows incumbent directors to maintain a "poison pill" defense that practically precludes a potential buyer from acquiring without management's consent a block of shares larger than that specified by the terms of the pill (commonly 10 to 20 percent). As a result, a buyer can purchase a large block of shares over the incumbents' objection only after inducing shareholders to replace the incumbents with a team of directors who favor the acquisition. When the target has a staggered board, supporters of an attractive acquisition offer must win two annual elections—longer than a hostile bidder can typically afford to wait.

The entrenching effect of staggered boards is costly to shareholders. In a recent empirical study, Alma Cohen and one of us find that, controlling for other relevant company characteristics, companies with a charter-based staggered board have a significantly lower value.[10] This study also provides evidence that staggered boards bring about, and do not merely reflect, lower firm value. Legal reform that would require or encourage firms to have all directors stand for election together thus could contribute significantly to shareholder wealth.

## Setting the Rules

Another way to reduce directors' ability to ignore shareholder interests is to remove the board's veto power over changes to the company's basic governance arrangements. These arrangements are set forth either in the rules of the state in which the company is incorporated or in the company's charter. Under long-standing corporate law, only the board—not a group of shareholders, however large—can initiate and bring to a shareholder vote a proposal to change the state of incorporation or to amend the corporate charter.

The federal securities laws give shareholders the power to express their sentiments in precatory shareholder resolutions, but these resolutions are nonbinding. In recent years, shareholders of companies with staggered boards have increasingly initiated proposals recommending annual election of all directors. However, boards often choose to ignore these proposals, even when they attract a majority of the shareholder vote.

Directors' control over the corporate agenda is often justified on grounds that the U.S. corporation is a completely "representative democracy" in which shareholders can act only through their representatives, the directors. In theory, if shareholders could easily replace directors, that power would be sufficient to induce directors not to stray from shareholders' wishes on major corporate issues.

As we have seen, however, the removal of directors is rather difficult under existing arrangements. It would be far from easy even under the SEC's proposed election reforms. Furthermore, shareholders may be pleased with management's general performance but still wish to put in place governance arrangements that restrict management's power or discretion in certain ways. Shareholders should be able to make a change in governance arrangements without concurrently having to replace the board.

The absence of shareholder power to initiate and approve changes in firms' basic corporate governance arrangements has, over time, tilted these arrangements excessively in management's favor. As new issues and circumstances have arisen, firms have tended to adopt charter amendments that address these changes efficiently only when the amendments were favored by management.[11] And states seeking to attract incorporating and reincorporating firms have had incentives to give substantial weight to management preferences, even at the expense of shareholder interests.[12]

Giving shareholders the power to initiate and approve by vote a proposal to reincorporate or to adopt a charter amendment could produce, in one bold stroke, a substantial improvement in the quality of corporate governance. Shareholder power to change governance arrangements would reduce the need for intervention from outside the firm by regulators, exchanges, or legislators.

Indeed, if shareholders had the power to set the ground rules of corporate governance, they could use it to address some of the problems we have discussed. They could establish rules that dismantle staggered boards or invigorate director elections. Shareholders could also adopt charter amendments that improve the process by which executive pay is set or place whatever limits they deem desirable on pay arrangements.

## Objections to Reducing Board Insulation

Management's supporters object strongly to any proposal that would decrease directors' insulation from shareholders and subject board members to the threat of removal. They also oppose giving shareholders the power to initiate and approve changes in the company's basic governance arrangements.

### Adverse Consequences?

Opponents of reform warn that giving shareholders the power to replace directors and change the corporate charter would have adverse consequences. They argue that such measures would lead to large-scale disruptions that would distract corporate management.[13] Should contested director elections become the norm, they suggest, companies would be forced to incur substantial out-of-pocket costs. More important, management's effort and attention would be diverted from productive activities.

But giving shareholders the power to intervene does not imply that they will use it on a regular basis. Shareholders will actually use such power only on those rare occasions in which management deviates substantially from the pursuit of shareholder interests and declines to correct itself despite growing shareholder dissatisfaction. Thus, the costs of actual contests will be incurred only in a small set of companies.

In contrast to the small number of cases in which costs will have to be incurred, the benefits of greater shareholder power will be system-wide. Recognizing shareholders' power to intervene, boards are likely to be more attentive to shareholder interests in the first instance. Tilting the balance of power in favor of shareholders is thus likely to improve the incentives and behavior of management in many publicly traded firms with dispersed ownership. The very viability of shareholder intervention would commonly make it unnecessary to use it.

Opponents also warn that reforms that reduce the board's insulation from shareholders would serve not shareholders' interests but those of "special interests."[14] In their view, greater shareholder power to place directors on the board would lead to the election of "special-interest" directors with labor, environmental, or social activist agendas; shareholder power to amend the charter would similarly operate to the benefit of special-interest groups. But shareholder power under these proposals could be exercised only by a vote of shareholders holding a majority of the voted stock, most of which is held by institutional shareholders. And most such institutions vote against management only on those issues where they feel management is acting in a way that severely hurts share-holder value.

Opponents of reform also argue that the board, in managing the corporation, has an informational advantage over even the most sophisticated shareholders.[15] But shareholders are aware of the board's informational advantage; past patterns indicate that institutional shareholders display much deference to boards in their voting decisions. The question is whether shareholders should be prevented from intervening on the rare occasions in which they wish to do so. Paternalistic tying of shareholders' hands seems unwarranted, especially given the concentration of stock in the hands of institutional investors. "Management," said the U.S. Supreme Court in one of its securities cases, "should not attribute to investors a child-like simplicity."[16]

Yet another objection focuses on the interests of long-term shareholders. Increased shareholder power, opponents argue, might cause management to focus "myopically" on producing short-term results that would avoid shareholder intervention.[17] This corporate myopia argument was invoked in the early debates on hostile takeovers, when it was raised to justify insulating management from hostile takeovers.[18] But there is no evidence that the myopia effect is sufficiently large to justify the costs of board insulation; indeed, the empirical evidence clearly indicates that firms with greater insulation from takeover have lower market value and worse operating performance.[19] In any event, myopia-based objections should at most call for giving shareholders the power to intervene only at certain intervals, or after sufficient delay, rather than at any time. Such objections cannot provide the basis for a system in which shareholders never have an opportunity, however long they wait, either to amend the corporate charter or to easily replace the board if they so choose.

Finally, the insulation of boards from shareholders, some opponents argue, is necessary so that boards can protect the interests of stakeholders such as employees.[20] But even though board insulation reduces directors' accountability to shareholders, it does not make directors accountable to stakeholders. Rather, it makes directors accountable to no one, protecting them in the event of poor performance that hurts *both* shareholders *and* stakeholders. Those interested in stakeholder protection, therefore, should not support the insulation of boards, but rather seek arrangements tailored specifically to stakeholders' concerns.

### Not Now?

Opponents of giving more power to shareholders also argue that, in any event, now is not the time to consider such a reform.[21] Recent reforms, they argue, can be expected to address past problems of corporate governance fully; at the minimum, they suggest, we should wait several years to see the consequences of these reforms before concluding that more is necessary.

As we have shown, however, even though recent reforms can be expected to improve matters, there is little basis for expecting them to fully address the corporate governance problems of the recent past. In particular, the director independence requirements cannot, by themselves, be relied on to ensure that directors serve as effective guardians of shareholder interests.

The story that we have told in this book is one that, we hope, will contribute to the recognition of the insufficiency of recent reforms. We have identified the myriad economic and social factors that have undermined directors' effectiveness in carrying out their important role of safeguarding shareholder interests. And we have shown that recent reforms cannot be expected to eliminate or outweigh these factors. Now is not the time to end the effort to reform corporate governance.

## Recognition and Reality

We ended chapter 15 by highlighting the effect that recognizing the problems of executive compensation can have on the reality of executive compensation. We would like to close by emphasizing the importance of recognizing the problems resulting from directors' insulation from shareholders. Recognition of these problems is a precondition for the reforms necessary to address them.

The power of the board, and its insulation from shareholders, is often viewed as an inevitable corollary of the modern corporation's widely dispersed ownership. But this power is partly due to the legal rules that insulate management from shareholder intervention. Changing these rules would reduce the extent to which boards can stray from shareholder interests and would much improve corporate governance.

The political obstacles to the necessary legal reforms are substantial, however. Corporate management has long been a powerful interest group in the politics of U.S. corporate law. The very control that the rules confer on management also gives it substantial power to fight changes in the status quo. As we discussed earlier, supporters of management, led by the Business Roundtable, have been putting up strong resistance even to the extremely mild proposal put forward by the SEC to allow shareholders to place a small number of shareholder-nominated candidates on the corporate ballot in some special circumstances.

For there to be changes in the allocation of power between management and shareholders, investors' demand for them must be sufficient to outweigh management's considerable ability to block reforms that chip away at its power and private benefits. This can happen only if investors and policymakers recognize the substantial costs that current arrangements impose—as well as the extent to which solving existing problems requires addressing the basic problem of board unaccountability. We hope that this book will contribute to such recognition.

# Notes

## Introduction

Epigraph: Kim Clark, "Corporate Scandals: Is It a Problem of Bad Apples, or Is It the Barrel?" Prepared remarks for the National Press Club, February 26, 2003, Harvard Business School.

1. Brian J. Hall and Kevin J. Murphy, "The Trouble with Stock Options," *Journal of Economic Perspectives* 17 (2003): 51.
2. Hall and Murphy, "The Trouble with Stock Options."
3. Janice Revell, "Mo' Money, Fewer Problems; Is It a Good Idea to Get Rid of the $1 Million CEO Pay Ceiling?" *Fortune*, March 31, 2003, 34.
4. Kevin J. Murphy, "Executive Compensation," in *Handbook of Labor Economics*, vol. 3, bk. 2, ed. Orley Ashenfelter and David Card, 2487 (New York: Elsevier, 1999). Murphy demonstrates graphically that the increase in academic papers on the subject of CEO pay outpaced the increase in total CEO pay during the late 1980s and early 1990s.
5. Graef S. Crystal, *In Search of Excess: The Overcompensation of American Executives* (New York: W. W. Norton, 1991); Robert A. G. Monks and Nell Minow, *Corporate Governance*, 3rd ed. (Oxford: Blackwell Publishing, 2001), 221–225.
6. For writings by legal scholars, see Linda J. Barris, "The Overcompensation Problem: A Collective Approach to Controlling Executive Pay," *Indiana Law Journal* 68 (1992): 59; Mark J. Loewenstein, "Reflections on Executive Compensation and a Modest Proposal for (Further) Reform," *Southern Methodist University Law Review* 50 (1996): 201; Carl T. Bogus, "Excessive Executive Compensation and the Failure of Corporate Democracy," *Buffalo Law Review* 41 (1993): 1; Eric W. Orts, "Shirking and Sharking: A Legal Theory of the Firm," *Yale Law and Policy Review* 16 (1996): 265–329; and Charles M. Yablon, "Bonus Questions—Executive Compensation in the Era of Pay for Performance," *Notre Dame Law Review* 75 (1999): 271.

For writings from an organizational or sociological perspective, see, for example, Michael Patrick Allen, "Power and Privilege in the Large Corporation: Corporate Control and Managerial Compensation," *American Journal of Sociology* 86 (1981): 1112–1123; Richard A. Lambert, David F. Larcker, and Keith Weigelt,

"The Structure of Organizational Incentives," *Administrative Science Quarterly* 38 (1993): 438–461; Sydney Finkelstein and Donald C. Hambrick, "Chief Executive Compensation: A Study of the Intersection of Markets and Political Processes," *Strategic Management Journal* 10 (1989): 121–134; Sydney Finkelstein and Donald C. Hambrick, "Chief Executive Compensation: A Synthesis and Reconciliation," *Strategic Management Journal* 9 (1988): 543–558; Charles A. O'Reilly III, Brian G. Main, and Graef S. Crystal, "CEO Compensation as Tournament and Social Comparison: A Tale of Two Theories," *Administrative Science Quarterly* 33 (1988): 257–274; Sydney Finkelstein, "Power in Top Management Teams: Dimensions, Measurement, and Validation," *Academy of Management Journal* 35 (1992): 505–538; James Wade, Charles A. O'Reilly III, and Ike Chandratat, "Golden Parachutes: CEOs and the Exercise of Social Influence," *Administrative Science Quarterly* 35 (1990): 587–603; and Mayer N. Zald, "The Power and Functions of Boards of Directors: A Theoretical Synthesis," *American Journal of Sociology* 75 (1969): 97–111.

7. Olivier Jean Blanchard, Florencio Lopez-de-Silanes, and Andrei Shleifer, "What Do Firms Do with Cash Windfalls?" *Journal of Financial Economics* 36 (1994): 337–360; David Yermack, "Good Timing: CEO Stock Option Awards and Company News Announcements," *Journal of Finance* 52 (1997): 449–476; and Marianne Bertrand and Sendhil Mullainathan, "Are CEOs Rewarded for Luck? The Ones without Principals Are," *Quarterly Journal of Economics* 116 (2001): 901–932.

8. See Lucian A. Bebchuk, Jesse M. Fried, and David I. Walker, "Managerial Power and Rent Extraction in the Design of Executive Compensation," *University of Chicago Law Review* 69 (2002): 753; and Lucian A. Bebchuk and Jesse M. Fried, "Executive Compensation as an Agency Problem," *Journal of Economic Perspectives* 17 (2003): 72.

9. For surveys from this perspective in the finance and economics literature, see, for example, John M. Abowd and David S. Kaplan, "Executive Compensation: Six Questions That Need Answering," *Journal of Economic Perspectives* 13 (1999): 145–168; Murphy, "Executive Compensation"; and John E. Core, Wayne Guay, and David F. Larcker, "Executive Equity Compensation and Incentives: A Survey," *Economic Policy Review* 9 (2003): 27–50.

   The arm's-length contracting view is also held by an important branch of legal scholarship. For early and well-known discussions of executive compensation by legal scholars, see Frank H. Easterbrook, "Managers' Discretion and Investors' Welfare: Theories and Evidence," *Delaware Journal of Corporate Law* 9 (1984): 540–571; and Daniel R. Fischel, "The Corporate Governance Movement," *Vanderbilt Law Review* 35 (1982): 1259–1292.

10. Michael C. Jensen and Kevin J. Murphy, "Performance Pay and Top-Management Incentives," *Journal of Political Economy* 98 (1990): 225–264; and Michael C. Jensen and Kevin J. Murphy, "CEO Incentives: It's Not How Much You Pay, but How," *Harvard Business Review* 68 (1990): 138–153.

11. For a classic statement of the view that such psychological motivations are critical, see Abraham H. Maslow, "A Theory of Human Motivation," *Psychology Review* 50 (1943): 370–396.

12. Clarence B. Randall, *The Executive in Transition* (New York: McGraw-Hill, 1967), 26.
13. Lucian A. Bebchuk and Yaniv Grinstein, "The Growth of Executive Pay," working paper, Harvard Law School and Cornell University, 2004.

## 1. The Official Story

Epigraph: Ira M. Millstein, "The Professional Board," *Business Lawyer* 50 (1995): 1428.
1. Rafael LaPorta, Florencio Lopez-de-Silanes, and Andrei Shleifer, "Corporate Ownership around the World," *Journal of Finance* 54 (1999): 471–517.
2. Adolf A. Berle Jr. and Gardiner C. Means, *The Modern Corporation and Private Property* (New York: Macmillan, 1932).
3. The standard reference is to Michael C. Jensen and William Meckling, "Theory of the Firm: Managerial Behavior, Agency Costs, and Ownership Structure," *Journal of Financial Economics* 3 (1976): 305–360.
4. Jensen and Meckling, "Theory of the Firm," 305–360; and Oliver Williamson, *The Economics of Discretionary Behavior: Managerial Objectives in a Theory of the Firm* (Englewood Cliffs, NJ: Prentice Hall, 1964).
5. Michael C. Jensen, "Agency Costs of Free Cash Flow, Corporate Finance, and Takeovers," *American Economic Review* 76 (1986): 323–329.
6. Andrei Shleifer and Robert W. Vishny, "Management Entrenchment: The Case of Manager-Specific Investments," *Journal of Financial Economics* 25 (1989): 123–140.
7. See, for example, Delaware General Corporate Law, sec. 141.
8. John E. Core, Wayne Guay, and David F. Larcker, "Executive Equity Compensation and Incentives: A Survey," *Economic Policy Review* 9 (2003): 27–50.
9. See *Brehm v. Eisner*, Delaware Supreme Court, 746 A.2d 244, 262–263 (2000).
10. Recent surveys of this work on executive compensation from an arm's-length contracting perspective include Kevin J. Murphy, "Executive Compensation," in *Handbook of Labor Economics*, vol. 3, bk. 2, ed. Orley Ashenfelter and David Card (New York: Elsevier, 1999), 2485–2563; and Core, Guay, and Larcker, "Executive Equity Compensation and Incentives," 27–50.
11. Classic works on the subject include J. A. Mirrlees, "The Optimal Structure of Incentives and Authority within an Organization," *Bell Journal of Economics* 7 (1976): 105–131; Bengt Holmstrom, "Moral Hazard and Observability," *Bell Journal of Economics* 10 (1979): 74–91; and Steven Shavell, "Risk Sharing and Incentives in the Principal and Agent Relationship," *Bell Journal of Economics* 10 (1979): 55–73. For a recent survey of the application of principal-agent theory to CEO compensation, see Murphy, "Executive Compensation."
12. See, for example, Michael C. Jensen and Kevin J. Murphy, "Performance Pay and Top-Management Incentives," *Journal of Political Economy* 98 (1990): 225–264.
13. See, for example, Lucian A. Bebchuk and Christine Jolls, "Managerial Value Diversion and Shareholder Wealth," *Journal of Law, Economics, and Organization* 15 (1999): 487–502.

14. Ira Kay, Ph.D., testimony before the Senate Finance Committee, April 2002, http://finance.senate.gov/hearings/testimony/041802iktest.pdf, 2 (accessed April 29, 2004).

15. See, for example, Franklin Snyder, "More Pieces of the Compensation Puzzle," *Delaware Journal of Corporate Law* (2003): 129–183.

16. See Jay W. Lorsch, "Compensating Corporate CEOs: A Process View," Harvard Business School working paper #99-013, 1998, 48.

## 2. Have Boards Been Bargaining at Arm's Length?

Epigraph: Adam Smith, *An Inquiry into the Nature and Causes of the Wealth of Nations* (New York: Modern Library, 1937), 107.

1. Stacey R. Kole, "The Complexity of Compensation Contracts," *Journal of Financial Economics* 43 (1997): 101.

2. Stacey Burke, Glenn Davis, Chris Loayza, Conor Murphy, and Sergio Schuchner, *Board Structure/Board Pay 2002* (Washington, DC: Investor Responsibility Research Center, 2002), 43.

3. Burke, Davis, Loayza, Murphy, and Schuchner, *Board Structure/Board Pay 2002*, 41.

4. *Internal Revenue Code*, sec. 162(m). The employees whose compensation is covered by this rule include the CEO or the individual acting in that capacity and the four most highly compensated officers other than the CEO, whose compensation must be reported under the Securities Exchange Act of 1934. See 26 CFR § 1.162-27(c)(2) (defining the employees covered under § 162(m)). Nonemployee directors who serve as consultants or who otherwise receive direct or indirect remuneration from the firm in a capacity other than that of directorship do not qualify as outside directors for the purposes of § 162(m). See 26 CFR § 1.162-27(e)(3).

5. Robert Charles Clark, *Corporate Law* (Boston: Little, Brown and Company, 1986), 194.

6. NASD Rule 4350; NYSE Listed Company Manual Rule 303A; American Stock Exchange Company Guide secs. 121, 801–809; SEC Release No. 34-48745 (November 4, 2003); and SEC Release No. 34-48863 (December 1, 2003).

7. AMEX creates an exception for "small business issuers," which are required only to have a board composed of at least 50 percent independent directors. American Stock Exchange Company Guide sec. 121B(2)(c).

8. Pearl Meyer & Partners, "Executive Pay Trends: Looking Forward and Looking Back" (2002): 3; and Garry Strauss, "Companies Pony Up to Keep Directors: Boards Seats Have Become Hot Seats," *USA Today*, November 21, 2002, B1.

9. UAL Corp Form 10-K (filed March 28, 2003): 104; and Starwood Hotels & Resorts Worldwide Inc. Form 10-K/A (filed July 7, 2003): 3.

10. Lucian A. Bebchuk and Marcel Kahan, "A Framework for Analyzing Legal Policy towards Proxy Contests," *California Law Review* 78 (1990): 1071–1135.

11. Lucian A. Bebchuk, "The Case for Shareholder Access to the Ballot," *Business Lawyer* 59 (2003): 43–66.

12. Brian G. M. Main, Charles A. O'Reilly III, and James Wade, "The CEO, the Board of Directors, and Executive Compensation: Economic and Psychological Perspectives," *Industrial and Corporate Change* 11 (1995): 302–303; Victor Brudney, "The Independent Director—Heavenly City or Potemkin Village?" *Harvard Law Review* 95 (1982): 610, n. 39; and Benjamin E. Hermalin and Michael S. Weisbach, "Endogenously Chosen Boards of Directors and Their Monitoring of the CEO," *American Economic Law Review* 88 (1998): 96–97. For a review of the economic literature on boards of directors, see Benjamin E. Hermalin and Michael S. Weisbach, "Boards of Directors as an Endogenously Determined Institution: A Survey of the Economic Literature," *Federal Reserve Bank of New York Economic Policy Review* 9 (2003): 7–26.

13. Shivdasani and Yermack report that in 1994, 78 percent of 341 publicly traded Fortune 500 firms had a nominating committee, and in 33 percent of those firms the CEO was a member of the nominating committee. Anil Shivdasani and David Yermack, "CEO Involvement in the Selection of New Board Members: An Empirical Analysis," *Journal of Finance* 54 (1999): 1834.

14. Burke, Davis, Loayza, Murphy, and Schuchner, *Board Structure/Board Pay 2002*, 49.

15. Main, O'Reilly, and Wade, "The CEO, the Board of Directors, and Executive Compensation"; and Cynthia A. Montgomery and Rhonda Kaufman, "The Board's Missing Link," *Harvard Business Review* 81 (2003): 89.

16. NASD Rule 4350; NYSE Listed Company Manual Rule 303A; American Stock Exchange Company Guide sec. 804; and SEC Release No. 34-48745 (November 4, 2003).

17. Daniel Nasaw, "Opening the Board: The Fight Is On to Determine Who Will Guide the Selection of Directors in the Future," *Wall Street Journal*, October 27, 2003, R8.

18. The Tyco CEO paid one director, Frank Walsh, a $20 million "finder's fee" for helping to arrange a deal. See Jeffrey Kranser, "Tyco Sues 2 Former Executives Accused of Pay Impropriety, a Coverup," *Boston Globe*, June 18, 2002, D1. WorldCom CEO Bernard Ebbers allowed Stiles A. Kellett Jr., the director who chaired the compensation committee, to rent a Falcon 20 jet for $1 a month plus $400 an hour plus minor expenses, when the standard rate for renting a corporate jet is at least several thousand dollars an hour. See Susan Pulliam, Jared Sandberg, and Deborah Solomon, "WorldCom Board Will Consider Rescinding Ebbers's Severance," *Wall Street Journal*, September 10, 2002, A1. The value of the lease was between $1.4 million and $3.4 million, and WorldCom's court-appointed monitor, Richard Breeden, recommended that Kellett repay at least $1.4 million. Christopher Stern, "WorldCom Director Urged to Leave," *Washington Post*, September 13, 2002, E01. Kellett eventually agreed to reimburse WorldCom at a rate of $3,000 per hour, requiring him to pay WorldCom $156,000 and to give up directors' fees and other amounts owed to him by WorldCom.

19. The examples in this paragraph are described in Gary Strauss, "Do Conflicts Cloud the Objectivity of Boards?" *USA Today*, March 5, 2002, 1A.

20. Victor Brudney and Allen Ferrell, "Corporate Speech and Citizenship: Corporate Charitable Giving," *University of Chicago Law Review* 69 (2002): 1197.

21. Strauss, "Do Conflicts Cloud the Objectivity of Boards?"

22. *In re Oracle Corp. Derivative Litigation*, 824 A.2d 917, 920–921 (Del. Ch. 2003).

23. There is evidence that executives and directors place value on having the firms donate to charitable causes favored by them. For example, the departing CEO of Ford, Jacques Nasser, extracted a commitment from Ford to endow a scholarship in his name at a school of his choice. See Joann S. Lublin, "Many Former Chief Executives Get Lush Perks and Fat Fees for Limited 'Consulting' Work," *Wall Street Journal*, September 13, 2002, B1.

24. Richard A. Oppel Jr., "Senate Panel Says Enron's Board Could Have Stopped High Risk Practices," *New York Times*, July 7, 2002, 1.

25. NYSE Listed Company Manual Rule 303A; NASD Rule 4350; and American Stock Exchange Company Guide sec. 121. In the text discussion that follows, we focus on the NYSE requirements because of the importance and prominence of this exchange.

26. NYSE Listed Company Manual Rule 303A.02(b)(ii). The NASDAQ and AMEX limit is $60,000. NASD Manual 4200(a)(14)(B); American Stock Exchange Company Guide sec. 121A(b).

27. Commentary to NYSE Listed Company Manual Rule 303A.02(b)(ii). NASDAQ's standard is stricter with respect to this issue. Directors whose immediate family members are employees of the company and who may qualify as independent directors under the NYSE standards may not be counted as independent under the NASDAQ standards. NASD Manual 4200(a)(14)(C).

28. NYSE Listed Company Manual Rule 303A(2)(b)(v). The figures used by AMEX and NASDAQ are $200,000 or 5 percent of gross revenues. American Stock Exchange Company Guide, sec. 121A(d); and NASD Manual 4200(a)(14)(D).

29. Commentary to NYSE Listed Company Manual Rule 303A(2)(b)(v).

30. Kevin Hallock, "Dual Agency: Corporate Boards with Reciprocally Interlocking Relationships," in *Executive Compensation and Shareholder Value: Theory and Evidence*, ed. Jennifer Carpenter and David Yermack (Boston: Kluwer Academic Publishers, 1999), 58. For an examination of the factors that make reciprocal CEO board membership more likely, see Eliezer M. Fich and Lawrence J. White, "Why Do CEOs Reciprocally Sit on Each Other's Boards?" working paper, New York University School of Business, 2001.

31. Ivan E. Brick, Oded Palmon, and John K. Wald, "CEO Compensation, Director Compensation, and Firm Performance: Evidence of Cronyism," working paper, Rutgers University Business School, September 2002, 29.

32. Main, O'Reilly, and Wade, "The CEO, the Board of Directors, and Executive Compensation." Similarly, CEO pay tends to be higher and the CEO is more

likely to have a golden parachute when a higher percentage of the outside directors has been appointed by the CEO.

33. Rakesh Khurana, *Searching for a Corporate Savior: The Irrational Quest for Charismatic CEOs* (Princeton, NJ: Princeton University Press, 2002), 83.

34. Khurana, *Searching for a Corporate Savior*, 84.

35. Melvin A. Eisenberg, "The Compensation of Chief Executive Officers and Directors of Publicly Held Corporations," *7th Annual Corporate Governance Institute*, SE39 ALI-ABA (1999): 117–118.

36. Main, O'Reilly, and Wade, "The CEO, the Board of Directors, and Executive Compensation," 304.

37. Burke, Davis, Loayza, Murphy, and Schuchner, *Board Structure/Board Pay 2002*, 47.

38. Graef S. Crystal, *In Search of Excess: The Overcompensation of American Executives* (New York: W. W. Norton, 1991).

39. Main, O'Reilly, and Wade, "The CEO, the Board of Directors, and Executive Compensation," 319–320.

40. In 2003, all but several of the 200 largest public industrial and service companies incorporated equity into board pay. Pearl Meyer & Partners, "2003 Director Compensation" (2003): 9; *http://www.execpay.com/ResDir.htm* (accessed June 23, 2004).

41. George P. Baker, Michael C. Jensen, and Kevin J. Murphy, "Compensation and Incentives: Practice vs. Theory," *Journal of Finance* 63 (1998): 614.

42. John E. Core, Robert W. Holthausen, and David F. Larcker, "Corporate Governance, Chief Executive Officer Compensation, and Firm Performance," *Journal of Financial Economics* 51 (1999): 371–406.

43. A case for increasing stock grants to independent directors is presented in Charles M. Elson, "Executive Over-Compensation—A Board-Based Solution," *Boston College Law Review* 34 (1993): 981–983.

44. Managers might well prefer it this way. There is some evidence that CEOs try to reduce the portion of director compensation that is equity based in order to further reduce the board's incentive to monitor the CEO's performance. See Harley E. Ryan Jr. and Roy A. Wiggins III, "Who Is in Whose Pocket? Director Compensation, Bargaining Power, and Barriers to Effective Monitoring," working paper, Louisiana State University and Bentley College, 2003.

45. Richard M. Cyert, Sok-Hyon Kang, and Praveen Kumar, "Corporate Governance, Takeovers, and Top-Management Compensation: Theory and Evidence," *Management Science* 48 (2002): 453–469.

46. Eugene F. Fama and Michael C. Jensen, "Separation of Ownership and Control," *Journal of Law and Economics* 26 (1983): 301–325.

47. See, for example, Geeta Anand, "Double Trouble: Ties to Two Firms Tainted by Scandal Haunt Top Doctor," *Wall Street Journal*, December 24, 2002, A1.

48. See, for example, Joshua Green, "Savage Business," *American Prospect* 13 (2002): 14–15.

49. See, for example, Main, O'Reilly, and Wade, "The CEO, the Board of Directors, and Executive Compensation," 302–303.

50. Jay W. Lorsch and Krishna G. Palepu, "Limits to Board Effectiveness," working paper, Harvard Business School, 2003, 3.

51. Khurana, *Searching for a Corporate Savior*, 81–118.

52. Judith Burns, "Everything You Wanted to Know about Corporate Governance . . . But Didn't Know to Ask," *Wall Street Journal*, October 27, 2003, R6.

53. Sidley Austin Brown & Wood LLP, "Best Practices Calendar for Corporate Boards and Committees" (March 2004): 1–2.

54. Patrick McGeehan, "Quick: What's the Boss Making?" *New York Times*, September 21, 2003, sec. 3, 1.

55. Crystal, *In Search of Excess*, 42–50.

56. Warren Buffett, letter to shareholders of Berkshire Hathaway, Inc., included in the Annual Report to the Shareholders of Berkshire Hathaway Inc., February 2004, 8; http://www.berkshirehathaway.com/letters/2003ltr.pdf (accessed April 30, 2004).

57. For an insider's account of the use of compensation consultants to justify executive pay, see Crystal, *In Search of Excess*.

58. This quote is reported in Warren Buffett, letter to shareholders, 8.

59. Carol J. Loomis, "This Stuff Is Wrong," *Fortune*, June 25, 2002, 74.

60. Stuart Gillan, "Has Pay for Performance Gone Awry: Views from a Corporate Governance Forum," *Research Dialogue* 68 (2001): 1–16.

61. For a recent study finding that CEO pay is higher in firms that use compensation consultants than in similar firms that do not, see Martin J. Conyon and Simon I. Peck, "Compensation Consultants and Executive Pay," working paper, The Wharton School, University of Pennsylvania, and Weatherhead School of Management, Case Western Reserve University, 2004, 3. Their study is based on UK data, but we conjecture that the same correlation would be found in U.S. data.

62. Commentary to NYSE Listed Company Manual Rule 303A(5)(b)(ii).

63. Kevin J. Murphy, "Explaining Executive Compensation: Managerial Power vs. the Perceived Cost of Stock Options," *University of Chicago Law Review* 69 (2002): 847.

64. Khurana, *Searching for a Corporate Savior*.

65. Michael S. Weisbach, "Outside Directors and CEO Turnover," *Journal of Financial Economics* 20 (1998): 453–454. More narrowly focused industry studies also find that the presence of inside directors reduces the likelihood that poorly performing CEOs will be fired. For example, Warren Boeker finds that the likelihood that a poorly performing CEO of a semiconductor firm will be replaced decreases as the percentage of inside directors increases. See Warren Boeker, "Power and Managerial Dismissal: Scapegoating at the Top," *Administrative Science Quarterly* 37 (1992): 400–418. Not surprisingly, firms in which the CEO is also chair of the board are less likely to fire the CEO for poor performance. Vidhan K. Goyal and Chul W. Park, "Board Leadership Structure and CEO Turnover," *Journal of Corporate Finance* 8 (2002): 49–66.

66. Denis B. K. Lyons, "CEO Casualties: A Battlefront Report," *Directors & Boards* (1999): 43–45.

67. Holman W. Jenkins, "Outrageous CEO Pay Revisited," *Wall Street Journal*, October 2, 2002, A17.
68. Narayanan Subramanian, Atreya Chakraborty, and Shahbaz Sheikh, "Performance Incentives, Performance Pressure, and Executive Turnover," working paper, Brandeis University, 2003.
69. Chris McNeil, Greg Niehaus, and Eric Powers, "Management Turnover in Subsidiaries of Conglomerates versus Stand-Alone Firms," working paper, School of Business, Penn State Erie, and Moore School of Business, University of South Carolina, 2003.
70. See, for example, Ira M. Millstein and Paul W. MacAvoy, "The Active Board of Directors and Performance of the Large Publicly Traded Corporation," *Columbia Law Review* 98 (1998): 1283–1321; and Mark J. Loewenstein, "The Conundrum of Executive Compensation," *Wake Forest Law Review* 35 (2000): 15.

### 3. Shareholders' Limited Power to Intervene

Epigraph: *Brehm v. Eisner*, 746 A.2d 244, 262 (Del. Sup. 2000).
1. Linda J. Barris, "The Overcompensation Problem: A Collective Approach to Controlling Executive Pay," *Indiana Law Review* 68 (1992): 82.
2. *Brehm v. Eisner*, 746 A.2d 244, 259–63 (Del. Sup. 2000).
3. *Zupnick v. Goizueta*, 698 A.2d 384 (Del. Ch. 1997).
4. *Steyner v. Meyerson*, C. A. No. 13139, 1995 WL 441999 (Del. Ch. 1995).
5. Mark J. Loewenstein, "Reflections on Executive Compensation and a Modest Proposal for (Further) Reform," *Southern Methodist University Law Review* 50 (1996): 201–223.
6. Randall S. Thomas and Kenneth J. Martin, "Litigating Challenges to Executive Pay: An Exercise in Futility?" *Washington University Law Quarterly* 79 (2001): 576–579.
7. *Bnehm v. Eisner*, 746 A.2d 244 (Del. Sup. 2000); *In re Walt Disney Co. Derivative Litig.*, 825 A.2d 275 (Del. Ch. 2003).
8. Telephone conversation on August 6, 2003, with Ally Monaco and Annick Dunning of the Investor Responsibility Research Center (IRRC). Annick Dunning conducted a study for the IRRC in which she found that only 40 percent of S&P 500 firms and 35 percent of S&P 1500 firms had stock option plans that were not approved by shareholders.
9. Randall S. Thomas and Kenneth J. Martin, "The Determinants of Shareholder Voting on Stock Option Plans," *Wake Forest Law Review* 35 (2000): 46–51.
10. For an example of proxy materials suggesting that the only effect of the shareholder vote will be to determine whether or not the firm can deduct executive compensation that the firm will pay in any event, see Finova Group Inc., Schedule 14A (filed on April 2, 1997); and Home Depot Schedule 14A (filed on April 19, 2002).
11. Recognition of this fact led the SEC in 2003 to require mutual funds to disclose all of their votes. See Investment Advisers Act Release No. 2106 (January 31, 2003); Final Rule: Disclosure of Proxy Voting Policies and Proxy Voting Records

by Registered Management Investment Companies; SEC, 7 CFR Parts 239, 249, 270, and 2; Release Nos. 33–8188, 34–47304, IC–25922; File No. S7–36–02; RIN 3235–AI64. Because investors base their choices of funds on investment performance, not on how funds vote in corporate governance matters, we do not expect this disclosure requirement to eliminate funds' promanagement bias in voting decisions. In our view, the most effective way to eliminate bias would be to require strictly confidential shareholder voting.

12. David Parthiban, Rahul Kochar, and Edward Levitas, "The Effect of Institutional Investors on the Level and Mix of CEO Compensation," *Academy of Management Journal* 41 (1998): 200–208.

13. Pui-Wing Tam, "Hewlett Sues, Seeking to Foil Compaq Deal," *Wall Street Journal*, March 29, 2002, A3.

14. Jennifer E. Bethel and Stuart L. Gillan, "The Impact of the Institutional and Regulatory Environment on Shareholder Voting," *Financial Management* 31 (2002): 29.

15. Stuart L. Gillan, "Option-Based Compensation: Panacea or Pandora's Box?" *Journal of Applied Corporate Finance* 14 (2001): 124.

16. Bethel and Gillan, "The Impact," 44.

17. See SEC Release No. 34–48108 (File Nos. SR–NYSE–2002–46 and SR–NASD–2002–140) (June 30, 2003); and SEC Release No. 34–48872 (File No. SR–Amex–2003–100) (December 3, 2003).

18. Thomas and Martin, "The Determinants," 58–59.

19. See Georgeson Shareholder, "Annual Corporate Governance Review" (2003): 3; and Brian R. Cheffins and Randall S. Thomas, "Should Shareholders Have a Greater Say over Executive Pay? Learning from the U.S. Experience," *Journal of Corporation Law Studies* 1 (2001): 301. Cheffins and Thomas report that in the 2000 proxy season, stockholders in 83 of the 1,000 leading U.S. public companies filed a precatory proposal relating to executive compensation.

20. Randall S. Thomas, and Kenneth J. Martin, "Should Labor Be Allowed to Make Shareholder Proposals?" *Washington Law Review* 73 (1998): 41, 68, 76.

21. Andrew Countryman, "Board Term Battle Heats Up: Shareholder Activists Pushing for Switch to Annual Elections," *Chicago Tribune*, June 16, 2003, 1.

22. Tom Petruno, "Activist Investors Making Inroads," *Los Angeles Times*, May 18, 2003, pt. 3, 1. According to data collected by Institutional Shareholder Services, until recently only about 10 percent of the resolutions receiving majority support were implemented. The percentage of implementation has increased, but is still about 30 percent. We are grateful to Patrick McGurn, vice president of Institutional Shareholder Services, for providing us with these figures.

## 4. The Limits of Market Forces

Epigraph: Frank H. Easterbrook, "Managers' Discretion and Investors' Welfare: Theories and Evidence," *Delaware Journal of Corporate Law* 9 (1984): 570.

1. Frank H. Easterbrook, "Managers' Discretion and Investors' Welfare"; Daniel R.

Fischel, "The 'Race to the Bottom' Revisited: Reflections on Recent Developments in Delaware's Corporation Law," *Northwestern University Law Review* 76 (1982): 916–920; and Eugene F. Fama, "Agency Problems and the Theory of the Firm," *Journal of Political Economy* 88 (1980): 289.

2. Lucian A. Bebchuk, "Federalism and the Corporation: The Desirable Limits on State Competition in Corporate Law," *Harvard Law Review* 105 (1992): 1461–1467; Lucian A. Bebchuk, "Limiting Contractual Freedom in Corporate Law: The Desirable Constraints on Charter Amendments," *Harvard Law Review* 102 (1989): 1840–1846; Lucian A. Bebchuk and Mark J. Roe, "A Theory of Path Dependence in Corporate Ownership and Governance," *Stanford Law Review* 52 (1999): 142–153. These works explain why market forces cannot ensure that insiders' reincorporation decisions, charter amendment decisions, and ownership structure decisions are those that are best for shareholders.

3. C. Edward Fee and Charles J. Hadlock, "Raids, Rewards, and Reputations in the Market for CEO Talent," *Review of Financial Studies* 16 (2003): 1327. The authors report that in a sample of 1,200 CEO hires during the period 1990–1998, only 26.5 percent were outside hires.

4. Melvin A. Eisenberg, "The Structure of Corporation Law," *Columbia Law Review* 89 (1989): 1495.

5. Fee and Hadlock, "Raids, Rewards, and Reputations," 1352.

6. Perry and Zenner report that in 1997, the median S&P 1500 CEO stood to gain or lose $11.50 per $1,000 of shareholder gain or loss. Tod Perry and Marc Zenner, "CEO Compensation in the 1990s: Shareholder Alignment or Shareholder Expropriation?" *Wake Forest Law Review* 35 (2000): 149. Similarly, Hall and Liebman have estimated that 1998 CEO-wealth-to-shareholder-value sensitivity was approximately $11 per $1,000, based on a firm with $1 billion market capitalization. Brian J. Hall and Jeffrey B. Liebman, "The Taxation of Executive Compensation," *Tax Policy and the Economy*, vol. 14, edited by James Poterba (Cambridge, MA: MIT Press, 2000), 6, fig. 1. CEO-wealth-to-shareholder-value sensitivity has been even lower in the past. Using earlier data from the period 1974–1986, Jensen and Murphy calculated a median CEO-wealth-to-shareholder-value sensitivity of $3.25 per $1,000, a figure that included a $0.30 per $1,000 adjustment for risk of dismissal. See Michael C. Jensen and Kevin J. Murphy, "Performance Pay and Top-Management Incentives," *Journal of Political Economy* 98 (1990): 261.

7. The importance of the market for corporate control as a source of discipline was first emphasized by Henry G. Manne, "Mergers and the Market for Corporate Control," *Journal of Political Economy* 73 (1965): 110–120.

8. Lucian Bebchuk, John Coates IV, and Guhan Subramanian, "The Powerful Antitakeover Force of Staggered Boards: Theory, Evidence, and Policy," *Stanford Law Review* 54 (2002): 887–951.

9. Marcel Kahan and Ed Rock, "How I Learned to Stop Worrying and Love the Pill: Adaptive Responses to Takeover Law," *University of Chicago Law Review* 69 (2002): 871–915.

10. Anup Agrawal and Ralph A. Walking, "Executive Careers and Compensation Surrounding Takeover Bids," *Journal of Finance* 49 (1994): 986. Their study examined Forbes 800 firms in the 1980s. They determined that takeover bids were more common in industries in which CEOs were overpaid, but found no significant difference between CEO compensation in firms that were takeover targets within these industries and CEO compensation in firms that were not.

11. See Lynn Stout, "The Unimportance of Being Efficient," *Michigan Law Review* 87 (1988): 645–647, for a discussion of the sources of capital for publicly traded firms.

12. To the extent that the firm uses debt financing, executive compensation arrangements that encourage excessive risk taking might increase the cost of debt. However, as in the case of equity financing, the increase in the cost of the debt would not prevent debt-financed expansion but would only reduce the value of existing shareholders' equity in the firm. Furthermore, managers would bear only a small fraction of this cost.

13. Easterbrook, "Managers' Discretion and Investors' Welfare."

14. Jean Tirole, *The Theory of Industrial Organization* (Cambridge, MA: MIT Press, 1988): 277–303.

## 5. The Managerial Power Perspective

Epigraph: Anonymous Fortune 500 CEO, interviewed in Carol J. Loomis, "This Stuff is Wrong," *Fortune*, June 25, 2002, 82.

1. The managerial power approach is in the spirit of the economics literature that focuses on certain agents' power within organizations and on the ability of these agents to extract rents. See, for example, Jack Hirshleifer, "Competition, Cooperation, and Conflict in Economics and Biology," *American Economic Review* 68 (1978): 238–243; Raghuram G. Rajan and Luigi Zingales, "Power in a Theory of the Firm," *Quarterly Journal of Economics* 113 (1998): 387–432; and Raghuram G. Rajan and Luigi Zingales, "The Firm as a Dedicated Hierarchy: A Theory of the Origin and Growth of Firms," *Quarterly Journal of Economics* 116 (2001): 805–851. However, most financial economists working in the particular context of executive compensation have largely assumed arm's-length contracting and have paid little attention to the role of managerial power.

2. For evidence that power is often distributed among two or more managers, see Sydney Finkelstein, "Power in Top Management Teams: Dimensions, Measurement, and Validation," *Academy of Management Journal* 35 (1992): 505–538.

3. James Wade, Charles A. O'Reilly III, and Timothy Pollock, "Overpaid CEOs and Underpaid Managers: Equity and Executive Compensation," working paper, University of Wisconsin–Madison, Stanford University, and University of Maryland, 2004, 27.

4. In some cases, an overpaid CEO might produce resentment among other top executives. In such a case, taking as given the CEO's compensation, overpaying

the other executives may reduce resentment of the CEO's pay, improve their working relationships with the CEO, and make shareholders better off. Even in such a case, providing other executives with rents would benefit the shareholders only given the rents captured by the CEO. The important point is that even when spillover rents benefit shareholders, the executives' pay arrangements will differ from those that would result under arm's-length contracting for all executives including the CEO.

5. Jay W. Lorsch and Elizabeth M. MacIver, *Pawns or Potentates? The Reality of America's Corporate Boards* (Boston: Harvard Business School Press, 1989), 23–31.

6. See Matthew Brelis, "GE, Welch Agree to Slash His Perks: Retired CEO Will Retain Office, Staff, Lose Many Benefits," *Boston Globe*, September 17, 2002, D1.

7. Linda C. Quinn, "Executive Compensation under the New SEC Disclosure Requirements," in Seventh Annual Corporate Law Symposium: Executive Compensation, *University of Cincinnati Law Review* 63 (1995): 770–771.

8. See, for example, Kevin J. Murphy, "Explaining Executive Compensation: Managerial Power vs. the Perceived Cost of Stock Options," *University of Chicago Law Review* 69 (2002): 847–869; Holman W. Jenkins Jr., "Business World: Outrageous CEO Pay Revisited," *Wall Street Journal*, October 2, 2002, A17.

9. Randall S. Thomas and Kenneth J. Martin, "The Effect of Shareholder Proposals on Executive Compensation," *University of Cincinnati Law Review* 67 (1999): 1021–1065.

10. Kenneth J. Martin and Randall S. Thomas, "When Is Enough, Enough? Market Reaction to Highly Dilutive Stock Option Plans and the Subsequent Impact on CEO Compensation," *Journal of Corporate Finance* (forthcoming).

11. Alexander Dyck and Luigi Zingales, "The Corporate Governance Role of the Media," working paper, Harvard Business School and the University of Chicago, 2002; and Alexander Dyck and Luigi Zingales, "Private Benefits of Control: An International Comparison," *Journal of Finance* 59 (2004): 537–600.

12. Robert Monks and Nell Minow, *Corporate Governance*, 2nd ed. (Cambridge, MA: Blackwell Publishing, 1995), 399–411.

13. Judith Dobrzynski, "CalPERS Is Ready to Roar, but Will CEOs Listen?" *BusinessWeek*, March 30, 1992, 44.

14. YiLin Wu, "The Impact of Public Opinion on Board Structure Changes, Director Career Progression, and CEO Turnover: Evidence from CalPERS' Corporate Governance Program," *Journal of Corporate Finance* 10 (2004): 199.

15. It has been reported that at least 65 percent of U.S. firms use compensation consultants. John M. Bizjak, Michael L. Lemmon, and Lalitha Naveen, "Has the Use of Peer Groups Contributed to Higher Levels of Executive Compensation?" Working paper, Portland State University, 2000, 10, 44.

16. James B. Wade, Joseph F. Porac, and Timothy G. Pollock, "Worth, Words, and the Justification of Executive Pay," *Journal of Organizational Behavior* 18 (1997): 657, 658.

17. Joseph F. Porac, James B. Wade, and Timothy G. Pollock, "Industry Categories and the Politics of the Comparable Firm in CEO Compensation," *Administrative Quarterly* 44 (1999): 112–144.

18. Kevin J. Murphy, "Politics, Economics, and Executive Compensation," *University of Cincinnati Law Review* 63 (1995): 736.

19. Bizjak, Lemmon, and Naveen, "Has the Use of Peer Groups," 2–3.

20. Kevin J. Murphy, "Executive Compensation," in *Handbook of Labor Economics*, vol. 3, bk. 2, ed. Orley Ashenfelter and David Card (New York: Elsevier, 1999), 2485, 2517–2518; Graef S. Crystal, *In Search of Excess: The Overcompensation of American Executives* (New York: W. W. Norton, 1991), 219; and Shawn Tully, "Raising the Bar," *Fortune*, June 8, 1998, 272.

21. Harvard Business School Dean Kim B. Clark, prepared remarks, National Press Club, February 26, 2003.

22. Murphy, "Explaining Executive Compensation"; and Brian J. Hall and Kevin J. Murphy, "The Trouble with Stock Options," *Journal of Economic Perspectives* 17 (2003): 64–65. See also Franklin Snyder, "More Pieces of the Compensation Puzzle," *Delaware Journal of Corporate Law* 28 (2003): 133.

23. Holman W. Jenkins Jr., "Business World: Outrageous CEO Pay Revisited," *Wall Street Journal*, October 2, 2002, A17.

24. See, for example, Brian Hall and Kevin J. Murphy, "The Trouble with Stock Options," 65.

25. Geoffrey Colvin, "The Great CEO Pay Heist," *Fortune*, June 25, 2001, 64.

26. Murphy, "Executive Compensation," 2493.

27. The 1929 crash led to the enactment in 1933 and 1934 of the nation's first securities laws. The recent crash has already led to the passing of the Sarbanes-Oxley Act of 2002.

28. See, for example, Melvin A. Eisenberg, "Corporate Law and Social Norms," *Columbia Law Review* 99 (1999): 1253–1292; and Symposium on Norms and Corporate Law, *University of Pennsylvania Law Review* 149 (2001): 1607–2191.

29. Andrew Balls, "Ill-judged Incentives: Share Options Are a Poor Way to Make Executives Act in Shareholders' Interests," *Financial Times*, November 12, 2002, 13.

30. Murphy, "Explaining Executive Compensation," 847; and Hall and Murphy, "The Trouble with Stock Options," 49–70.

## 6. The Relationship between Power and Pay

Epigraph: John E. Core, Robert W. Holthausen, and David F. Larcker, "Corporate Governance, Chief Executive Compensation, and Firm Performance." *Journal of Financial Economics* 51 (1999): 372.

1. Core, Holthausen, and Larcker, "Corporate Governance, Chief Executive Compensation, and Firm Performance," 372–373.

2. David Yermack, "Higher Market Valuation of Companies with a Small Board of Directors," *Journal of Financial Economics* 40 (1996): 205.

3. Core, Holthausen, and Larcker, "Corporate Governance, Chief Executive Compensation, and Firm Performance," 372–373.

4. Core, Holthausen, and Larcker, "Corporate Governance, Chief Executive Compensation, and Firm Performance," 372–373.

5. Vidhan K. Goyal and Chul W. Park, "Board Leadership Structure and CEO Turnover," *Journal of Corporate Finance* 8 (2002): 49–66.

6. Richard Cyert, Sok-Hyon Kang, and Praveen Kumar, "Corporate Governance, Takeovers, and Top-Management Compensation: Theory and Evidence." *Management Science* 48 (2002): 453–469; James Wade, Charles A. O'Reilly III, and Ike Chandratat, "Golden Parachutes, CEOs, and the Exercise of Social Influence," *Administrative Science Quarterly* 35 (1990): 592–593; Martin J. Conyon and Kevin J. Murphy, "The Prince and the Pauper? CEO Pay in the U.S. and the U.K.," *Economic Journal* 110 (2000): 640–671; and Core, Holthausen, and Larcker, "Corporate Governance, Chief Executive Compensation, and Firm Performance," 371–406.

7. Core, Holthausen, and Larcker, "Corporate Governance, Chief Executive Compensation, and Firm Performance," 372–373; and Cyert, Kang, and Kumar, "Corporate Governance, Takeovers, and Top-Management Compensation," 453–469.

8. Harley E. Ryan Jr. and Roy A. Wiggins III, "Who Is in Whose Pocket? Director Compensation, Board Independence, and Barriers to Effective Monitoring," working paper, Louisiana State University and Bentley College, 2003, 25.

9. Kevin Hallock, "Reciprocally Interlocking Boards of Directors and Executive Compensation," *Journal of Financial and Quantitative Analysis* 32 (1997): 332.

10. Brian G. Main, Charles A. O'Reilly III, and James Wade, "The CEO, the Board of Directors, and Executive Compensation: Economic and Psychological Perspectives," *Industrial and Corporate Change* 11 (1995): 293–332.

11. Harry A. Newman and Haim A. Mozes, "Does the Composition of the Compensation Committee Influence CEO Compensation Practices?" *Financial Management* 28 (1999): 41–53.

12. Cyert, Kang, and Kumar, "Corporate Governance, Takeovers, and Top-Management Compensation," 453–469.

13. Andrei Shleifer and Robert W. Vishny, "Large Shareholders and Corporate Control," *Journal of Political Economy* 94 (1986): 461–688.

14. Cyert, Kang, and Kumar, "Corporate Governance, Takeovers, and Top-Management Compensation," 453–469.

15. Core, Holthausen, and Larcker, "Corporate Governance, Chief Executive Compensation, and Firm Performance," 372–373; and Richard A. Lambert, David F. Larcker, and Keith Weigelt, "The Structure of Organizational Incentives," *Administrative Science Quarterly* 38 (1993): 438–461.

16. Donald C. Hambrick and Sydney Finkelstein, "The Effects of Ownership Structure on Conditions at the Top: The Case of CEO Pay Raises," *Strategic Management Journal* 16 (1995): 175–193; and Henry L. Tosi Jr. and Luis R. Gomez-Mejia, "The Decoupling of CEO Pay and Performance: An Agency Theory Perspective," *Administrative Science Quarterly* 34 (1989): 181.

17. Marianne Bertrand and Sendhil Mullainathan, "Are CEOs Rewarded for Luck? The Ones without Principals Are," *Quarterly Journal of Economics* 116 (2001): 929.

18. Marianne Bertrand and Sendhil Mullainathan, "Agents With and Without Principals," *American Economics Review* 90 (2000): 205.

19. Jay C. Hartzell and Laura T. Starks, "Institutional Investors and Executive Compensation," *Journal of Finance* 58 (2003): 2351–2374. See also Parthiban David, Rahul Kochar, and Edward Levitas, "The Effect of Institutional Investors on the Level and Mix of CEO Compensation," *Academy of Management Journal* 41 (1998): 200–208.

20. David, Kochar, and Levitas, "The Effect of Institutional Investors on the Level and Mix of CEO Compensation," 200–208.

21. Kenneth A. Borokhovich, Kelly R. Brunarski, and Robert Parrino, "CEO Contracting and Anti-Takeover Amendments," *Journal of Finance* 52 (1997): 1503–1513.

22. Anup Agrawal and Charles R. Knoeber, "Managerial Compensation and the Threat of Takeover," *Journal of Financial Economics* 47 (1998): 219.

23. Shijun Cheng, Venky Nagar, and Madhav V. Rajan, "Identifying Control Motives in Managerial Ownership: Evidence from Antitakeover Regulation," *Review of Financial Studies* (forthcoming).

24. Marianne Bertrand and Sendhil Mullainathan, "Is There Discretion in Wage Setting? A Test Using Takeover Legislation," *Rand Journal of Economics* 30 (1999): 535; Gerald T. Garvey and Gordon Hanka, "Capital Structure and Corporate Control: The Effect of Antitakeover Statutes on Firm Leverage," *Journal of Finance* 54 (1999): 519, 520; and Paul A. Gompers, Joy L. Ishii, and Andrew Metrick, "Corporate Governance and Equity Prices," *Quarterly Journal of Economics* 118 (2003): 107–155.

25. Gompers, Ishii, and Metrick, "Corporate Governance and Equity Prices," 107–155.

26. Kevin J. Murphy, "Explaining Executive Compensation: Managerial Power versus the Perceived Cost of Stock Options," *University of Chicago Law Review* 69 (2002): 853.

27. Robert Parrino, "CEO Turnover and Outside Succession: A Cross-Sectional Analysis," *Journal of Financial Economics* 46 (1997): 168.

28. Bertrand and Mullainathan, "Agents With and Without Principals," 205.

## 7. Managerial Influence on the Way Out

Epigraph: Corporate lawyer interviewed in Suzanne Koudsi, "First, Why CEOs Are Paid so Much to Beat It," *Fortune*, May 29, 2000, 34–35.

1. Mattel proxy statement filed with SEC, April 28, 2000, 24–25.

2. Joann S. Lublin, "As Their Companies Crumbled, Some CEOs Got Big-Money Payouts," *Wall Street Journal*, February 26, 2002, B1.

3. Rakesh Khurana, *Searching for a Corporate Savior: The Irrational Quest for Charismatic CEOs* (Princeton, NJ: Princeton University Press, 2002), 3–4.

4. Dan Sabbagh, "Orange Chief Received $70m in Two Severance Payments," *Times* (London), March 12, 2003, 25.
5. Jay C. Hartzell, Eli Ofek, and David Yermack, "What's in It for Me? CEOs Whose Firms Are Acquired," *Review of Financial Studies* 17 (2004): 37–61.
6. The story told in this paragraph is more fully covered in Andrew Ross Sorkin, "Those Sweet Trips to the Merger Mall," *New York Times*, April 7, 2002, sec. 3, 1.
7. Sorkin, "Those Sweet Trips to the Merger Mall."
8. Hartzell, Ofek, and Yermack, "What's in It for Me?"
9. Julie Wulf, "Do CEOs in Mergers Trade Power for Premium? Evidence from 'Mergers of Equals,'" *Journal of Law, Economics and Organization* 20 (2004): 60–101.
10. "Retired Kodak CEO Received 47% Boost in His Bonus in 1999," *Wall Street Journal*, March 14, 2000, A8.
11. Justin Fox, "The Amazing Stock Option Sleight of Hand," *Fortune*, June 25, 2001, 86–92.
12. Joann S. Lublin, "Executive Pay under the Radar," *Wall Street Journal*, April 11, 2002, B7.
13. Lublin, "Executive Pay under the Radar," B7.
14. Gary Strauss, "CEOs Cash In after Tenure," *USA Today*, April 25, 2002, money section, B1.

## 8. Retirement Benefits

Epigraph: Joann S. Lublin, "How CEOs Retire In Style: Many Former Chief Executives Get Lush Perks and Fat Fees for Limited Consulting Work," *Wall Street Journal*, September 13, 2002, B1.
1. We borrow the term "stealth compensation" from Robert Monks, who used it to refer to executives' stock option compensation because that form of payment is not expensed on the firm's income statement. Robert A. G. Monks, *The Emperor's Nightingale: Restoring the Integrity of the Corporation in the Age of Shareholder Activism* (Boston: Addison-Wesley, 1999), 59–62.
2. To illustrate how the tax subsidy provided to a qualified plan operates, consider the following examples involving a hypothetical firm and employee. Assume that both face a 40 percent tax rate on all of their income, including capital gains. And assume that both are able to earn, between the preretirement period and retirement period, a pretax return of 100 percent on their investments.

    Example 1: The employee invests for retirement outside a qualified plan. Suppose the firm pays the employee $100 in the preretirement period. The firm deducts $100 from its taxable income, reducing its tax liability by $40. The employee pays $40 in taxes, takes the aftertax income of $60, and invests it. The $60 grows to $120 by the retirement period—a gain of $60. This $60 gain triggers a tax liability of $24 (40 percent of $60), leaving the employee with $96 ($60 + $36) when the employee retires.

    Example 2: The firm invests for the employee's retirement under a qualified plan. Now suppose the firm contributes the $100 to a qualified pension plan in the preretirement period. The firm again deducts $100 from its taxable income, reducing its tax liability by $40. The $100 grows to $200 by the time of the employee's retirement—a gain of $100. The $200 is distributed to the employee, who pays a tax of $80 (40 percent of $200), leaving the employee with $120, or $24 more than in Example 1, in which the employee had received $100 from the firm in the preretirement period and saved for retirement. The gain to the employee does not come at the expense of the employer: in both examples, the employer incurs an aftertax cost of $60 in the preretirement period.

3. Clark Consulting reports that approximately 70 percent of responding firms use SERPs. Clark Consulting, "Executive Benefits: A Survey of Current Trends: 2003 Results," 26.

4. A firm can shelter from taxation the investment income on funds set aside for financing executive pensions by investing these funds in life insurance policies on the lives of its executives and other employees. However, because of the fees that must be paid to the insurance company, this tax-sheltering mechanism involves significant costs, which are borne by the company rather than the executive. If, on the other hand, the executive received the funds to begin with, the executive would also be able to shelter the investment returns from taxation by purchasing a variable annuity, at no cost to the company.

5. To illustrate the effect of a SERP on the tax burdens of the parties, consider the following example and explanation, which builds on the examples provided in note 2. Assume again that both the firm and the executive face a 40 percent tax rate on all of their income, including capital gains. And assume that both are able to earn, between the preretirement and retirement periods, a pretax return of 100 percent on their investments.

Example 3: The firm invests for the executive's retirement under a nonqualified plan. Suppose a firm seeks to use a SERP to give an executive the same retirement payment that it gives the employee in example 2 using a qualified plan. As in the case of the employee, the firm sets aside $100 to fund the executive's pension, which grows to $200 by the time the executive retires. The $200 is distributed to the executive, who, like the employee, pays a 40 percent tax on the retirement distribution—a tax of $80. This leaves the executive, like the employee in example 2, with $120, $24 more than the employee in example 1 made.

Now consider the effect of the SERP on the firm. In examples 1 and 2, discussed in note 2, the firm reduces its tax liability by $40 in the preretirement period when it pays the worker $100 or contributes $100 to the worker's qualified pension plan. In example 3, the firm reduces its tax liability by $80 in the retirement period when it pays the executive $200. However, the firm must add to its taxable income in the retirement period the $100 gain on the funds it previously invested for the executive's retirement, and this *increases* the firm's tax liability in the retirement period by $40. The net effect of the $200 payment to the executive and the $100 gain is to reduce the firm's tax liability by $40 during the retirement period.

Had the firm reduced its tax liability by \$40 in the preretirement period, rather than during the retirement period, it could have invested the \$40 and earned a pretax return of \$40 (100 percent) by the retirement period. That \$40 would also have been taxed at 40 percent, leaving the firm with \$64. But by reducing its tax liability in the retirement period, the firm has only an extra \$40, \$24 less. The firm is thus worse off than in example 2, in which it received the same \$40 reduction in its tax liability in the preretirement period. The \$24 gain to the executive from the use of a nonqualified plan designed to put the executive in the same position as an employee under a qualified retirement plan comes at the expense of the firm.

6. For an explanation of the tax effects of using arrangements such as SERPs to defer compensation under various scenarios, see Myron S. Scholes, Mark A. Wolfson, Merle Erickson, Edward L. Maydew, and Terry Shevlin, *Taxes and Business Strategy: A Planning Approach*, 2nd ed. (Upper Saddle River, NJ: Prentice Hall, 2002), 181–185.

7. The tax efficiency of a SERP will also be affected by expected changes in the firm's (or the executive's) tax rate change over time. For example, if the firm is losing money and thus unable to get a current tax benefit by deducting executive compensation in the current period, but is expected to be subject to a higher tax rate in the future, deferring an executive's compensation will be tax efficient, all else being equal.

8. Clark Consulting, "Executive Benefits: A Survey of Current Trends: 2003 Results," 26.

9. Steven Balsam, *An Introduction to Executive Compensation* (San Diego, CA: Academic Press, 2002): 175.

10. See, for example, Mike Blahnik, "For CEO Pensions, Rank Has Its Privileges," *Star Tribune* (Minneapolis, MN), May 18, 2003, 1A.

11. See International Business Machines Schedule 14A (filed on March 12, 2001): 18.

12. To take another example, GE's former CEO, Jack Welch, left his firm with an annual pension of almost \$10 million. See Paul Hodgson, "Golden Parachutes and Cushioned Landings," The Corporate Library (February 2003): 14. The large actuarial value of the stream of promised pension payments never appeared in the firm's compensation tables.

13. Cynthia Richson, quoted in Liz Pulliam Weston, "Despite Recession, Perks for Top Executives Grow," *Los Angeles Times*, February 1, 2002, A1.

14. See Glenn Howatt, "HealthPartners Ex-CEO Reaped Board's Favors: Secret Deals Contributed to \$5.5 Million Package," *Minneapolis* (MN) *Star Tribune*, January 17, 2003, A1. The *Star Tribune* reported that the HealthPartners board adopted a SERP for the CEO "after receiving assurances that the supplemental retirement plan wouldn't have to be reported to the public" and "rejecting a suggestion that awards in the plan be tied to company performance."

15. In addition, firms are required to file a letter with the Labor Department indicating the number of executive pension plans and the number of participants. However, not all firms comply with this requirement. Ellen E. Schultz, "Big Send-

Off: As Firms Pare Pensions for Most, They Boost Those for Executives," *Wall Street Journal*, June 20, 2001, A1.

16. See Joann S. Lublin, "Executive Pay under the Radar," *Wall Street Journal*, April 11, 2002, B7; and Anne Fisher, "Proxies: The Treasure Is Still Buried," *Fortune*, June 8, 1998, 285.

17. Financial Accounting Standard no. 132 (revised 2003).

18. Financial Accounting Standard no. 87 (1985).

19. Schultz, "Big Send-Off."

20. In June 2004, the U.S. House of Representatives passed the American Jobs Creation Act of 2004, which penalizes firms using certain types of trusts to protect deferred compensation from the firms' creditors. The U.S. Senate passed a similar bill in May 2004.

21. Clark Bardes Consulting reported in 2001 that 86 percent of firms responding to a survey use security devices to protect SERPs to the greatest extent possible. See Clark Bardes Consulting, "Executive Benefits: A Survey of Current Trends: 2001 Results," 33; http://www.clarkconsulting.com/knowledgecenter/articles/benefits/20020305.pdf (accessed June 23, 2004); Ron Suskind, "More Executives Get Pension Guarantees to Protect against Takeovers, Failures," *Wall Street Journal*, July 5, 1991, B1; and Theo Francis and Ellen Schultz, "As Workers Face Pension Cuts, Executives Get Rescued," *Wall Street Journal*, April 3, 2003, C1.

22. Francis and Schultz, "As Workers Face Pension Cuts."

23. Francis and Schultz, "As Workers Face Pension Cuts."

24. Suskind, "More Executives Get Pension Guarantees."

25. Suskind, "More Executives Get Pension Guarantees."

26. Clark Consulting reports that close to 93 percent of firms responding to a survey said they had such plans in 2002. Clark Consulting, "Executive Benefits," 2.

27. For example, when Sears, Roebuck, and Company executives postpone bonuses and long-term incentive pay, they receive an additional contribution equal to 20 percent of the amount deferred. Ellen E. Schultz and Theo Francis, "Well-Hidden Perk Means Big Money for Top Executives," *Wall Street Journal*, October 11, 2002, A1, A9.

28. Liz Pulliam Weston, "Despite Recession," A1.

29. Lublin, "Executive Pay under the Radar."

30. To illustrate how the tax subsidy provided to a 401(k) operates, consider the following examples involving a hypothetical firm and employee. As in the SERP examples found in note 2 (examples 1 and 2), assume that both the firm and the employee face a 40 percent tax rate on all of their income. Assume also that both are able to earn, between the preretirement and retirement periods, a pretax return of 100 percent on their investments.

Example 4: The employee saves outside the 401(k) plan. Suppose the firm pays the employee $100 in the preretirement period. The firm deducts $100 from its taxable income, reducing its tax liability by $40. The employee pays $40 in taxes, and invests the aftertax income of $60 in an ordinary, nonqualified investment account. By the retirement period, the $60 grows to $120—a gain of $60. The employee pays a tax of $24 on the gain (40 percent of $60), leading to an aftertax gain of $36. The employee is thus able to withdraw a total of $96 ($60 + $36).

Example 5: The employee saves under a 401(k) plan. Now suppose that the employee contributes $100 of compensation income to a 401(k) account. The firm again deducts $100 from its taxable income, reducing its tax liability by $40. The $100 grows to $200 by the time the employee withdraws the funds from the 401(k) account. The employee pays a tax of $80 (40 percent of $200), leaving the employee with $120—$24 more than in example 4, where the employee received $100 from the firm in the preretirement period and saved the money outside the 401(k) plan. The $24 gain to the employee does not come at the expense of the employer. In both example 4 and example 5, the employer pays the employee $100 in the preretirement period, thereby reducing its taxable income by $100 and its tax liability by $40.

31. Internal Revenue Code, sec. 402(g)(1)(B).

32. A company can shelter from taxation investment income on funds set aside for financing executive pensions by investing these funds in insurance policies on the lives of its executives and other employees, but this will impose other costs on the firm. See note 4.

33. To illustrate the effect of executive deferred-compensation arrangements on the tax burdens of the parties, consider the following example and explanation, which refer to examples 4 and 5 provided in note 30.

Example 6: The firm offers the executive deferred compensation outside a 401(k) plan. Assume, as in examples 4 and 5, that both the firm and the executive face a 40 percent tax rate on all of their income, including capital gains. And assume that both are able to earn, between the preretirement and retirement periods, a pretax return of 100 percent on their investments.

Suppose the firm seeks to use deferred compensation to give an executive the same (100 percent) return that the firm provides the employee in example 5 using a 401(k) plan. As in the case of the employee, the firm sets aside $100, which grows to $200 by the time the executive withdraws the deferred compensation and the buildup credited to the designated amount of deferred compensation. The $200 is distributed to the executive. Like the employee, the executive pays 40 percent tax on the retirement distribution—a tax of $80. This leaves the executive, like the employee in example 5, with $120, or $24 more than the employee saving on his own ended up with in example 4.

Now let us consider the effect of the executive's deferred compensation arrangement on the firm. In examples 4 and 5, the firm reduces its tax liability by $40 in the preretirement period when it pays the worker $100 or contributes $100 to the worker's qualified pension plan. In example 6, the firm reduces its tax liability by $80 in the retirement period when it pays the executive $200. However, the firm must add to its taxable income in the retirement period the $100 generated to boost the executive's withdrawal payout from $100 to $200— which in turn increases the firm's tax liability by $40. The net effect of the $100 gain and the $200 payment to the executive is to reduce the firm's tax liability by $40 during the retirement period. The firm is thus worse off than in example 2, where it received the same reduction in its tax liability in the preretirement period.

Had the firm reduced its tax liability by $40 in the earlier period, it could have invested the $40 and earned a pretax return of $40 (100 percent) by the retirement period. The $40 would have been taxed at 40 percent, leaving the firm with $64. By reducing its tax liability in the retirement period, the firm has only an extra $40, or $24 less. Thus, the $24 gain to the executive from the use of a deferred-compensation arrangement designed to put the executive in the same position as an employee under a qualified 401(k) comes at the expense of the firm.

34. For an explanation of the tax effects of deferred compensation under various scenarios, see Scholes, Wolfson, Erickson, Maydew, and Shevlin, *Taxes and Business Strategy*, 181–185.

35. Internal Revenue Code sec. 1

36. Internal Revenue Code sec. 11. As in the case of SERPs, a firm can reduce the tax cost of deferred compensation by using company-owned life insurance. Under this strategy, the firm uses aftertax dollars to buy insurance on the lives of its executives and other employees. Part of the premium is invested, increasing the "cash value" of the policy. The policy is then cashed out when funds are needed to pay deferred compensation. The tax savings come from life insurance policies' capacity to shelter from taxes the buildup of the cash value. However, because the insurance company charges fees, the use of a life insurance policy to avoid taxes gives rise to transaction costs. A 1996 study found that 70 percent of the 1,000 largest firms did not use insurance for funding deferred compensation, which suggests that these costs can be quite high. See Christopher Drew and David Cay Johnston, "Special Tax Breaks Enrich Savings of Many in the Ranks of Management," *New York Times*, October 13, 1996, sec. 1, 1.

37. Clark Consulting, "Executive Benefits," 2.

38. "Tax Deferred Pay for Executives," *New York Times*, October 18, 1996, A36.

39. According to Coca-Cola's annual reports to shareholders, it paid taxes on its income in every year of Goizueta's tenure except 1992.

40. Gretchen Morgenson, "Executive Pay, Hiding Behind Small Print," *New York Times*, February 8, 2004, sec. 3, 1.

41. The Corporate Library, "The Use of Company Aircraft," special report (2001).

42. Lublin, "Executive Pay under the Radar"; and Gary Strauss, "CEOs Cash In after Tenure," *USA Today*, April 25, 2002, money section, B1.

43. See http://contracts.corporate.findlaw.com/agreements/fleetboston/murray.emp .2001.10.10.html (accessed May 12, 2004).

44. Joann S. Lublin, "Many Former Chief Executives Get Lush Perks and Fat Fees for Limited 'Consulting' Work," *Wall Street Journal*, September 13, 2002, B1.

45. This misperception led one compensation consultant to label jet use as "an efficient way of delivering something of value to the executive." Yale D. Tauber, quoted in Lublin, "Executive Pay under the Radar."

46. We thank Marc Abramowitz and Yitz Applbaum for useful discussions on the cost of operating corporate jets.

47. The Corporate Library, "The Use of Company Aircraft."

48. Ira Kay, cited in Strauss, "CEOs Cash In after Tenure."

49. Lublin, "Many Former Chief Executives Get Lush Perks."

50. Strauss, "CEOs Cash In after Tenure."

51. Strauss, "CEOs Cash In after Tenure."

52. Joann S. Lublin, "How CEOs Retire in Style," *Wall Street Journal*, September 13, 2002, B1.

53. The examples and quotations in this paragraph are taken from Lublin, "How CEOs Retire in Style."

54. Of course, there are cases where even these outlays are hidden by the provision of in-kind value rather than cash. For departing CEO Hugh McColl's continuing "advice and counsel," Bank of America is providing him or members of his family with 150 hours of flying time on corporate aircraft. See Strauss, "CEOs Cash In after Tenure." This perk has a value of $500,000 or more.

## 9. Executive Loans

Epigraph: Conseco, Inc., Definitive Notice and Proxy, Schedule 14A, April 21, 1999, 17.

1. Gary Strauss, "Execs Reap Benefits of Cushy Loans," *USA Today*, December 24, 2002, 1B.

2. 15 U.S.C. 78m (k); and David S. Hilzenrath and Helen Dewar, "Senate Votes to Curb Insider Lending," *Washington Post*, July 13, 2002, A13.

3. Paul Hodgson, "My Big Fat Corporate Loan," The Corporate Library, 2002, 1.

4. Andrew Backover, "Questions on Ebbers Loans May Aid Probes," *USA Today*, November 6, 2002, money section, 3B.

5. Dana Cimilluca, "Former Worldcom CEO Ebbers Misses Loan Payment," *Toronto Star*, May 17, 2003, C4.

6. The loans made by this company are described in Gary Strauss, "Don't Bother Paying Us Back, Many Boards Tell CEOs," *USA Today*, November 13, 2001, 1B.

7. Debra Sparks, "The Mother of All Stock Option Plans," *BusinessWeek*, November 23, 1998, 158.

8. Sparks, "The Mother of All Stock Option Plans," 158.

9. Star Staff Report, "7 Ex-Conseco Officials Face Separate Suits on Loans," *Indianapolis Star*, May 8, 2004, C1.

10. Rob Kaiser, "Comdisco Loans Re-Examined: 106 Former Execs at Bankrupt Firm Press for Relief," *Chicago Tribune*, August 11, 2002, C1.

11. Hodgson, "My Big Fat Corporate Loan," 1.

12. Hodgson, "My Big Fat Corporate Loan," 3.

13. Kathleen M. Kahle and Kuldeep Shastri, "Executive Loans," *Journal of Financial and Quantitative Analysis*. Kahle and Shastri estimate that the average stock loan, which typically is offered to executives at a below-market interest rate, has his-

torically cost a firm borrowing in the corporate debt markets $2 in interest for every $1 in interest savings made available to the executives.

14. Kahle and Shastri, "Executive Loans," 9.

15. Kahle and Shastri, "Executive Loans," 5.

16. Kathleen M. Kahle and Kuldeep Shastri report that in the period 1996–2000, 12.6 percent of executive loans in their sample were forgiven, and the interest was forgiven in another 10.2 percent of the cases. See Kahle and Shastri, "Executive Loans," 9. However, most of this activity took place before NASDAQ crashed. Given the decline in stock market prices during the subsequent period of 2000–2002, the rate of forgiveness in this period is likely to have been higher.

17. Hodgson, "My Big Fat Corporate Loan," 2.

18. Ralph King, "Insider Loans: Everyone Was Doing It," *Business 2.0* (November 2002): 82.

19. Hodgson, "My Big Fat Corporate Loan," 2.

20. See David Leonhardt, "It's Called a 'Loan,' But It's Far Sweeter," *New York Times*, February 3, 2002, 1.

21. We discuss further the relative lack of restrictions on insider trading in chapter 14.

22. Leonhardt, "It's Called A 'Loan,' But It's Far Sweeter"; and Joann S. Lublin, "Executive Pay Under the Radar: As CEOs Reported Salaries and Bonuses Get Pinched, Many Chiefs Are Finding Hidden Ways to Increase Their Compensation," *Wall Street Journal*, April 11, 2002, B7.

## 10. Non-Equity-Based Compensation

1. A well-known, forceful appeal for providing executives with large amounts of performance-based compensation was made by Michael Jensen and Kevin J. Murphy in 1990. Michael C. Jensen and Kevin J. Murphy, "Performance Pay, and Top-Management Incentives," *Journal of Political Economy* 98 (1990): 225–264.

2. Paul Hodgson, "What Really Happened to CEO Pay in 2002?" The Corporate Library 2003, 8.

3. See Kevin J. Murphy, "Executive Compensation," in *Handbook of Labor Economics*, vol. 3, bk. 2, ed. Orley Ashenfelter and David Card (New York: Elsevier, 1999), 2535.

4. See Charles P. Himmelberg and R. G. Hubbard, "Incentive Pay and the Market for CEOs: An Analysis of Pay-for-Performance Sensitivity," working paper, Columbia University and the National Bureau of Economic Research, 2000, 19.

5. Olivier Jean Blanchard, Florencio Lopez-de-Silanes, and Andrei Shleifer, "What Do Firms Do with Cash Windfalls?" *Journal of Financial Economics* 36 (1994): 358–359.

6. Marianne Bertrand and Sendhil Mullainathan, "Are CEOs Rewarded for Luck? The Ones without Principals Are," *Quarterly Journal of Economics* 116 (2001): 901–932.

7. Murphy, "Executive Compensation," 2537.

8. In some firms, such as McDermott, shareholder pressure led the firm to remove pension income from earnings for purposes of bonus calculation. Ellen E. Shultz, "McDermott Alters Its Pay Formulas for Top Executives," *Wall Street Journal*, February 25, 2002, A2.

9. Bethany McLean, "That Old Financial Magic: How Do You Grow Earnings Five Times Faster Than Revenues? Just Watch," *Fortune*, February 18, 2002, 70.

10. Floyd Norris, "Pension Folly: How Losses Become Profits," *New York Times*, April 26, 2002, C1.

11. Jesse Drucker and Theo Francis, "Pensions Fall—Not CEO's Bonus," *Wall Street Journal*, June 18, 2003, C1.

12. Carol J. Loomis, "This Stuff Is Wrong," *Fortune*, June 25, 2002, 73–84.

13. Kevin J. Murphy and Paul Oyer, "Discretion in Executive Incentive Contracts: Theory and Evidence," working paper, University of Southern California Marshall School of Business and Stanford University Graduate School of Business, 2003.

14. Richard Trigauz, "Great Disconnect," *St. Petersburg Times*, May 26, 2002, 1H; Louis Lavelle, "Executive Pay," *BusinessWeek*, April 15, 2002, 84; and David Leonhardt, "Coke Rewrote Rules, Aiding Its Boss," *New York Times*, April 7, 2002, sec. 3, 6.

15. Jesse Drucker, "AT&T Wireless Eases Bonus Rules," *Wall Street Journal*, April 15, 2003, B3.

16. Gretchen Morgenson, "The Rules on Bosses' Pay Seem Written with Pencil," *New York Times*, May 25, 2003, sec. 3, 1.

17. Yaniv Grinstein and Paul Hribar, "CEO Compensation and Incentives—Evidence from M&A Bonuses," *Journal of Financial Economics*.

18. Andrew Ross Sorkin, "Those Sweet Trips to the Merger Mall," *New York Times*, April 7, 2002, sec. 3, 1.

19. See El Paso Corp Schedule 14A (filed March 18, 2002): 10.

20. See SBC Communications Schedule 14A (filed February 14, 1998): 23.

21. Bernard S. Black, "Bidder Overpayment in Takeovers," *Stanford Law Review* 41 (1989): 597.

22. Fred J. Weston, Juan A. Siu, and Brian A. Johnson, *Takeovers, Restructuring, and Corporate Governance*, 3rd ed. (Upper Saddle River, NJ: Prentice Hall, 2001), 200, 221.

23. Sara B. Moeller, Frederik P. Schlingemann, and Rene M. Stulz, "Do Shareholders of Acquiring Firms Gain from Acquisitions?" Working paper, Southern Methodist University, University of Pittsburgh, and Ohio State University, 2003, 9.

24. David Henry, "Mergers: Why Most Big Deals Don't Pay Off," *BusinessWeek*, October 14, 2002, 60, 62.

25. Grinstein and Hribar, "CEO Compensation and Incentives."

26. One compensation consultant said that it is only fair to "award CEOs willing to take the risk to make bet on your company, bet your career transactions." See Sorkin, "Those Sweet Trips to the Merger Mall." But isn't that what running the firm is all about?

27. Sorkin, "Those Sweet Trips to the Merger Mall."

28. This section draws on a report by Paul Hodgson of The Corporate Library. See Paul Hodgson, "Golden Hellos," The Corporate Library, 2002.

29. Gretchen Morgenson, "Conseco Shares Slide on News of Rating Drop and Departure," *New York Times*, January 5, 2002, C1.

30. Al Lewis, "Global Crossing's Revolving Door Pure Platinum," *Denver Post*, February 17, 2002, K-01.

31. Patrick McGeehan, "Top Executives' Lucrative Deals Tie the Hands That Pay Them," *New York Times*, June 28, 2003, B1.

32. Jeremy Kahn, "Suddenly Some Perks Aren't Worth the Pain," *Fortune*, November 11, 2002.

33. Paul Hodgson, "My Big Fat Corporate Loan," The Corporate Library, 2002, 5.

34. Liz Pulliam Weston, "Despite Recession, Perks for Top Executives Grow," *Los Angeles Times*, February 1, 2002, A1.

35. IRS Notice 2002–8.

36. Dean Foust and Louis Lavelle, "CEO Pay: Nothing Succeeds like Failure," *BusinessWeek*, September 11, 2000, 46.

37. McGeehan, "Top Executives' Lucrative Deals."

38. Paul Hodgson, "Golden Parachutes and Cushion Landings," The Corporate Library, 2003, 7.

39. Hodgson, "Golden Parachutes and Cushioned Landings," 7.

40. Paul Hodgson, "Paying CEOs to Stay at Home," The Corporate Library, 2003, 1.

41. Steven Balsam, *An Introduction to Executive Compensation* (San Diego, CA: Academic Press, 2002), 86–87.

42. Balsam, *An Introduction to Executive Compensation*, 110.

## 11. Windfalls in Conventional Options

Epigraph: Alfred Rappaport. "New Thinking on How to Link Executive Pay with Performance," *Harvard Business Review* 77 (1999): 92.

1. Kevin J. Murphy, "Executive Compensation," in *Handbook of Labor Economics*, vol. 3, bk. 2, ed. Orley Ashenfelter and David Card (New York: Elsevier, 1999), 2490; and David Yermack, "Do Corporations Award CEO Stock Options Effectively?" *Journal of Financial Economics* 39 (1995): 238.

2. See, for example, Clifford Holderness, Randall Kroszner, and Dennis Sheehan, "Were the Good Old Days That Good? Evolution of Managerial Stock Ownership and Corporate Governance since the Great Depression," *Journal of Finance* 54 (1999): 435–469; John J. McConnell and Henri Servaes, "Additional Evidence on Equity Ownership and Corporate Value," *Journal of Financial Economics* 27 (1990): 595–612; and Randall Morck, Andrei Shleifer, and Robert Vishny, "Management Ownership and Market Valuation," *Journal of Financial Economics* 20 (1988): 293–315.

3. Michel A. Habib and Alexander P. Ljungqvist, "Firm Value and Managerial Incentives: A Stochastic Frontier Approach." Forthcoming. *Journal of Business.*

4. David Leonhardt, "Report on Executive Pay: Will Today's Huge Rewards Devour

Tomorrow's Earnings?" *New York Times*, April 2, 2000, sec. 3, 1. The only other study focusing exclusively on the use of options, albeit in an earlier period, also suggests that option plans may not be designed efficiently. An analysis of companies that adopted executive stock option plans between 1978 and 1982 determined that cumulative abnormal returns declined subsequently for two thirds of the sample, that return on assets (ROA) declined absolutely and adjusted for industry, that R&D expenditure decreased, and that perquisite consumption increased. See Richard A. DeFusco, Robert R. Johnson, and Thomas S. Zorn, "The Association between Executive Stock Option Plan Changes and Managerial Decision Making," *Financial Management* 20 (1991): 40.

5. The "informativeness principle" was introduced in Bengt Holmstrom, "Moral Hazard and Observability," *Bell Journal of Economics* 10 (1979): 74–91.

6. The study by SCA Consulting is reported in Simon Patterson and Peter Smith, "How to Make Top People's Pay Reflect Performance," *Sunday Times (London)*, August 9, 1998, business section, 12.

7. James J. Angel and Douglas M. McCabe, "Market-Adjusted Options for Executive Compensation," *Global Business and Economics Review* 4 (2002): 14.

8. For an analysis suggesting that indexed options could not screen out *all* market or industry effects, see Lisa K. Meulbroek, "Executive Compensation Using Relative-Performance-Based Options: Evaluating the Structure and Costs of Indexed Options," working paper, Harvard Business School, 2001, 1–3. Meulbroek shows that an option with an exercise price tied to a market or industry index does not completely filter out market or industry effects, and she offers an alternative mechanism designed to do so.

9. See Alfred Rappaport, "New Thinking on How to Link Executive Pay with Performance," *Harvard Business Review* 77 (1999): 91–101. See also Mark A. Clawson and Thomas C. Klein, "Indexed Stock Options: A Proposal for Compensation Commensurate with Performance," *Stanford Journal of Law, Business & Finance* 3 (1997): 31–50.

10. See Shane A. Johnson and Yisong S. Tian, "The Value and Incentive Effects of Non-Traditional Executive Stock Option Plans," *Journal of Financial Economics* 57 (2000): 25–26. For a detailed analysis of the incentive effects and valuation of indexed options, see Shane A. Johnson and Yisong S. Tian, "Indexed Executive Stock Options," *Journal of Financial Economics* 57 (2000): 35.

11. Kevin J. Murphy, "Explaining Executive Compensation: Managerial Power vs. the Perceived Cost of Stock Options," *University of Chicago Law Review* 69 (2002): 863.

12. There are other possible benefits to indexing that we have not discussed. For example, it has been argued that indexing the exercise price of options could reduce the executive's exposure to market risk. See Bengt Holmstrom, "Moral Hazard in Teams," *Bell Journal of Economics* 13 (1982): 328–330. In any event, our focus is not on the riskiness of conventional options but rather on the fact that the random noise associated with them has significant positive value for executives.

13. Brian J. Hall, "A Better Way to Pay CEOs?" in *Executive Compensation and Share-*

*holder Value*, ed. Jennifer Carpenter and David Yermack (Boston: Kluwer Academic Publishers, 1999), 43.

14. Shawn Tully, "Raising the Bar," *Fortune*, June 8, 1998, 272.

15. Tully, "Raising the Bar."

16. See Joann S. Lublin, "Why the Get-Rich-Quick Days May be Over," *Wall Street Journal*, April 14, 2003, R3.

17. Tully, "Raising the Bar."

## 12. Excuses for Conventional Options

Epigraph: John M. Abowd and David S. Kaplan, "Executive Compensation: Six Questions That Need Answering," *Journal of Economic Perspectives* 13 (1999): 157.

1. Kevin J. Murphy, "Executive Compensation," in *Handbook of Labor Economics*, vol. 3, bk. 2, ed. Orley Ashenfelter and David Card (New York: Elsevier, 1999), 21; and Brian J. Hall and Jeffrey B. Liebman, "The Taxation of Executive Compensation," in *Tax Policy and the Economy*, vol. 14, ed. James Poterba (Cambridge, MA: MIT Press, 2000), 11.

2. APB Opinion No. 25. See also Ronald L. Groves, *Executive Compensation* ¶ 214.04 at 498 (CCH Tax Transactions Library, 1992).

3. To the extent that managers' bonuses are based on reported earnings, higher earnings also are rewarded with increased bonuses. But presumably if the board were sophisticated enough to use indexed options, it would understand that the bonus formula would need to be adjusted to reflect the accounting effect of these options.

4. Indeed, there is evidence that stock prices are affected slightly by whether option expenses are recognized or merely disclosed. See Hassan Espahbodi, Pouran Espahbodi, Zabihollah Rezaee, and Hassan Tehranian, "Stock Price Reaction and Value Relevance of Recognition versus Disclosure: The Case of Stock Based Compensation," *Journal of Accounting and Economics* 33 (2002): 343–373.

5. Jennifer Reingold, "Commentary: An Option Plan Your CEO Hates," *BusinessWeek*, February 28, 2000, 82; and James P. Miller, "Indexing Concept Aims at Fairness," *Chicago Tribune*, May 4, 2003, C1.

6. Frederic W. Cook & Co., "Update on Stock Option Accounting Debate," July 30, 2002. http://www.fwcook.com/alert_letters/7-30-02UpdateSOAcctingDebate .pdf (accessed June 23, 2004).

7. See http://www.tiaa-cref.org/pubs/html/admin_resource/article2.html (accessed May 30, 2004).

8. Andrew Hill, "Emotions Run High in Fight over US Stock Option Costs," *Financial Times*, January 31, 2003, 20.

9. Georgeson Shareholder, "2003 Annual Corporate Governance Review," 2003, 7. http://www.georgesonshareholder.com/pdf/2003%20a.wrapup.pdf (accessed June 23, 2004).

10. See Financial Accounting Standards Board, "Exposure Draft: Proposed Statement of Financial Accounting Standards," March 31, 2004, http://www.fasb.org/draft/ ed_share-based_payment.pdf (accessed May 23, 2004).

11. Financial Accounting Standards Board, "Statement of Financial Accounting Standards," no. 123 (October 1995), 23–25.

12. Graef S. Crystal, *In Search of Excess: The Overcompensation of American Executives* (New York: W. W. Norton, 1991), 234.

13. Financial Accounting Standards Board, "Statement of Financial Accounting Standards," no. 123 (October 1995), 14.

14. Linda Barris, "The Overcompensation Problem: A Collective Approach to Controlling Executive Pay," *Indiana Law Journal* 68 (1992): 73.

15. Justin Fox, "The Only Option (for Stock Options, That Is): Pretending They Are Free Didn't Work. Expensing Them May Be the Silver Bullet We're Looking For," *Fortune*, August 12, 2002, 110.

16. According to a study by compensation consultant Pearl Meyer & Partners, 6.9 percent of the options that firms grant to employees are given to the CEO, and another 8.6 percent are given to other top executives. See Pearl Meyer & Partners, "Equity Stake: Study of Management Equity Participation in the Top 200 Corporations," 2001, 14.

17. Patricia M. Dechow, Amy P. Hutton, and Richard G. Sloan, "Economic Consequences of Accounting for Stock-Based Compensation," *Journal of Accounting Research* 34 (1996): 1–20.

18. Surya N. Janakiraman, Richard A. Lambert, and David F. Larcker, "An Empirical Investigation of the Relative Performance Evaluation Hypothesis," *Journal of Accounting Research* 30 (1992): 66.

19. 17 CFR § 229.402 (2001).

20. Janakiraman, Lambert, and Larcker, "An Empirical Investigation," 66–67.

21. Ronald A. Dye, "Relative Performance Evaluation and Project Selection," *Journal of Accounting Research* 30 (1992): 28.

22. See Rajesh K. Aggarwal and Andrew A. Samwick, "Executive Compensation, Strategic Competition, and Relative Performance Evaluation: Theory and Evidence," *Journal of Finance* 54 (1999): 2000.

23. Murphy, "Executive Compensation," 2538, table 9.

24. Saul Levmore, "Puzzling Stock Options and Compensation Norms," *University of Pennsylvania Law Review* 149 (2001): 1922–1923, 1930. Options with performance-conditioned vesting could have similar effects.

25. Charles P. Himmelberg and R. Glenn Hubbard, "Incentive Pay and the Market for CEOs: An Analysis of Pay-for-Performance Sensitivity," working paper, Columbia University and the National Bureau of Economics Research, 2000, 1–3. See also Paul Oyer, "Why Do Firms Use Incentives That Have No Incentive Effects?" Forthcoming. *Journal of Finance*.

26. Himmelberg and Hubbard, "Incentive Pay and the Market for CEOs," 1–3.

27. C. Edward Fee and Charles J. Hadlock, "Raids, Rewards, and Reputations in the Market for CEO Talent," *Review of Financial Studies* 16 (2003): 1347.

28. Kevin J. Murphy, "Explaining Executive Compensation: Managerial Power versus the Perceived Cost of Stock Options," *University of Chicago Law Review* 69 (2002): 863.

29. John E. Core, Wayne Guay, and David F. Larcker, "Executive Equity Compen-

sation and Incentives: A Survey," *Economic Policy Review* 9 (2003): 12–13; Gerald Garvey and Todd Milbourn, "Incentive Compensation When Executives Can Hedge the Market: Evidence of Relative Performance Evaluation in the Cross Section," *Journal of Finance* 58 (2003): 1557–1581; and Li Jin, "CEO Compensation, Diversification, and Incentives," *Journal of Financial Economics* 66 (2002): 29–63.

30. David M. Schizer, "Tax Constraints on Indexed Options," *University of Pennsylvania Law Review* 149 (2001): 1942–1943. As the discussion should make clear, one could also argue that the tax advantage of conventional options is a partial explanation for the lack of options with performance-conditioned vesting.

31. 26 USC § 162m (1994).

32. Schizer, "Tax Constraints on Indexed Options," 1942–1943. Although there are technical grounds to deny a deduction for indexed options under Section 162(m), there is a good chance that a taxpayer could get a favorable ruling from the government on this issue. For a discussion, see David M. Schizer, "Reducing the Tax Costs of Indexed Options," *Tax Notes* 96 (2002): 1375.

## 13. More on Windfalls in Equity-Based Compensation

Epigraph: Warren Buffett quoted in Shawn Tully, "Raising the Bar," *Fortune*, June 8, 1998: 272.

1. See Kevin J. Murphy, "Performance Standards in Incentive Contracts," *Journal of Accounting and Economics* 30 (2001): 273; and Richard A. DeFusco, Robert R. Johnson, and Thomas S. Zorn, "The Effect of Executive Stock Option Plans on Stockholders and Bondholders," *Journal of Finance* 45 (1990): 617.

2. See, for example, Tom Nohel and Steven Todd, "Stock Options and Managerial Incentives to Invest," *Journal of Derivatives Accounting* 1 (2004): 29–46.

3. Nohel and Todd, "Stock Options and Managerial Incentives to Invest."

4. Chongwoo Choe, "Leverage, Volatility, and Executive Stock Options," *Journal of Corporate Finance* 9 (2003): 593.

5. See Kevin J. Murphy, "Executive Compensation," in *Handbook of Labor Economics*, vol. 3, bk. 2, ed. Orley Ashenfelter and David Card (New York: Elsevier, 1999), 70, table 5.

6. Brian J. Hall and Kevin J. Murphy, "Stock Options for Undiversified Executives," *Journal of Accounting and Economics* 33 (2002): 23. Other economists have also acknowledged that this pattern is inconsistent with arm's-length contracting. See, for example, Yisong S. Tian, "Optimal Contracting, Incentive Effects, and the Valuation of Executive Stock Options," working paper, York University, 2001, 40. Hall and Murphy do try to come up with an advantage for at-the-money options. They conduct numerical simulations in an attempt to derive optimal exercise prices, using various assumptions about the shape of managerial utility functions, managerial wealth, stock market returns, and the volatility of the firm's stock. Under a range of parameters, they show that the exercise price that maximizes

pay-for-performance sensitivity is usually in a range that includes the current market price. See Brian J. Hall and Kevin J. Murphy, "Optimal Exercise Prices for Executive Stock Options," *American Economic Association Proceedings* 90 (2000): 213; and Hall and Murphy, "Stock Options for Undiversified Executives," 3–42. However, their analysis cannot explain why, as they report, 94 percent of option grants are at-the-money. First, there is no evidence that the utility functions they use—which are designed to make their calculations tractable—correspond to those of actual managers. Second, the analysis does not take into account the incentive effects of the options on managerial behavior. Third, even if their parameters corresponded to the situations of actual CEOs and incentive effects could be ignored, their parameters generate a range of optimal exercise prices, some of which, under certain conditions, are out-of-the-money. Yet, almost all option grants are at-the-money.

7. Gretchen Morgenson, "After I.B.M.'s Option Overhaul," *New York Times*, February 29, 2004, sec. 3, 1.
8. Morgenson, "After I.B.M.'s Option Overhaul," sec. 3, 1.
9. Paul L. Gilles, "Alternatives for Stock Options," *HR Magazine*, January 1999, 40–48.
10. See Brian J. Hall, "A Better Way to Pay CEOs?" in *Executive Compensation and Shareholder Value*, ed. Jennifer Carpenter and David Yermack (Boston: Kluwer Academic Publishers, 1999): 43; Nohel and Todd, "Stock Options and Managerial Incentives to Invest"; Shane A. Johnson and Yisong S. Tian, "The Value and Incentive Effects of Non-Traditional Executive Stock Option Plans," *Journal of Financial Economics* 57 (2000): 3–34; and Richard A. Lambert, David F. Larcker, and Robert E. Verrecchia, "Portfolio Considerations in Valuing Executive Compensation," *Journal of Accounting Research* 29 (1991): 129–149.
11. See Michel A. Habib and Alexander P. Ljungqvist, "Firm Value and Managerial Incentives: A Stochastic Frontier Approach," working paper, London School of Business and Stern School of Business, New York University, 2003.
12. Hall, "A Better Way to Pay CEOs?" 43.
13. This example is presented by Steven Balsam in *An Introduction to Executive Compensation* (San Diego, CA: Academic Press, 2002), 151.
14. Joe Cheung, "Valuation of 'Razorback' Executive Stock Options: A Simulation Approach," working paper, The University of Auckland, 2002.
15. Internal Revenue Code, Section 162(m).
16. Deborah Solomon, "SEC Probes Options Grants Made as Company News Boosts Stock," *Wall Street Journal*, March 30, 2004, 1.
17. David Aboody and Ron Kasznik, "CEO Stock Option Awards and the Timing of Corporate Voluntary Disclosures," *Journal of Accounting and Economics* 29 (2000): 73–100; Steven Balsam, Huajing Chen, and Srinivasan Sankaraguruswamy, "Earnings Management Prior to Stock Option Grants," working paper, Temple University Department of Accounting, 2003; and David Yermack, "Good Timing: CEO Stock Option Awards and Company News Announcements," *Journal of Finance* 52 (1997): 449–477.

18. This finding is consistent with evidence that there are abnormal price declines shortly before options are awarded. See Keith Chauvin and Cathy Shenoy, "Stock Price Decreases Prior to Executive Stock Option Grants," *Journal of Corporate Finance: Contracting, Governance, and Organization* 7 (2001): 53–76.

19. Balsam, Chen, and Sankaraguruswamy, "Earnings Management Prior to Stock Option Grants."

20. Menachem Brenner, Rangarajan K. Sundaram, and David Yermack, "Altering the Terms of Executive Stock Options," *Journal of Financial Economics* 57 (2000): 110. According to the Investor Responsibility Research Center (IRRC), 3 percent of 1,189 firms surveyed by the IRRC repriced options in 1998. See Kathy B. Ruxton, *Executive Pay, 1998: Chief Executive Officer Compensation at S&P Super 1,500 Companies as Reported in 1998* (Investor Responsibility Research Center, 1999), 2.

21. Brenner, Sundaram, and Yermack, "Altering the Terms of Executive Stock Options," 112.

22. Thomas A. Ratcliffe, "New Guidance in Accounting for Stock-Based Compensation: FASBIN No. 44," *National Public Accountant* 46 (2001): 28.

23. Brian J. Hall and Thomas Knox, "Managing Option Fragility," working paper no. 02–19, Harvard Business School, Negotiations, Organizations and Markets Unit, 2002, 3.

24. See Justin Fox, "Amazing Stock Option Sleight of Hand," *Fortune*, June 25, 2001, 86.

25. Viral V. Acharya, Kose John, and Rangarajan K. Sundaram, "On the Optimality of Resetting Executive Stock Options," *Journal of Financial Economics* 57 (2000): 67.

26. Li Jin and Lisa Meulbroek, "Do Underwater Executive Stock Options Still Align Incentives? The Effect of Stock Price Movements on Managerial Incentive-Alignment," working paper, Harvard Business School, 2001, 39–40.

27. See Mary Ellen Carter and Luann J. Lynch, "The Effect of Stock Option Repricing on Employee Turnover," working paper, The Wharton School, University of Pennsylvania, and University of Virginia Darden Graduate School of Business, 2003, 4.

28. P. Jane Saly, "Repricing Executive Stock Options in a Down Market," *Journal of Accounting and Economics* 16 (1994): 326.

29. A. Martinez, "Moving the Goal Posts: Options Re-pricing Gives Companies a Powerful Tool to Retain Workers; Critics See It as Rewarding Failure," *Wall Street Journal*, April 9, 1998, R4; J. A. Byrne, "How to Reward Failure: Reprice Stock Options," *BusinessWeek*, October 12, 1998, 50; and James E. Heard, "Executive Compensation: Perspective of the Institutional Investor," *University of Cincinnati Law Review* 63 (1995): 749. The Council of Institutional Investors, Corporate Governance Policies, lists as a core principle that underwater options should not be repriced or replaced without shareholder approval. See http://www.cii.org/dcwascii/web.nsf/doc/policies_iv.cm (accessed March 17, 2004).

30. In one study, the strike price was reduced but remained above the repricing-date

market price in about 20 percent of the repricing cases examined. See Brenner, Sundaram, and Yermack, "Altering the Terms of Executive Stock Options," 112.

31. Perhaps nervous about public outrage, some executives and boards have limited the benefit from repricing by using an exercise price slightly higher than the repricing-date stock price. See Donald M. Chance, Raman Kumar, and Rebecca B. Todd, "The 'Re-pricing' of Executive Stock Options," *Journal of Financial Economics* 57 (2000): 148.

32. Brenner, Sundaram, and Yermack, "Altering the Terms of Executive Stock Options," 121.

33. Chance, Kumar, and Todd, "The 'Re-pricing' of Executive Stock Options," 131; and Mary Ellen Carter and Luann J. Lynch, "An Examination of Executive Stock Option Re-pricing," *Journal of Financial Economics* 61 (2001): 209.

34. Sandra Renfro Callaghan, P. Jane Saly, and Chandra Subramaniam, "The Timing of Option Re-pricing," working paper, Texas Christian University, University of St. Thomas, and University of Texas at Arlington, 2003.

35. See Timothy G. Pollock, Harold M. Fischer, and James B. Wade, "The Role of Power and Politics in Repricing Executive Options," *Academy of Management Journal* 45 (2002): 1178.

36. As will be explained, there are several variations on the reload theme. For example, some reload plans provide additional reload options to replace shares that would have to be sold to pay the tax that is due on exercise.

37. Thomas Hemmer, Steve Matsunaga, and Terry Sherlin, "Optimal Exercise and the Cost of Granting Employee Stock Options with a Reload Provision," *Journal of Accounting Research* 36 (1998): 234.

38. P. Jane Saly, Ravi Jagannathan, and Steven J. Huddart, "Valuing the Reload Feature of Executive Stock Options," *Accounting Horizons* 12 (1999): 220.

39. The *Wall Street Journal* reported that in 1999, 21 of 40 reload firms surveyed issued additional options to replace shares set aside to pay taxes on option exercise. See Christopher Gay, "Hard to Lose: 'Reload' Options Promote Stock Ownership among Executives; But Critics Say They're a Lot More Costly than Shareholders Realize," *Wall Street Journal*, April 8, 1999, R6.

40. See Saly, Jagannathan, and Huddart, "Valuing the Reload Feature," 220. A few companies deviate from the standard reload design in other ways. Some issue a new option for every option exercised, rather than for each share surrendered in exercising the options. Others extend the term of the new options issued beyond the maturity date of the initial options. See Gay, "Hard to Lose." Both practices add value for executives.

41. Heard, "Executive Compensation," 749, 759.

42. See Gay, "Hard to Lose"; and Jennifer Reingold, "Nice Option if You Can Get It," *BusinessWeek*, May 4, 1998, 111.

43. One group of economists examined S&P 1500 data from 1993 to 1995 and found that executives with relatively low stock holdings retain about 30 percent of the shares received on exercise of their options, while relatively high-ownership executives sold all of their shares. See Eli Ofek and David Yermack, "Taking Stock:

Equity-Based Compensation and the Evolution of Managerial Ownership," *Journal of Finance* 55 (2000): 1377–1378.

44. See, for example, Joann S. Lublin, "With Options Tainted, Companies Award Restricted Stock," *Wall Street Journal*, March 3, 2003, B1.

45. Lublin, "With Options Tainted."

46. Restricted stock may well create another problem because of the zero exercise price. While many of the shareholders are diversified, managers are likely to have a significant fraction of their wealth tied up in the equity instruments they get as compensation. If managers have large holdings of stock, they may tend to be more conservative than they would be in the interests of their diversified shareholders. Because options with a positive exercise price make managers focus more on the upside, they tend to counteract executives' tendency to be too conservative.

47. Brian J. Hall and Kevin J. Murphy, "The Trouble with Stock Options," *Journal of Economic Perspective* 17 (2003): 60.

## 14. Freedom to Unwind Equity Incentives

Epigraph: Eli Ofek and David Yermack, "Taking Stock: Equity-Based Compensation and the Evolution of Managerial Ownership," *Journal of Finance* 55 (1997): 1367–1384.

1. The argument in this paragraph is more fully developed in Oren Bar-Gill and Lucian Bebchuk, "The Costs of Permitting Managers to Sell Shares," working paper, Harvard Law School, 2003.

2. David M. Schizer, "Executives and Hedging: The Fragile Legal Foundation of Incentive Compatibility," *Columbia Law Review* 100 (2000): 468–472.

3. Jennifer N. Carpenter, "The Exercise and Valuation of Executive Stock Options," *Journal of Financial Economics* 48 (1998): 139.

4. Paul L. Gilles, "Alternatives for Stock Options," *HR Magazine*, January 1999, 40–48; Steven Huddart, "Employee Stock Options," *Journal of Accounting and Economics* 18 (1994): 207–231; and Ofek and Yermack, "Taking Stock," 1376–1377.

5. Ellen E. Schultz and Theo Francis, "Fair Shares? Why Company Stock Is a Burden for Many and Less So for a Few," *Wall Street Journal*, November 27, 2001, A1; Greg Ip, "Collars Give Insiders Way to Cut Risk," *Wall Street Journal*, September 17, 1997, C1, C3; Stuart Weinberg, "Insiders Hedge with Zero-Cost Collars," *Wall Street Journal*, August 7, 2002, B5; and Randall Smith and Jesse Eisinger, "The Insiders' Magic Way to Sell," *Wall Street Journal*, March 19, 2004, C1.

6. J. Carr Bettis, John M. Bizjak, and Michael L. Lemmon, "Managerial Ownership, Incentive Contracting, and the Use of Zero-Cost Collars and Equity Swaps by Corporate Insiders," *Journal of Financial and Quantitative Analysis* 36 (2001): 345–370.

7. A study by Stewart Schwab and Randall Thomas of 375 CEO employment contracts collected by The Corporate Library found that none restricted the CEO from hedging his or her unvested stock options. See Stewart J. Schwab and Randall S. Thomas, "What Do CEOs Bargain For? An Empirical Study of Key

Legal Components of CEO Contracts," working paper, Cornell Law School and Vanderbilt Law School, 2004, 5.

8. Schwab and Thomas, "What Do CEOs Bargain For?" 13.

9. Schizer, "Executives and Hedging," 442–443.

10. Ofek and Yermack, "Taking Stock," 1376.

11. John E. Core and David F. Larcker, "Performance Consequences of Mandatory Increases in Executive Stock Ownership," *Journal of Financial Economics* 64 (2002): 322.

12. American Express Schedule 14A (filed on March 16, 2001): 25.

13. American Express Schedule 14A filings from 1993 to 2000.

14. American Express Schedule 14A (filed on March 10, 2000), 27, as reported in Steven Balsam, *An Introduction to Executive Compensation* (San Diego, CA: Academic Press, 2002), 211.

15. See Joann S. Lublin, "Why the Get-Rich-Quick Days May Be Over," *Wall Street Journal*, April 14, 2003, R3.

16. See Lublin, "Why the Get-Rich-Quick Days May be Over."

17. For a full discussion of this issue, see Jesse M. Fried, "Reducing the Profitability of Corporate Insider Trading through Pretrading Disclosure," *Southern California Law Review* 71 (1998): 334–348, 364.

18. Fried, "Reducing the Profitability of Corporate Insider Trading," 322–323; and H. Nejat Seyhun, *Investment Intelligence from Insider Trading* (Cambridge, MA: MIT Press, 1998). Managers can also boost their insider trading profits by using share repurchases to buy the public's shares indirectly at a low price. See Jesse M. Fried, "Insider Signaling and Insider Trading with Repurchase Tender Offers," *University of Chicago Law Review* 67 (2000): 421–477; and Jesse M. Fried, "Open Market Repurchases: Signaling or Managerial Opportunism," *Theoretical Inquiries in Law* 2 (2001): 865–894.

19. See Jesse M. Fried, "Insider Abstention," *Yale Law Journal* 113 (2003): 486–491.

20. See 17 C.F.R. Section 240.10b5-1.

21. See, for example, Steven E. Bochner and Leslie A. Hakala, "Implementing Rule 10b5-1 Stock Trading Plans," *Insights* 15 (2001): 2.

22. For a survey of the evidence, see Fried, "Reducing the Profitability of Corporate Insider Trading," 303–392. In the latter half of the 1980s, insiders were able to use inside information to make about $5 billion annually in extra trading profits.

23. Randall Smith and Danielle Sessa, "Ameritrade Says Insiders' Sales Must Now Be Announced First," *Wall Street Journal*, March 17, 1999, C3.

24. Fried, "Reducing the Profitability of Corporate Insider Trading," 345.

25. J. Carr Bettis, Jeffrey L. Coles, and Michael L. Lemmon, "Corporate Policies Restricting Trading by Insiders," *Journal of Financial Economics* 57 (2000): 192.

26. Kumar Sivakumar and Gregory Waymire, "Insider Trading Following Material News Events: Evidence from Earnings," *Financial Management* 23 (1994): 23–32. For an explanation of why trading windows do not completely prevent executives from trading on inside information, see Fried, "Reducing the Profitability of Corporate Insider Trading," 346.

27. For example, an executive of Micro Warehouse Inc., which permits executives to trade only during a nine-day period that begins five days after each quarterly earnings announcement, sold $2.4 million of stock in late April/early May, a month before an announcement about disappointing second-quarter earnings drove the share price down by more than 60 percent. See Bridget O'Brian, "Insider Selling of a Stock Headed South May Mean Others Should Also Bail Out," *Wall Street Journal*, July 17, 1996, C14.

28. Andrew Hill, "Inside Track," *Financial Times* (London), August 2, 2002, 10.

29. Henny Sender and Rebecca Blumenstein, "Questing the Books: Global Crossing Creditors Review Sales, Swaps," *Wall Street Journal*, February 25, 2002, A6.

30. Mark Gimein, "You Bought, They Sold," *Fortune*, September 2, 2002, 64–65.

31. William S. Lerach, "Plundering America: How American Investors Got Taken for Trillions by Corporate Insiders," *Stanford Journal of Law, Business and Finance* 8 (2002): 103.

32. Jennifer N. Carpenter and Barbara Remmers, "Executive Stock Option Exercises and Inside Information," *Journal of Business* 74 (2001): 513–534.

33. See Bin Ke, Steven Huddart, and Kathy Petroni, "What Insiders Know about Future Earnings and How They Use It: Evidence from Insider Trades," *Journal of Accounting and Economics* 35 (2003): 315–346.

34. See Messod Beneish, Eric Press, and Mark E. Vargus, "The Relation between Incentives to Avoid Debt-Covenant Default and Insider Trading," working paper, Indiana University, 2001.

35. David Leonhardt, "It's Called a 'Loan,' But It's Far Sweeter," *New York Times*, February 3, 2002, sec. 3, 11; and David Leonhardt, "Executives Beyond Enron Took Months to Report Sales," *New York Times*, February 11, 2002, C1.

36. Shijun Cheng, Venky Nagar, and Madhav V. Rajan, "Do Delayed Insider Disclosures Convey Information about Future Earnings?" working paper, University of Michigan Business School, 2002.

37. Alex Berenson, "2 Tyco Officials Sold Stock by Returning It to Company" *New York Times*, January 30, 2002, C1.

38. Sarbanes-Oxley Act, sec. 403(a).

39. SEC Release No. 33–8230 (May 7, 2003).

40. Section 306(a) of the Sarbanes-Oxley Act also prohibits officers and directors from trading in the firm's securities during pension fund "blackout periods," in which the firm's employees are unable to switch their retirement account funds among investment options (which usually include the firms stock). However, blackout periods are not triggered by the existence of inside information on which executives and other employees could profitably trade. Rather, they are typically imposed by the pension plan administrator whenever it changes investment alternatives, the frequency of portfolio valuations, or the plan trustee (or other service provider). Therefore, it is far from clear that this prohibition will significantly reduce managers' ability to trade profitably on inside information.

41. A formal model of these perverse incentives is developed in Bar-Gill and Bebchuk, "The Costs of Permitting Managers to Sell Shares."

42. Daniel Bergstresser and Thomas Philippon, "CEO Incentives and Earnings Management: Evidence from the 1990s," working paper, Harvard Business School and Massachusetts Institute of Technology, 2003; Messod D. Beneish, "Incentives and Penalties Related to Earnings Overstatements That Violate GAAP," *Accounting Review* 74 (1999): 425–457; and Bin Ke, "The Influence of Equity-Based Compensation on CEOs' Incentives to Report Strings of Consecutive Earnings Increases," working paper, Pennsylvania State University, 2003.

43. Beneish, "Incentives and Penalties," 425–457. Another study found that top managers of firms that experienced accounting irregularities and were subsequently subject to SEC enforcement actions had exercised their options in the preceding period at a higher rate than top managers of other firms. See Simi Kedia and Natasha Burns, "Do Executive Stock Options Generate Incentives for Earnings Management? Evidence from Accounting Restatements," working paper, Harvard Business School, 2003.

44. Scott L. Summers and John T. Sweeney, "Fraudulently Misstated Financial Statements and Insider Trading: An Empirical Analysis," *Accounting Review* 73 (1998): 131–146.

45. Shane A. Johnson, Harley E. Ryan, and Yisong S. Tian, "Executive Compensation and Corporate Fraud," working paper, Louisiana State University and York University, 2003.

46. Merle Erickson, Michelle Hanlon, and Edward Maydew, "How Much Will Firms Pay for Earnings That Do Not Exist? Evidence of Taxes Paid on Allegedly Fraudulent Earnings," *Accounting Review*.

47. See Section 304 of the Sarbanes-Oxley Act of 2002.

## 15. Improving Executive Compensation

Epigraph: SEC Chairman William Donaldson, quoted in Lori Calabro, "Above Board," *CFO Magazine* (October 2003), http://www.cfo.com/article/1,5309,10801%7C0%7CM%7C706%7C,00.html (accessed June 23, 2004).

1. Jesse M. Fried, "Reducing the Profitability of Corporate Insider Trading through Pretrading Disclosure," *Southern California Law Review* 71 (1998): 303–392.

2. Reg. S-K, Item 402 (17 CFR 229.402).

3. See NYSE Corp. Gov. Rules Sec. 303A.05.

4. See, for example, TIAA-CREF, "Policy Statement on Corporate Governance," http://www.tiaa-cref.org/pubs/html/governance_policy (accessed March 16, 2004).

5. NASD Rule 4350; NYSE Listed Company Manual Rule 303A; SEC Release No. 34–48108 (June 3, 2003).

6. See, for example, Andrew Countryman, "Investors Get Say on Equity Pay; SEC Mandates Stockholder Vote," *Chicago Tribune*, July 1, 2003, C3; and Amy Strahan Butler, "S.E.C. Passes Rule Changes for Options," *New York Times*, July 1, 2003, C3.

7. See Wachtell, Lipton, Rosen, and Katz, "Stock Plan Design for the Upcoming Proxy Season," January 21, 2004.

8. See Council of Institutional Investors, "Council Policies—Director and Management Compensation," http://www.cii.org/dcwascii/web.nsf/doc/policies_iv.cm (accessed June 23, 2004).

## 16. Improving Corporate Governance

Epigraph: Chancellor William Allen, writing in *Blasius v. Atlas*, 564 A.2d 651, 659 (Del. Ch. 1988).

1. See Lucian A. Bebchuk, "The Case for Shareholder Access to the Ballot," *Business Lawyer* 59 (2003): 43–66, reprinted in Lucian A. Bebchuk, ed., *Shareholder Access to the Corporate Ballot* (Cambridge, MA: Harvard University Press, 2004); and Lucian A. Bebchuk, "The Case for Allocating More Power to Shareholders, *Harvard Law Review* (forthcoming).

2. For two recent comprehensive statements by supporters of the current allocation of power between management and shareholders, see Martin Lipton and Steven A. Rosenblum, "Election Contests in the Company's Proxy: An Idea Whose Time Has Not Come," *Business Lawyer* 59 (2003): 67–94, reprinted in Bebchuk, *Shareholder Access to the Corporate Ballot*; and John J. Castellani and Amy L. Goodman, "The Case against the SEC Director Election Proposal," in Bebchuk, *Shareholder Access to the Corporate Ballot*.

3. Charles M. Elson, "The Duty of Care, Compensation, and Stock Ownership," *University of Cincinnati Law Review* 63 (1994): 690–692.

4. *Unocal Corp. v. Mesa Petroleum Co.*, 493 A. 2d 946, 949 (Del. 1985); quoting *Aronson v. Lewis*, 473 A. 2d 805, 811 (Del. 1984).

5. Bebchuk, "The Case for Shareholder Access to the Ballot," *Business Lawyer* 59 (2003): 43–66.

6. During the seven-year period, 215 contested proxy solicitations took place, an average of about 30 a year. The majority of the contested solicitations, however, did not involve attempts to replace the board with a new team that would run the firm differently for the benefit of its current shareholders. About a quarter of the cases did not involve the choice of directors at all, but were about other matters, such as proposed bylaw amendments. There was also a roughly similar number of contests over director election in connection with attempts by a hostile bidder to replace the board to make a hostile takeover possible or attempts to open or restructure a closed-end fund.

7. Letter from Henry A. McKinnell, Ph.D., chairman and CEO, Pfizer Inc., and chairman, The Business Roundtable, to Jonathan G. Katz, secretary, SEC (December 22, 2003), http://www.sec.gov/rules/proposed/s71903/s71903-381.pdf (accessed March 16, 2004). The main points of this comment letter are put forward in a subsequent paper by the president of the Business Roundtable and one of its lawyers. See Castellani and Goodman, "The Case against the SEC Director Election Proposal."

8. Lucian Bebchuk and Marcel Kahan, "A Framework for Analyzing Legal Policy towards Proxy Contests," *California Law Review* 78 (1990): 1071–1136.

9. Letter from Lucian A. Bebchuk to Jonathan G. Katz, secretary, SEC (December 22, 2003), http://www.sec.gov/rules/proposed/s71903/labebchuk122203.htm (accessed March 16, 2004).

10. See Lucian Bebchuk and Alma Cohen, "The Costs of Entrenched Boards," Harvard Law School, working paper, 2003, http://www.law.harvard.edu/faculty/bebchuk/ (accessed March 16, 2004).

11. For a discussion of this problem, see Lucian Bebchuk and Assaf Hamdani, "Optimal Defaults for Corporate Law Evolution," *Northwestern Law Review* 96 (2002): 489–520.

12. For an analysis of how boards' power over incorporation decisions provides states with incentives to provide rules that favor managers, see Lucian A. Bebchuk, "Federalism and the Corporation: The Desirable Limits on State Competition in Corporate Law," *Harvard Law Review* 105 (1992): 1435–1510; and Lucian A. Bebchuk and Allen Ferrell, "Federalism and Takeover Law: The Race to Protect Managers from Takeovers," *Columbia Law Review* 99 (1999): 1168–1199. For empirical evidence that firms' incorporation decisions provide states seeking incorporations with incentives to adopt antitakeover statutes that protect managers, see Lucian A. Bebchuk and Alma Cohen, "Firms' Decision Where to Incorporate," *Journal of Law and Economics* 46 (2003): 383–425.

13. Lipton and Rosenblum, "Election Contests in the Company's Proxy," 83–85.

14. Lipton and Rosenblum, "Election Contests in the Company's Proxy," 82.

15. Lipton and Rosenblum, "Election Contests in the Company's Proxy," 77.

16. 485 U.S. 224, 234 (1988), quoting *Flamm v. Eberstadt*, 814 F. 2d 1169, 1175 (7th Cir. 1987).

17. Lipton and Rosenblum, "Election Contests in the Company's Proxy," 87.

18. Martin Lipton, "Takeover Bids in the Target's Boardroom," *Business Lawyer* 35 (1979): 101–134; and Jeremy C. Stein, "Takeover Threats and Managerial Myopia," *Journal of Political Economy* 96 (1988): 61–80.

19. Paul A. Gompers, Joy L. Ishii, and Andrew Metrick, "Corporate Governance and Equity Prices," *Quarterly Journal of Economics* 118 (2003): 107–155; and Bebchuk and Cohen, "The Costs of Entrenched Boards."

20. Lipton and Rosenblum, "Election Contests in the Company's Proxy," 76.

21. Lipton and Rosenblum, "Election Contests in the Company's Proxy," 94.

# References

Aboody, David, and Ron Kasznik. 2000. "CEO Stock Option Awards and the Timing of Corporate Voluntary Disclosures." *Journal of Accounting and Economics* 29: 73–100.

Abowd, John M., and David S. Kaplan. 1999. "Executive Compensation: Six Questions That Need Answering." *Journal of Economic Perspectives* 13: 145–168.

Acharya, Viral V., Kose John, and Rangarajan K. Sundaram. 2000. "On the Optimality of Resetting Executive Stock Options." *Journal of Financial Economics* 57: 65–101.

Aggarwal, Rajesh K., and Andrew A. Samwick. 1999. "Executive Compensation, Strategic Competition, and Relative Performance Evaluation: Theory and Evidence." *Journal of Finance* 54: 1999–2043.

Agrawal, Anup, and Charles R. Knoeber. 1998. "Managerial Compensation and the Threat of Takeover." *Journal of Financial Economics* 47: 219–239.

Agrawal, Anup, and Ralph A. Walkling. 1994. "Executive Careers and Compensation Surrounding Takeover Bids." *Journal of Finance* 49: 985–1014.

Allen, Michael Patrick. 1981. "Power and Privilege in the Large Corporation: Corporate Control and Managerial Compensation." *American Journal of Sociology* 86: 1112–1123.

Angel, James J., and Douglas M. McCabe. 2002. "Market-Adjusted Options for Executive Compensation." *Global Business and Economics Review* 4: 1–23.

Baker, George P., Michael C. Jensen, and Kevin J. Murphy. 1998. "Compensation and Incentives: Practice vs. Theory." *Journal of Finance* 63: 614.

Balsam, Steven. 2002. *An Introduction to Executive Compensation*. San Diego, CA: Academic Press.

Balsam, Steven, Huajing Chen, and Srinivasan Sankaraguruswamy. 2003. "Earnings Management Prior to Stock Option Grants." Working paper, Temple University, Department of Accounting.

Bar-Gill, Oren, and Lucian A. Bebchuk. 2003. "The Costs of Permitting Managers to Sell Shares." Working paper, Harvard Law School.

Barris, Linda J. 1992. "The Overcompensation Problem: A Collective Approach to Controlling Executive Pay." *Indiana Law Journal* 68: 59–100.

Bebchuk, Lucian A. 1989. "Limiting Contractual Freedom in Corporate Law: The

Desirable Constraints on Charter Amendments." *Harvard Law Review* 102: 1820–1860.

———. 1992. "Federalism and the Corporation: The Desirable Limits on State Competition in Corporate Law." *Harvard Law Review* 105: 1435–1510.

———. 2003. "The Case for Shareholder Access to the Ballot." *Business Lawyer* 59: 43–66.

———. Forthcoming. "The Case for Allocating More Power to Shareholders." *Harvard Law Review*.

Bebchuk, Lucian A., John Coates IV, and Guhan Subramanian. 2002. "The Powerful Antitakeover Force of Staggered Boards: Theory, Evidence, and Policy." *Stanford Law Review* 54: 887–951.

Bebchuk, Lucian A., and Alma Cohen. 2003. "The Costs of Entrenched Boards." Working paper, Harvard Law School.

———. 2003. "Firms' Decision Where to Incorporate." *Journal of Law and Economics* 46: 383–425.

Bebchuk, Lucian A., and Allen Ferrell. 1999. "Federalism and Takeover Law: The Race to Protect Managers from Takeovers." *Columbia Law Review* 99: 1168–1199.

Bebchuk, Lucian A., and Jesse M. Fried. "Executive Compensation as an Agency Problem." *Journal of Economic Perspectives* 17 (2003): 71–92.

Bebchuk, Lucian A., Jesse M. Fried, and David I. Walker. "Managerial Power and Rent Extraction in the Design of Executive Compensation." *University of Chicago Law Review* 69 (2002): 751–846.

Bebchuk, Lucian A. and Yaniv Grinstein. 2004. "The Growth of Executive Pay." Working paper, Harvard Law School.

Bebchuk, Lucian A., and Assaf Hamdani. 2002. "Optimal Defaults for Corporate Law Evolution." *Northwestern Law Review* 96: 489–520.

Bebchuk, Lucian A., and Christine Jolls. 1999. "Managerial Value Diversion and Shareholder Wealth." *Journal of Law, Economics, and Organization* 15: 487–502.

Bebchuk, Lucian A., and Marcel Kahan. 1990. "A Framework for Analyzing Legal Policy towards Proxy Contests." *California Law Review* 78: 1071–1135.

Bebchuk, Lucian A., and Mark J. Roe. 1999. "A Theory of Path Dependence in Corporate Ownership and Governance." *Stanford Law Review* 52: 127–170.

Beneish, Messod D. 1999. "Incentives and Penalties Related to Earnings Overstatements that Violate GAAP." *Accounting Review* 74: 425–457.

Beneish, Messod D., Eric Press, and Mark E. Vargus. 2001. "The Relation between Incentives to Avoid Debt-Covenant Default and Insider Trading." Working paper, Indiana University.

Bergstresser, Daniel, and Thomas Philippon. 2002. "CEO Incentives and Earnings Management." Working paper, Harvard Business School and Massachusetts Institute of Technology.

Berle, Adolph A. Jr., and Gardiner C. Means. *The Modern Corporation and Private Property*. New York: Macmillan, 1932.

Bertrand, Marianne, and Sendhil Mullainathan. 1999. "Is There Discretion in Wage Setting? A Test Using Takeover Legislation." *Rand Journal of Economics* 30: 535–554.

———. 2000. "Agents With and Without Principals." *American Economics Review* 90: 203–208.

———. 2001. "Are CEOs Rewarded for Luck? The Ones without Principals Are." *Quarterly Journal of Economics* 116: 901–932.

Bethel, Jennifer E., and Stuart L. Gillan. 2002. "The Impact of the Institutional and Regulatory Environment on Shareholder Voting." *Financial Management* 31: 29–54.

Bettis, J. Carr, John M. Bizjak, and Michael L. Lemmon. 2001. "Managerial Ownership, Incentive Contracting, and the Use of Zero-Cost Collars and Equity Swaps by Corporate Insiders." *Journal of Financial and Quantitative Analysis* 36: 345–371.

Bettis, J. Carr, Jeffrey L. Coles, and Michael L. Lemmon. 2000. "Corporate Policies Restricting Trading by Insiders." *Journal of Financial Economics* 57: 191–220.

Bizjak, John M., Michael L. Lemmon, and Lalitha Naveen. 2000. "Has the Use of Peer Groups Contributed to Higher Levels of Executive Compensation?" Working paper, Portland State University, University of Utah, and Arizona State University.

Black, Bernard S. 1989. "Bidder Overpayment in Takeovers." *Stanford Law Review* 41: 597–660.

Blanchard, Olivier Jean, Florencio Lopez-de-Silanes, and Andrei Shleifer. 1994. "What Do Firms Do with Cash Windfalls?" *Journal of Financial Economics* 36: 337–360.

Bochner, Steven E. and Leslie A. Hakala. 2001. "Implementing Rule 10b5-1 Stock Trading Plans." *Insights* 15: 2.

Boeker, Warren. 1992. "Power and Managerial Dismissal: Scapegoating at the Top." *Administrative Science Quarterly* 37: 400–418.

Bogus, Carl T. 1993. "Excessive Executive Compensation and the Failure of Corporate Democracy." *Buffalo Law Review* 41: 1–83.

Borokhovich, Kenneth A., Kelly R. Brunarski, and Robert Parrino. 1997. "CEO Contracting and Anti-Takeover Amendments." *Journal of Finance* 52: 1495–1517.

Brenner, Menachem, Rangarajan K. Sundaram, and David Yermack. 2000. "Altering the Terms of Executive Stock Options." *Journal of Financial Economics* 57: 103–128.

Brick, Ivan E., Oded Palmon, and John K. Wald. 2002. "CEO Compensation, Director Compensation, and Firm Performance: Evidence of Cronyism." Working paper, Rutgers University Business School.

Brudney, Victor. 1982. "The Independent Director—Heavenly City or Potemkin Village?" *Harvard Law Review* 95: 597–659.

Brudney, Victor, and Allen Ferrell. 2002. "Corporate Speech and Citizenship: Corporate Charitable Giving." *University of Chicago Law Review* 69: 1191–1218.

Burke, Stacey, Glenn Davis, Chris Loayza, Conor Murphy, and Sergio Schuchner. 2002. "The Structure and Compensation of Boards of Directors at S&P Super 1500 Companies." In *Board Structure/Board Pay 2002*. Washington, DC: Investor Responsibility Research Center.

Calabro, Lori. "Above Board," 2003. *CFO Magazine* (October), http://www.cfo.com/article/1,5309,10801|0|M|706|,00.html (accessed June 23, 2004).

Callaghan, Sandra Renfro, P. Jane Saly, and Chandra Subramaniam. 2000. "The Timing of Option Repricing." Working paper, Texas Christian University, University of St. Thomas, and University of Texas at Arlington.

Carpenter, Jennifer N. 1998. "The Exercise and Valuation of Executive Stock Options." *Journal of Financial Economics* 48: 127–158.

Carpenter, Jennifer N., and Barbara Remmers. 2001 "Executive Stock Option Exercises and Inside Information." *Journal of Business* 74: 513–534.

Carter, Mary Ellen, and Luann J. Lynch. 2001. "An Examination of Executive Stock Option Re-pricing." *Journal of Financial Economics* 61: 207–225.

———. 2003. "The Effect of Stock Option Repricing on Employee Turnover." Working paper, The Wharton School, University of Pennsylvania, and University of Virginia Darden Graduate School of Business, 4.

Castellani, John J., and Amy L. Goodman. 2004. "The Case against the SEC Director Election Proposal." In *Shareholder Access to the Corporate Ballot*, edited by Lucian A. Bebchuk. Cambridge, MA: Harvard University Press.

Chance, Don M., Raman Kumar, and Rebecca B. Todd. 2000. "The 'Re-pricing' of Executive Stock Options." *Journal of Financial Economics* 57: 129–154.

Chauvin, Keith, and Cathy Shenoy. 2001. "Stock Price Decreases Prior to Executive Stock Option Grants." *Journal of Corporate Finance: Contracting, Governance, and Organization* 7: 53–76.

Cheffins, Brian R., and Randall S. Thomas. 2001. "Should Shareholders Have a Greater Say over Executive Pay? Learning from the U.S. Experience." *Journal of Corporation Law Studies* 1: 227–315.

Cheng, Shijun, Venky Nagar, and Madhav V. Rajan. 2002. "Do Delayed Insider Disclosures Convey Information about Future Earnings?" Working paper, University of Michigan Business School.

———. Forthcoming. "Identifying Control Motives in Managerial Ownership: Evidence from Antitakeover Regulation." *Review of Financial Studies*.

Cheung, Joe. 2002. "Valuation of 'Razorback' Executive Stock Options: A Simulation Approach." Working paper, University of Auckland, New Zealand.

Choe, Chongwoo. 2003. "Leverage, Volatility, and Executive Stock Options." *Journal of Corporate Finance* 9: 591–609.

Clark, Kim. 2003. "Corporate Scandals: Is It a Problem of Bad Apples, or Is It the Barrel?" Prepared remarks for the National Press Club, February 26, 2003, Harvard Business School.

Clark, Robert C. 1986. *Corporate Law*. Boston: Little, Brown and Company.

Clark Bardes Consulting. n.d. "Executive Benefits: A Survey of Current Trends: 2001 Results." http://www.clarkconsulting.com/knowledgecenter/articles/benefits/20020305.pdf (accessed June 23, 2004).

Clark Consulting 2003. "Executive Benefits: A Survey of Current Trends: 2003 Results."

Clawson, Mark A., and Thomas C. Klein. 1997. "Indexed Stock Options: A Proposal for Compensation Commensurate with Performance." *Stanford Journal of Law, Business and Finance* 3: 31–50.

Conyon, Martin J., and Kevin J. Murphy. 2000. "The Prince and the Pauper? CEO Pay in the U.S. and the U.K." *Economic Journal* 110: F640–F671.

Conyon, Martin J., and Simon I. Peck. 2004. *Compensation Consultants and Executive Pay.* Working paper, The Wharton School, University of Pennsylvania, and Weatherhead School of Management, Case Western Reserve University.

Core, John E., Wayne Guay, and David F. Larcker. 2003. "Executive Equity Compensation and Incentives: A Survey." *Economic Policy Review* 9: 27–50.

Core, John E., Robert W. Holthausen, and David F. Larcker. 1999. "Corporate Governance, Chief Executive Officer Compensation, and Firm Performance." *Journal of Financial Economics* 51: 371–406.

Core, John E., and David F. Larcker. 2002. "Performance Consequences of Mandatory Increases in Executive Stock Ownership." *Journal of Financial Economics* 64: 317–340.

Corporate Library, The. 2001. "The Use of Company Aircraft." Special report.

Crystal, Graef S. 1991. *In Search of Excess: The Overcompensation of American Executives.* New York: W. W. Norton.

Cyert, Richard M., Sok-Hyon Kang, and Praveen Kumar. 2002. "Corporate Governance, Takeovers, and Top-Management Compensation: Theory and Evidence." *Management Science* 48: 453–469.

David, Parthiban, Rahul Kochar, and Edward Levitas. 1998. "The Effect of Institutional Investors on the Level and Mix of CEO Compensation." *Academy of Management Journal* 41: 200–208.

DeChow, Patricia M., Amy P. Hutton, and Richard G. Sloan. 1996. "Economic Consequences of Accounting for Stock-Based Compensation." *Journal of Accounting Research* 34: 1–20.

DeFusco, Richard A., Robert R. Johnson, and Thomas S. Zorn. 1990. "The Effect of Executive Stock Option Plans on Stockholders and Bondholders." *Journal of Finance* 45: 617–627.

———. 1991. "The Association between Executive Stock Option Plan Changes and Managerial Decision Making." *Financial Management* 20: 36–43.

Dyck, Alexander, and Luigi Zingales. 2002. "The Corporate Governance Role of the Media." Working paper, Harvard Business School and the University of Chicago.

———. 2004. "Private Benefits of Control: An International Comparison." *Journal of Finance* 59: 537–600.

Dye, Ronald A. 1992. "Relative Performance Evaluation and Project Selection." *Journal of Accounting Research* 30: 27–52.

Easterbrook, Frank H. 1984. "Managers' Discretion and Investors' Welfare: Theories and Evidence." *Delaware Journal of Corporate Law* 9: 540–571.

Eisenberg, Melvin A. 1989. "The Structure of Corporation Law." *Columbia Law Review* 89: 1461–1489.

———. 1999a. "The Compensation of Chief Executive Officers and Directors of Publicly Held Corporations." *7th Annual Corporate Governance Institute* (SE 39 ALI-ABA), 103–138.

———. 1999b. "Corporate Law and Social Norms." *Columbia Law Review* 99: 1253–1292.

Elson, Charles M. 1993. "Executive Over-Compensation—A Board-Based Solution." *Boston College Law Review* 34: 937–996.

———. 1995. "The Duty of Care, Compensation, and Stock Ownership." *University of Cincinnati Law Review* 63: 649–711.

Erickson, Merle, Michelle Hanlon, and Edward Maydew. Forthcoming. "How Much Will Firms Pay for Earnings That Do Not Exist? Evidence of Taxes Paid on Allegedly Fraudulent Earnings." *Accounting Review.*

Espahbodi, Hassan, Pouran Espahbodi, Zabihollah Rezaee, and Hassan Tehranian. 2002. "Stock Price Reaction and Value Relevance of Recognition versus Disclosure: The Case of Stock Based Compensation." *Journal of Accounting and Economics* 33: 343–373.

Fama, Eugene F. 1980. "Agency Problems and the Theory of the Firm." *Journal of Political Economy* 88: 288–307.

Fama, Eugene F., and Michael C. Jensen. 1983. "Separation of Ownership and Control." *Journal of Law and Economics* 26: 301–325.

Fee, C. Edward, and Charles J. Hadlock. 2003. "Raids, Rewards, and Reputations in the Market for CEO Talent." *Review of Financial Studies* 16: 1315–1357.

Fich, Eliezer M., and Lawrence J. White. Forthcoming. "Why Do CEOs Reciprocally Sit on Each Other's Boards?" *Journal of Corporate Finance.*

Finkelstein, Sydney. 1992. "Power in Top Management Teams: Dimensions, Measurement, and Validation." *Academy of Management Journal* 35: 505–538.

Finkelstein, Sydney, and Donald C. Hambrick. 1988. "Chief Executive Compensation: A Synthesis and Reconciliation." *Strategic Management Journal* 9: 543–558.

———. 1989. "Chief Executive Compensation: A Study of the Intersection of Markets and Political Processes." *Strategic Management Journal* 10: 121–134.

Fischel, Daniel R. 1982. "The Corporate Governance Movement." *Vanderbilt Law Review* 35: 1259–1292.

———. 1982. "The Race to the Bottom Revisited: Reflection on Recent Development in Delaware's Corporation Law." *Northwestern University Law Review* 76: 913–945.

Fried, Jesse M. 1998. "Reducing the Profitability of Corporate Insider Trading through Pretrading Disclosure." *Southern California Law Review* 71: 303–392.

———. 2000. "Insider Signaling and Insider Trading with Repurchase Tender Offers." *University of Chicago Law Review* 67: 421–477.

———. 2001. "Open Market Repurchases: Signaling or Managerial Opportunism." *Theoretical Inquiries in Law* 2: 865–894.

———. 2003. "Insider Abstention." *Yale Law Journal* 113: 455–492.

Garvey, Gerald T., and Gordon Hanka. 1999. "Capital Structure and Corporate Control: The Effect of Antitakeover Statutes on Firm Leverage." *Journal of Finance* 54: 519–546.

Garvey, Gerald T., and Todd Milbourn. 2003. "Incentive Compensation When Executives Can Hedge the Market: Evidence of Relative Performance Evaluation in the Cross Section." *Journal of Finance* 58: 1557–1581.

Georgeson Shareholder. 2003. "Annual Corporate Governance Review." http://www
.georgesonshareholder.com/pdf/2003%20a.wrapup.pdf (accessed June 23, 2004).

Gillan, Stuart L. 2001a. "Has Pay for Performance Gone Awry: Views from a Corporate Governance Forum." *Research Dialogue* 68: 1–16.

———. 2001b. "Option-Based Compensation: Panacea or Pandora's Box?" *Journal of Applied Corporate Finance* 14: 115–128.

Gompers, Paul A., Joy L. Ishii, and Andrew Metrick. 2003. "Corporate Governance and Equity Prices." *Quarterly Journal of Economics* 118: 107–155.

Goyal, Vidhan K., and Chul W. Park. 2002. "Board Leadership Structure and CEO Turnover." *Journal of Corporate Finance* 8: 49–66.

Green, Joshua. 2002. "Savage Business." *American Prospect* 13: 14–15.

Grinstein, Yaniv, and Paul Hribar. Forthcoming. "CEO Compensation and Incentives—Evidence from M&A Bonuses." *Journal of Financial Economics.*

Groves, Ronald L. 1992. *Executive Compensation.* CCH Tax Transactions Library.

Habib, Michel A., and Alexander P. Ljungqvist. Forthcoming. "Firm Value and Managerial Incentives: A Stochastic Frontier Approach." *Journal of Business.*

Hall, Brian J. 1999. "A Better Way to Pay CEOs?" In *Executive Compensation and Shareholder Value: Theory and Evidence,* edited by Jennifer Carpenter and David Yermack. Boston: Kluwer Academic Publishers.

Hall, Brian J., and Thomas Knox. 2002, May. "Managing Option Fragility." Working paper no. 02–19, Harvard Business School, Negotiations, Organizations and Markets Unit.

Hall, Brian J., and Jeffrey B. Liebman. 1998. "Are CEO's Really Paid like Bureaucrats?" *Quarterly Journal of Economics* 113: 653–691.

———. 2000. "The Taxation of Executive Compensation." In *Tax Policy and the Economy,* edited by James Poterba. Vol. 14. Cambridge, MA: MIT Press.

Hall, Brian J., and Kevin J. Murphy. 2000. "Optimal Exercise Prices for Executive Stock Options." *American Economic Association Proceedings* 90: 209–214.

———. 2002. "Stock Options for Undiversified Executives." *Journal of Accounting and Economics* 33: 3–42.

———. 2003. "The Trouble with Stock Options." *Journal of Economic Perspectives* 17: 49–70.

Hallock, Kevin. 1997. "Reciprocally Interlocking Boards of Directors and Executive Compensation." *Journal of Financial and Quantitative Analysis* 32: 331–344.

———. 1999. "Dual Agency: Corporate Boards with Reciprocally Interlocking Relationships." In *Executive Compensation and Shareholder Value,* edited by J. Carpenter and D. Yermack. Boston: Kluwer Academic Publishers.

Hambrick, Donald C., and Sydney Finkelstein. 1995. "The Effects of Ownership Structure on Conditions at the Top: The Case of CEO Pay Raises." *Strategic Management Journal* 16: 175–193.

Hartzell, Jay C., Eli Ofek, and David Yermack. 2004. "What's in It for Me? CEOs Whose Firms Are Acquired." *Review of Financial Studies* 17: 37–61.

Hartzell, Jay C., and Laura T. Starks. 2003. "Institutional Investors and Executive Compensation." *Journal of Finance* 58: 2351–2374.

Heard, James E. 1995. "Executive Compensation: Perspective of the Institutional Investor." *University of Cincinnati Law Review* 63: 749–767.

Hemmer, Thomas, Steve Matsunaga, and Terry Shevlin. 1998. "Optimal Exercise and the Cost of Granting Employee Stock Options with a Reload Provision." *Journal of Accounting Research* 36: 231–255.

Hermalin, Benjamin E., and Michael S. Weisbach. 1998. "Endogenously Chosen Boards of Directors and Their Monitoring of the CEO." *American Economic Law Review* 88 (March): 96–118.

———. 2003. "Boards of Directors as an Endogenously Determined Institution: A Survey of the Economic Literature." *Federal Reserve Bank of New York Economic Policy Review* 9: 7–26.

Himmelberg, Charles P., and R. Glenn Hubbard. 2000. "Incentive Pay and the Market for CEOs: An Analysis of Pay-for-Performance Sensitivity." Working paper, Columbia University and the National Bureau of Economic Research.

Hirshleifer, Jack. 1978. "Competition, Cooperation, and Conflict in Economics and Biology." *American Economic Review* 68: 238–243.

Hodgson, Paul. 2002. "Golden Hellos." The Corporate Library.

———. 2002. "My Big Fat Corporate Loan." Study by the Corporate Library.

———. 2003. "Golden Parachutes and Cushioned Landings." The Corporate Library.

———. 2003. "Paying CEOs to Stay at Home." The Corporate Library.

———. 2003. "What Really Happened to CEO Pay in 2002." The Corporate Library.

Holderness, Clifford, Randall Kroszner, and Dennis Sheehan. 1999. "Were the Good Old Days That Good? Evolution of Managerial Stock Ownership and Corporate Governance since the Great Depression." *Journal of Finance* 54: 435–469.

Holmstrom, Bengt. 1979. "Moral Hazard and Observability." *Bell Journal of Economics* 10: 74–91.

———. 1982. "Moral Hazard in Teams." *Bell Journal of Economics* 13: 324–340.

Huddart, Steven. 1994. "Employee Stock Options." *Journal of Accounting and Economics* 18: 207–231.

Janakiraman, Surya N., Richard A. Lambert, and David F. Larcker. 1992. "An Empirical Investigation of the Relative Performance Evaluation Hypothesis." *Journal of Accounting Research* 30: 53–69.

Jensen, Michael C. 1986. "Agency Costs of Free Cash Flow, Corporate Finance, and Takeovers." *American Economic Review* 76: 323–329.

Jensen, Michael C., and Kevin J. Murphy. 1990. "CEO Incentives: It's Not How Much You Pay, but How." *Harvard Business Review* 68: 138–153.

———. 1990. "Performance, Pay and Top-Management Incentives." *Journal of Political Economy* 98: 225–264.

Jensen, Michael C., and William Meckling. 1976. "Theory of the Firm: Managerial Behavior, Agency Costs, and Ownership Structure." *Journal of Financial Economics* 3: 305–360.

Jin, Li. 2002. "CEO Compensation, Diversification, and Incentives." *Journal of Financial Economics* 66: 29–63.

Jin, Li, and Lisa Meulbroek. 2001. "Do Underwater Executive Stock Options Still Align Incentives? The Effect of Stock Price Movements on Managerial Incentive-Alignment." Working paper, Harvard Business School.

Johnson, Shane A., Harley E. Ryan, and Yisong S. Tian. 2003. "Executive Compensation and Corporate Fraud." Working paper, Louisiana State University and York University.

Johnson, Shane, and Yisong S. Tian. 2000. "Indexed Executive Stock Options." *Journal of Financial Economics* 57: 35–64.

———. 2000. "The Value and Incentive Effects of Non-Traditional Executive Stock Option Plans." *Journal of Financial Economics* 57: 3–34.

Kahan, Marcel, and Ed Rock. 2002. "How I Learned to Stop Worrying and Love the Pill: Adaptive Responses to Takeover Law." *University of Chicago Law Review* 69: 871–915.

Kahle, Kathleen M., and Kuldeep Shastri. Forthcoming. "Executive Loans." *Journal of Financial and Quantitative Analysis*.

Ke, Bin. 2003. "The Influence of Equity-Based Compensation on CEOs' Incentives to Report Strings of Consecutive Earnings Increases." Working paper, Pennsylvania State University.

Ke, Bin, Steven Huddart, and Kathy Petroni. 2003. "What Insiders Know about Future Earnings and How They Use It: Evidence from Insider Trades." *Journal of Accounting and Economics* 35: 315–346.

Kedia, Simi, and Natasha Burns. 2003. "Do Executive Stock Options Generate Incentives for Earnings Management? Evidence from Accounting Restatements." Working paper, Harvard Business School.

Khurana, Rakesh. 2002. *Searching for a Corporate Savior: The Irrational Quest for Charismatic CEOs*. Princeton, NJ: Princeton University Press.

Kole, Stacey R. 1997. "The Complexity of Compensation Contracts." *Journal of Financial Economics* 43: 79–104.

Lambert, Richard A., David F. Larcker, and Robert E. Verrecchia. 1991. "Portfolio Considerations in Valuing Executive Compensation." *Journal of Accounting Research* 29: 129–149.

Lambert, Richard A., David F. Larcker, and Keith Weigelt. 1993. "The Structure of Organizational Incentives." *Administrative Science Quarterly* 38: 438–461.

La Porta, Rafael, Florencio Lopez-de-Silanes, and Andrei Shleifer. 1999. "Corporate Ownership around the World." *Journal of Finance* 54: 471–517.

Lerach, William S. 2002. "Plundering America: How American Investors Got Taken for Trillions by Corporate Insiders." *Stanford Journal of Law, Business and Finance* 8: 69–126.

Levinsohn, Alan. 2001. "A Garden of Stock Options Helps Harvest Talent." *Strategic Finance* 82: 81–82.

Levmore, Saul. 2001. "Puzzling Stock Options and Compensation Norms." *University of Pennsylvania Law Review* 149: 1901–1940.

Lipton, Martin. 1979. "Takeover Bids in the Target's Boardroom." *Business Lawyer* 35: 101–134.

Lipton, Martin, and Steven A. Rosenblum. 2003. "Election Contests in the Company's Proxy: An Idea Whose Time Has Not Come." *Business Lawyer* 59: 67–94.

Loewenstein, Mark J. 1996. "Reflections on Executive Compensation and a Modest Proposal for (Further) Reform." *Southern Methodist University Law Review* 50: 201–223.

———. 2000. "The Conundrum of Executive Compensation." *Wake Forest Law Review* 35: 1–30.

Lorsch, Jay W. 1998. "Compensating Corporate CEOs: A Process View." Harvard Business School working paper #99–013.

Lorsch, Jay W., and Elizabeth M. MacIver. 1989. *Pawns or Potentates? The Reality of America's Corporate Boards*. Boston: Harvard Business School Press.

Lorsch, Jay W., and Krishna G. Palepu. 2003. "Limits to Board Effectiveness." Working paper, Harvard Business School.

Lyons, Denis B. K. 1999. "CEO Casualties: A Battlefront Report." *Directors & Boards* (summer): 43–45.

Main, Brian G. M., Charles A. O'Reilly III, and James Wade. 1995. "The CEO, the Board of Directors, and Executive Compensation: Economic and Psychological Perspectives." *Industrial and Corporate Change* 11: 292–332.

Manne, Henry G. 1965. "Mergers and the Market for Corporate Control." *Journal of Political Economy* 73: 110–120.

Martin, Kenneth J., and Randall S. Thomas. Forthcoming. "When Is Enough, Enough? Market Reaction to Highly Dilutive Stock Option Plans and the Subsequent Impact on CEO Compensation." *Journal of Corporate Finance*.

McConnell, John J., and Henri Servaes. 1990. "Additional Evidence on Equity Ownership and Corporate Value." *Journal of Financial Economics* 27: 595–612.

McNeil, Chris, Greg Niehaus, and Eric Powers. 2003. "Management Turnover in Subsidiaries of Conglomerates versus Stand-Alone Firms." Working paper, School of Business, Penn State Erie, and Moore School of Business, University of South Carolina.

Meulbroek, Lisa K. 2001. "Executive Compensation Using Relative-Performance-Based Options: Evaluating the Structure and Costs of Indexed Options." Working paper, Harvard Business School.

Millstein, Ira M. 1995. "The Professional Board." *Business Lawyer* 50: 1427–1443.

Millstein, Ira M., and Paul W. MacAvoy. 1998. "The Active Board of Directors and Performance of the Large Publicly Traded Corporation." *Columbia Law Review* 98: 1283–1321.

Mirrlees, James A. 1976. "The Optimal Structure of Incentives and Authority within an Organization." *Bell Journal of Economics* 7: 105–131.

Moeller, Sara B., Frederik P. Schlingemann, and Rene M. Stulz. 2003. "Do Shareholders of Acquiring Firms Gain from Acquisitions?" Working paper, Southern Methodist University, University of Pittsburgh, and Ohio State University.

Monks, Robert A. G. 1999. *The Emperor's Nightingale: Restoring the Integrity of the Corporation in the Age of Shareholder Activism*. Boston: Addison-Wesley Publishing.

Monks, Robert A. G., and Nell Minow. 1995. *Corporate Governance*, 2nd ed. Cambridge, MA: Blackwell Publishing.

———. 2001. *Corporate Governance*, 3rd ed. Oxford: Blackwell Publishing.

Montgomery, Cynthia A., and Rhonda Kaufman. 2003. "The Board's Missing Link." *Harvard Business Review* 81: 86–93.

Morck, Randall, Andrei Shleifer, and Robert Vishny. 1988. "Management Ownership and Market Valuation." *Journal of Financial Economics* 20: 293–315.

Murphy, Kevin J. 1995. "Politics, Economics, and Executive Compensation." *University of Cincinnati Law Review* 63: 713–746.

———. 1999. "Executive Compensation." In *Handbook of Labor Economics*, edited by Orley Ashenfelter and David Card. Vol. 3, bk. 2. New York: Elsevier.

———. 2000. "Performance Standards in Incentive Contracts." *Journal of Accounting and Economics* 30: 245–278.

———. 2002. "Explaining Executive Compensation: Managerial Power vs. the Perceived Cost of Stock Options." *University of Chicago Law Review* 69: 847–869.

Murphy, Kevin J., and Paul Oyer. 2003. "Discretion in Executive Incentive Contracts." Working paper, University of Southern California Marshall School of Business and Stanford University Graduate School of Business.

Newman, Harry A., and Haim A. Mozes. 1999. "Does the Composition of the Compensation Committee Influence CEO Compensation Practices?" *Financial Management* 28: 41–53.

Nohel, Tom, and Steven Todd. 2004. "Stock Options and Managerial Incentives to Invest." *Journal of Derivatives Accounting* 1: 29–46.

Ofek, Eli, and David Yermack. 1997. "Taking Stock: Equity-Based Compensation and the Evolution of Managerial Ownership." *Journal of Finance* 55: 1367–1384.

O'Reilly III, Charles A., Brian G. Main, and Graef S. Crystal. 1988. "CEO Compensation as Tournament and Social Comparison: A Tale of Two Theories." *Administrative Science Quarterly* 33: 257–274.

Orts, Eric W. 1998. "Shirking and Sharking: A Legal Theory of the Firm." *Yale Law and Policy Review* 16: 265–329.

Oyer, Paul. Forthcoming. "Why Do Firms Use Incentives That Have No Incentive Effects?" *Journal of Finance*.

Parrino, Robert. 1997. "CEO Turnover and Outside Succession: A Cross-Sectional Analysis." *Journal of Financial Economics* 46: 165–197.

Parthiban, David, Rahul Kochar, and Edward Levitas. 1998. "The Effect of Institutional Investors on the Level and Mix of CEO Compensation." *Academy of Management Journal* 41: 200–208.

Pearl Meyer & Partners. 2001. "Equity Stake: Study of Management Equity Participation in the Top 200 Corporations: 2001."

———. 2002. "Executive Pay Trends: Looking Forward and Looking Back." *USA Today*, November 21, B1.

———. 2003. "2003 Director Compensation." http://www.execpay.com/ResDir.htm (accessed June 23, 2004).

Perry, Tod, and Marc Zenner. 2000. "CEO Compensation in the 1990s: Shareholder Alignment or Shareholder Expropriation?" *Wake Forest Law Review* 35: 123–152.

Pollock, Timothy G., Harald M. Fischer, and James B. Wade. 2002. "The Role of Power and Politics in Repricing Executive Options." *Academy of Management Journal* 45: 1172–1182.

Porac, Joseph F., James B. Wade, and Timothy G. Pollock. 1999. "Industry Categories and the Politics of the Comparable Firm in CEO Compensation." *Administrative Quarterly* 44: 112–144.

Quinn, Linda C. 1995. "Executive Compensation under the New SEC Disclosure Requirements." In Seventh Annual Corporate Law Symposium: Executive Compensation. *University of Cincinnati Law Review* 63: 769–815.

Rajan, Raghuram G., and Luigi Zingales. 1998. "Power in a Theory of the Firm." *Quarterly Journal of Economics* 113: 387–432.

———. 2001. "The Firm as a Dedicated Hierarchy: A Theory of the Origin and Growth of Firms." *Quarterly Journal of Economics* 116: 805–851.

Randall, Clarence B. *The Executive in Transition.* New York: McGraw-Hill, 1967.

Rappaport, Alfred. 1999. "New Thinking on How to Link Executive Pay with Performance." *Harvard Business Review* 77: 91–101.

Ratcliffe, Thomas A. 2001. "New Guidance in Accounting for Stock-Based Compensation: FASBIN No. 44." *National Public Accountant* 46: 28–30.

Ruxton, Kathy B. 1999. *Executive Pay, 1998: Chief Executive Officer Compensation at S&P Super 1,500 Companies as Reported in 1998.* Vol. 2. Washington DC: Investor Responsibility Research Center.

Ryan, Harley E. Jr., and Roy A. Wiggins III. Forthcoming. "Who Is in Whose Pocket? Director Compensation, Bargaining Power and Barriers to Effective Monitoring." *Journal of Financial Economics.*

Saly, P. Jane. 1994. "Repricing Executive Stock Options in a Down Market." *Journal of Accounting and Economics* 16: 325–356.

Saly, P. Jane, Ravi Jagannathan, and Steven J. Huddart. 1999. "Valuing the Reload Feature of Executive Stock Options." *Accounting Horizons* 12: 219–240.

Schizer, David M. 2000. "Executives and Hedging: The Fragile Legal Foundation of Incentive Compatibility." *Columbia Law Review* 100: 440–504.

———. 2001. "Tax Constraints on Indexed Options." *University of Pennsylvania Law Review* 149: 1941–1954.

———. 2002. "Reducing the Tax Costs of Indexed Options." *Tax Notes* 96: 1375–1382.

Scholes, Myron S., Mark A. Wolfson, Merle Erickson, Edward L. Maydew, and Terry Shevlin. 2002. *Taxes and Business Strategy: A Planning Approach*, 2nd ed. Upper Saddle River, NJ: Prentice Hall.

Schwab, Stewart J., and Randall S. Thomas. 2004. "What Do CEOs Bargain For? An Empirical Study of Key Legal Components of CEO Contracts." Working paper, Cornell Law School and Vanderbilt Law School.

Seyhun, H. Nejat. 1998. *Investment Intelligence from Insider Trading.* Cambridge, MA: MIT Press.

Shavell, Steven. 1979. "Risk Sharing and Incentives in the Principal and Agent Relationship." *Bell Journal of Economics* 10: 55–73.

Shivdasani, Anil, and David Yermack. 1999. "CEO Involvement in the Selection of New Board Members: An Empirical Analysis." *Journal of Finance* 54: 1829–1853.

Shleifer, Andrei, and Robert W. Vishny. 1986. "Large Shareholders and Corporate Control." *Journal of Political Economy* 94: 461–488.

———. 1989. "Management Entrenchment: The Case of Manager-Specific Investments." *Journal of Financial Economics* 25: 123–140.

Sivakumar, Kumar, and Gregory Waymire. 1994. "Insider Trading Following Material News Events: Evidence from Earnings." *Financial Management* 23: 23–32.

Smith, Adam. 1776. *An Inquiry into the Nature and Causes of the Wealth of Nations.* Reprint, New York: Modern Library, 1937.

Snyder, Franklin. 2003. "More Pieces of the Compensation Puzzle." *Delaware Journal of Corporate Law* 28: 129–183.

Stein, Jeremy C. 1988. "Takeover Threats and Managerial Myopia." *Journal of Political Economy* 96: 61–80.

Stout, Lynn. 1988. "The Unimportance of Being Efficient." *Michigan Law Review* 87: 613–709.

Strauss, Gary. 2002. "Companies Pony Up to Keep Directors: Boards Seats Have Become Hot Seats." *USA Today*, November 21, B1.

Subramanian, Narayanan, Atreya Chakraborty, and Shahbaz Sheikh. 2003. "Performance Incentives, Performance Pressure, and Executive Turnover." Working paper, Brandeis University.

Summers, Scott L., and John T. Sweeney. 1998. "Fraudulently Misstated Financial Statements and Insider Trading: An Empirical Analysis." *Accounting Review* 73: 131–146.

Symposium on Norms and Corporate Law. 2001. *University of Pennsylvania Law Review* 149: 1607–2191.

Thomas, Randall S., and Kenneth J. Martin. 1998. "Should Labor Be Allowed to Make Shareholder Proposals?" *Washington Law Review* 73: 41–80.

———. 1999. "The Effect of Shareholder Proposals on Executive Compensation." *University of Cincinnati Law Review* 67: 1021–1065.

———. 2000. "The Determinants of Shareholder Voting on Stock Option Plans." *Wake Forest Law Review* 35: 31–82.

———. 2001. "Litigating Challenges to Executive Pay: An Exercise in Futility?" *Washington University Law Quarterly* 79: 593–613.

Tian, Yisong S. 2001. "Optimal Contracting, Incentive Effects and the Valuation of Executive Stock Options." Working paper, York University.

Tirole, Jean. 1988. "The Theory of Industrial Organization." Cambridge, MA: MIT Press.

Tosi, Henry L., and Luis R. Gomez-Mejia. 1989. "The Decoupling of CEO Pay and Performance: An Agency Theory Perspective." *Administrative Science Quarterly* 34: 169–189.

Wade, James, Charles A. O'Reilly III, and Ike Chandratat. 1990. "Golden Parachutes:

CEOs and the Exercise of Social Influence." *Administrative Science Quarterly* 35: 587–603.

Wade, James, Charles A. O'Reilly III, and Tim Pollock. 2004. "Overpaid CEOs and Underpaid Managers: Equity and Executive Compensation." Working paper, University of Wisconsin–Madison, Stanford University, and University of Maryland.

Wade, James B., Joseph F. Porac, and Timothy G. Pollock. 1997. "Worth, Words, and the Justification of Executive Pay." *Journal of Organizational Behavior* 18: 641–664.

Weisbach, Michael S. 1988. "Outside Directors and CEO Turnover." *Journal of Financial Economics* 20: 431–460.

Weston, Fred J., Juan A. Siu, and Brian A. Johnson. 2001. *Takeovers, Restructuring, and Corporate Governance.* 3rd ed. Upper Saddle River, NJ: Prentice Hall.

Williamson, Oliver. 1964. *The Economics of Discretionary Behavior: Managerial Objectives in a Theory of the Firm.* Englewood Cliffs, NJ: Prentice Hall.

Wu, YiLin. 2004. "The Impact of Public Opinion on Board Structure Changes, Director Career Progression, and CEO Turnover: Evidence from CalPERS' Corporate Governance Program." *Journal of Corporate Finance* 10: 199–227.

Wulf, Julie. 2004. "Do CEOs in Mergers Trade Power for Premium? Evidence from 'Mergers of Equals.'" *Journal of Law, Economics & Organization* 20 (2004): 60–101.

Yablon, Charles M. 1999. "Bonus Questions—Executive Compensation in the Era of Pay for Performance." *Notre Dame Law Review* 75: 271–308.

Yermack, David. 1995. "Do Corporations Award CEO Stock Options Effectively?" *Journal of Financial Economics* 39: 237–269.

———. 1996. "Higher Market Valuation of Companies with a Small Board of Directors." *Journal of Financial Economics* 40: 185–211.

———. 1997. "Good Timing: CEO Stock Option Awards and Company News Announcements." *Journal of Finance* 52: 449–477.

Zald, Mayer N. 1969. "The Power and Functions of Boards of Directors: A Theoretical Synthesis." *American Journal of Sociology* 75: 97–111.

# Index

Aboody, David, 164, 247
Abowd, John, 147, 218
Acharya, Viral, 248
Acquisitions
    Payments to acquiring firm CEOs, 127–130
    Payments to target firm CEOs, 89–92
ADC Communications Corp., 131
Aetna Corp., 131
Agency costs
    Definition of, 15–17
    Use of executive compensation to reduce, 17–20
Aggarwal, Rajesh, 245
Agrawal, Anup, 56, 228, 232
Allen, Michael Patrick, 217
Allen, Ronald, 109
Allen, William, 201
American Express Corp., 177, 178, 251
American Stock Exchange (AMEX) listing requirements, 11, 24
Ameritrade Corp., 180, 181
Angel, James, 140, 243
Annunziata, Robert, 131
AOL Time Warner Corp., 109, 182
Apple Computer Corp., 73, 161
Arm's length bargaining (contracting)
    Approach to studying executive compensation, 18
    Definition of, 17–18
    See also "Official" story of executive compensation
Ashenfelter, Orley, 217, 219, 230, 240, 242, 244, 246
AT&T Wireless Corp., 127
At-the-money options
    Managerial power and, 162–164

Manipulating the exercise price of, 163–164
Use of, 159–162

Baker, George, 223
Balsam, Steven, 164, 235, 242, 247, 251
Bank of America Corp., 28, 128, 239
Bank One Corp., 88, 149
Barad, Jill, 88, 133
Bar-Gill, Oren, 250, 252
Barris, Linda, 217, 225, 245
Bebchuk, Lucian, 218, 219, 220, 221, 227, 250, 252, 254, 255
Beneish, Messod, 184, 252, 253
Bergstresser, Daniel, 253
Berkshire Hathaway Corp., 224
Berle Jr., Adolph, 15, 219
Bertrand, Marianne, 83, 86, 123, 218, 232, 240
Bethel, Jennifer, 226
Bettis, J. Carr, 250, 251
Bizjak, John, 71, 229, 230, 250
Black, Bernard, 241
Blanchard, Oliver Jean, 123, 218, 240
Board of directors
    Effect of size and independence on pay, 80–81
    Election of, 25–27, 207–212
    Key role of, 17, 24
    Nomination to, 25–27
    Reducing insulation from shareholders, 206–215
    Staggered boards, 55, 211–212
    See also Compensation committees; Directors; Nomination committees
Bochner, Steven, 251

**271**